The Rolling Stones
and Philosophy

Popular Culture and Philosophy® Series Editor: George A. Reisch

IN PREPARATION:

For full details of all Popular Culture and Philosophy® books, visit www.opencourtbooks.com.

Popular Culture and Philosophy®

The Rolling Stones and Philosophy

It's Just a Thought Away

Edited by

LUKE DICK and GEORGE A. REISCH

OPEN COURT
Chicago and LaSalle, Illinois

Volume 64 in the series, Popular Culture and Philosophy®, edited by George A. Reisch

To order books from Open Court, call toll-free 1-800-815-2280, or visit our website at www.opencourtbooks.com.

Open Court Publishing Company is a division of Carus Publishing Company.

Copyright © 2011 by Carus Publishing Company

First printing 2012

Library of Congress Cataloging-in-Publication Data

The Rolling Stones and philosophy : it's just a thought away / edited by Luke Dick and George A. Reisch.
        p. cm. — (Popular culture and philosophy ; v. 64)
    Includes bibliographical references and index.
    ISBN 978-0-8126-9758-2 (trade paper : alk. paper)
    1. Rolling Stones. 2. Music and philosophy. 3. Rock music—England—History and criticism. I. Dick, Luke, 1979- II. Reisch, George A., 1962-
    ML421.R64R643 2011
    782.42166092'2—dc23
                                                    2011031893

Contents

It's Only Philosophy but We Like It

GEORGE A. REISCH

When it comes to philosophy, Keith Richards is an excellent guitar player. Keith himself would probably agree because, according to him, "rock and roll starts from the neck down." "The minute rock and roll reaches the head, forget it," he told his biographer when talking about the famous Live Aid concert of 1985. And that's something to be thankful for—"it's a few moments when you can forget about nukes and racism and all the other evils God's kindly thrown upon us."[1]

But if rock and roll, Richards-style, is all about your crotch and not your mind, why did he call his autobiography *Life*? Obviously there's some trademark Richards irony in that choice. There he is on the jacket cover, the rock star with a legendary reputation for life-saving blood transfusions, sporting a skull-ring and lighting his seven-hundred thousandth some-odd cigarette (figure two packs a day for fifty years) next to the word "life." Irony aside, Keith would say it's simply because that's what his book's about. And there's no doubt that Keith has lived *intensely*. He's been pursued by fans who adore him and cops and politicians who hate him. He's thrived at the pinnacle of rock star success and hit bottom (and bounced a few times). He's rubbed elbows and traded riffs with the greatest of musicians and songwriters, dated, married, or bedded some of the most beautiful women in the world, and glimmered alongside rock's greatest vocalist, even when the twins weren't speaking or writing classic albums together.

---

[1] Victor Bokris, *Keith Richards: The Biography*, Da Capo, p. 344.

Had he gone for double entendre instead of irony, he could have called the book *History*. Along with The Beatles (though, more about *them* later), Keith, Mick, and the rest were front-row-center participants in some of the massive cultural changes happening in the 1960s in the wake of the free speech and civil rights movements and, of course, the British Invasion. Thirty years later, they were still on top of things. On August 17th, 1990, Keith and Mick and the band started up a stadium full of Czechoslovakian Stones fans who had endured over twenty years of Soviet occupation during which The Stones and other bands were not permitted to play. After Keith's opening riff, these Czechs spent two hours "jumping, clapping, shouting, dancing and singing along, surprising themselves" according to Eduard Freisler, there with his dad as a teenager, who watched The Stones officially liberate his father and his country from Soviet rules and attitudes.

With posters around the stadium declaring "The Rolling Stones roll in, Soviet army rolls out" (*New York Times*, August 17th, 2010) you might say that if The Stones and what they represent had not helped defeat communism in the Cold War, they obviously outlasted it and got over the obstacle it put in their way. But that's what Keith and The Stones are good at. They survived the death of their founder Brian Jones, the disaster at Altamont, the shadow of The Beatles (who were always a little more respectable and successful), drug arrests, near bankruptcy, disco, "artistic differences," romantic jealousy, enough cigarettes, drinks, and drugs to bury weaker constitutions, and of course the big guns of heroin that almost put Keith in a Canadian jail and sooner rather than later, we all figured in the 1970s, would make Keith history.

Yet all of this life and all this history, Keith would have us believe, has nothing to do with philosophy? Philosophy involves many things, but one is an attitude and an approach to life that puts things in a certain framework and perspective. Keith's book is exemplary, for there is no doubt it could have been a much darker, more depressing, and even tragic book about the darker sides of human nature. It could have been about greed, jealousy, insecurity, and addiction, or Spinal-Tap stories about managers stealing money and publishing rights. Or it could have been a sad display of old rockers trying to settle old scores before the spotlights finally go out. Life is often like that, and anyone who's closely observed the long career of The Stones knows it. But Keith's *Life* is optimistic and uplifting. It has a distinctive focus and a mental discipline that says *scholar* or *philosopher* more than it says world's greatest rock star. But *Life* is full of surprises—like the fact that Keith owns what sounds like a world-class collection of books (and guitars).

Don't Trust Anyone Over ~~Seventy~~ Seventy-Five

The focus that keeps Keith's life and his book on track is music. Even after four decades, he writes about the opening riffs of "Brown Sugar" and "Satisfaction" with the enthusiasm of a proud father, with the same joy he had in 1970 or 1965. About those moments on stage when his and Ronnie's guitars start to weave and flow so perfectly that he's not sure who's playing what, Keith writes like a mystic struggling to find words for something that is magical, indescribable, and life-sustaining. It seems me that as long as Keith can still sing, play, and perform, even if sex and cigarettes and drinks were no longer available, he'd keep rolling ahead in search of union with his musical divine. For him it towers over whatever it is he and Mick are not talking about, whatever financial and legal problems the band faced in the 1970s and 1980s, and it probably glowed at the end of the tunnels he crawled out of during his detoxes.

Talk about shining a light—The Stones and their music have been a beacon in the life of anyone old enough to appreciate their longevity. Not a beacon that you should necessarily go toward or follow (most of us don't have the talent or the guts). But a beacon that shines valuable light in this crazy world. You don't have to have kicked heroin, after all, or have been a not-from-these-parts kind of guy with long hair arrested in the deep South to see the ongoing career of The Rolling Stones as a reassuring fixture—especially as time goes by and new wrinkles, new aches and pains, and which-concert-was-that? moments come more and more often. As time and The Stones keep rolling on, they become less a rock band, regardless of how popular and influential, and more something else like an institution, a cherished piece of furniture, or a rock that we all need to lean on. If not for music, coke, or sympathy, just to stay upright and above the fray.

As I write, it's been almost fifty years since The Stones first played together as The Rolling Stones. That puts us, as well as them, in new territory for rock'n'roll. No other band, not even The Who and their generation, so effectively pegged the new sound to youth. With their clothes, their attitudes, and the frightening energy of their amped-up rhythm and blues, adults of the early Sixties can be forgiven for wondering if these five hooligans really were the harbinger of civilization's demise. Even The Beatles, after all, respectfully adapted the eternal verities of melody, harmony, arrangement, and classical instruments in some of their songs. But while The Beatles were winning over their fans and their fans' grandparents with "Yesterday" or "Eleanor Rigby," Mick, Keith, and Brian laughed at the very idea of common ground between generations by releasing "Lady Jane"—a song that, despite the courtly sounds of Brian's dulcimer and Mick's schoolboy rhymes about the wives of Henry the Eighth, is nonetheless an ode to female genitalia. Long before the Sex Pistols impolitely poked their guitars at the Queen and her "fascist regime," The Stones had punked not only their elders but Britannia's royal history.

So it's hard to imagine watching The Stones in the Sixties and Seventies and thinking that they would still be at it forty years later when the youth that seemed so much a part of their presence and their spirit had left them. But The Stones, and Keith in particular, have proven us wrong time and again—a fact that, all by itself, should make the philosopher in Keith and in all of us sit up and take notice.

Trying, Philosophically

In an interview during their 1969 American tour, Mick was asked if he's yet found satisfaction. In reply, he distinguished between different kinds of satisfaction, just like a young philosopher should. He replied, "financially dissatisfied, sexually satisfied, and philosophically trying." The *New York Times* reporter who quoted Jagger ended his report there, adding that "some of his fellow performers grinned." (November 28th, 1969). Apparently, no one was expecting such a precise, thoughtful answer, much less Mick's agreement with the interviewer's suggestion that from "(I Can't Get No) Satisfaction" onward, the work of The Stones may be more than an assortment of popular songs to be played on the radio to accompany advertisements for cigarettes and laundry detergent. Looking for satisfaction can be, and maybe *ought* to be, a life-long quest.

Was Mick's reply another put on? Another performance? Keith would probably insist it was, but then again he and Mick don't always agree. On this point, the writers in this book step in. Obviously, and even despite their Sgt. Pepper-ish explorations of the late Sixties (such as "2000 Light Years from Home") The Stones are not philosophers grappling with the meaning of life or existence in terms that are familiar from Philosophy 101 or even *Dark Side of the Moon*. But while Keith may be right that rock "starts from the neck down," Mick was right to suggest that it doesn't always stay there. It didn't for The Stones. Many of their best songs and albums, the ones that established them as a cultural force to rival The Beatles, moved up into philosophical territory of one kind or another. Think of the politics in "Street Fighting Man," "Sweet Black Angel" and "Sweet Neo Con," or the existentialism buried in "Paint it, Black," "You Can't Always Get What You Want" and "Nineteenth Nervous Breakdown" (a song which Pink Floyd, and certainly Syd Barrett, could have written). And what about "Sympathy for the Devil" that perfectly marries Keith's neckdown energy to Mick's literary sensibilities? This is no longer just about shaking your hips or getting your rocks off. It's about the arc and meaning of human history, and Mick's cheeky but dead-serious suggestion that everything you were taught about the metaphysics of evil in Christianity is mistaken.

Still, the bulk of The Stones' songs, and some of their best, are simply about people, relationships, romance, and sex. They mean just to entertain, and not to provoke or shock their listeners. But even then, we'd be wrong to think there is nothing at all of neck-up importance. Think again of that concert in Prague shortly after the collapse of the Soviet Union and imagine telling those Czech citizens that The Rolling Stones are mere entertainers, on a par with the entertainers and folkheros of whom Moscow approved. They'd look at you like they'd just seen Brian Jones. While the aura of glamour and celebrity may have obscured it in the West, in the Soviet-controlled East The Stone's individualism, creativity, iconoclasm—their celebration of the pursuit of "satisfaction"—were marks of a dangerous liberal philosophy from which Moscow intended to protect its satellites with radio-jamming antennas and, if necessary, guns and tanks.

Those first chords of "Start Me Up" that night were about *much* more than sparks flying between a guy and a girl. These were sparks of a freedom that would allow a band like The Stones to play in public and allow people to buy their records and listen to them as much as they want, even if they think it's only Rock and Roll. That night The Stones were a two-thousand-year echo of Socrates in Greece, condemned to death for teaching and discussing unpopular ideas and reaching unpopular conclusions. Socrates's revenge, despite his drinking the hemlock, was his reputation and his influence that long outlasted the regime that killed him.

The Stones and their fans had similarly outlasted their oppressors. "From that point on," Freisler wrote about his father, sobbing with joy after the last encore, "no one would tell him how he should think, how he should feel. He had seen The Rolling Stones with his own eyes. And it felt so good." Some satisfaction, at last.

I

One Thought
(to the Body)

1
The Glimmer Twins

RANDALL E. AUXIER

Sometimes it seems ordained by the gods that certain pairs of people just have to go through the proverbial threescore and ten *together*, the whole damn thing. You know what I'm talking about because you've known people, especially certain couples, who play in the sandbox, date, marry, divorce, remarry, divorce again, and still end up together. Full disengagement isn't among the options, even when they no longer *want* to be entangled. Is it a cosmic joke of some kind? If that occasional feature of human life, alone, isn't weird enough, the phenomenon becomes still more interesting when the entangled pair is famous and artistic. Mick and Keith are not only December's Children. They're destiny's children.

The fact that they were a Stone's throw from each other in the unassuming burb of Dartford, and schoolmates (if not quite friends) even before they hooked up in their teens, adds a bit of romance to our way of imagining their destiny. That also isn't a bad place to start wondering. It invites speculation, for instance, on what might have been if they had been on different buses on a particular day (the point at which the collaboration *really began*). The world with no Rolling Stones? How could that be, and how far-reaching the consequences? I don't know about you, but I can't easily work out how my own life would be different with no Stones. They have been so pervasive as a presence for so long, supplying the soundtrack of my entire life and probably yours too, well, I just don't know. Many of my ideas, especially about rock music, but about a full range of aesthetic topics, used The Stones as a model. Anyway, I don't think I can quite believe in destiny, but cosmic entanglement I have seen first hand. So it's hard to grasp how long the Jagger-Richards tentacles might be, but hardly any part of the world is wholly out of the reach of their collaboration.

When it comes to Mick and Keith, on the one hand, it seems sort of inevitable that two kids with such similar drives and musical tastes, and occupying almost the same space, would eventually hook up, but *meeting* isn't quite enough. The circumstances of meeting needed to be such as to open rather than close the doors. Earlier encounters between Jagger and Richards had failed to produce that "moment of recognition." In the days before The Stones formed, any number of events might have taken them in different directions. And so, in that light, it all seems quite evitable. (My computer actually recognizes that word, so I am deprived of my snarky moment of creative rebellion by the Microsoft Corporation; maybe some things are evitable, but not Microsoft, I add chalantly.)

Pretty Pairs

What makes this more than a matter of idle curiosity is that just this entangled duo turned out to be the Glimmer Twins, the most culturally important *genuine* collaboration in music in the second half of the twentieth century. Lennon and McCartney didn't really collaborate on their songwriting— more of a corporation there than a co-operation, a good business deal. We could certainly take The Beatles as a whole to be a crucial collaboration, but they were not entangled for life, and at the core of that whole effort, John and Paul were mostly writing their songs individually. It's different from the Mick-and-Keith nexus. The kind of creative collaboration that intrigues me goes all the way down and all the way up, which includes dipping into the ether and pulling out the songs together, not just individually, then taking whatever is found forward into recording, performance, and through decades of response and repetition. A song can't "exist" more completely than do some of the Jagger-Richards classics.

When a full-bodied collaboration comes up in the domain of music, at least during the brief 120 years since the "song" became the dominant musical unit, we usually find that one half of the pair writes the music, the other writes the lyrics. The Gershwins, Rodgers-Hart (later Hammerstein), Lerner-Loewe, and, from a later day, John-Taupin or even Garcia-Hunter would be the other pairs one might mention. But fewer were full collaborations, with both members contributing both lyrics and music, and also taking the music from bottom to top. Page-Plant and Waters-Gilmour come to mind along with the Glimmer Twins as partners who also made a living sharing the stage, *presenting* what they had created. And these collaborations were more than songwriting, entering into every phase of the creation of commercial music.

Of those three pairs, the Glimmer Twins were the most enduring and successful, but I'm aware that to say they were the most important, as artists, can be disputed. It's really tough to imagine any commercial music more important, artistically speaking, than Pink Floyd's, and no single project of The Stones had the impact of either *Dark Side of the Moon* or *The Wall*. The artistic impact of Zeppelin's body of work is also very serious, if not as focused or sustained as the Waters-Gilmour creations. What I will say is that while I think the fruits of the Waters-Gilmour partnership are more intense and deeper, I do not believe their overall impact on the world, as artists, was greater, nor do I find their creative process very intriguing, for reasons you may or may not find compelling. But instead of dissecting Waters and Gilmour, let me put it in more positive terms.

I'll just blurt it out: the reason The Stones pair is more interesting, from a philosophical and human point of view, is because it's so very clear that Mick and Keith actually always *loved* each other, being far more than friends and something closer to brothers, nay, actual twin sons of different mothers, as Mick once said. Except they are also a bit like a married couple at the same time, or so it appears when one sees them bickering. Yet, even that characterization sort of understates the matter, if some of the biographers are to be believed. Christopher Andersen basically claims that Mick was *in love* with Keith and depicts a Jones-Jagger-Richards love triangle when the three shared a flat on Edith Grove, in the early days. This triangle was the beginning of a lifetime of jealousies, any time someone else moved in to take Keith away from Mick, or Mick away from Keith, there was going to be trouble.

Frankly, I don't know what to believe about any of that, and I don't much care, but a lot of what people like Andersen say seems to be confirmed in Keith's autobiography. What I'm talking about between them might or might not involve lust, and I wouldn't be surprised if lust is part of the story. It certainly *does* involve jealousy of various kinds. The creative process for artists is inseparable from *eros*, as I understand that ancient idea. Still, there's more to *eros* than sexual desire—it can be directed in many ways—but if *eros* comes to be expressed by artists in sexual activity, no one ought to be surprised. And if that sort of desire is the close companion of jealousy, and perhaps also envy, well, we all know how stories like that go. Things get ugly sometimes. It's not as if The Stones were renowned for their wisdom, maturity, restraint, and circumspection.

My point is that the obvious depth of Mick's and Keith's relationship makes their creative process all the more fascinating (and perhaps easier to understand). Waters and Gilmour had a hard time ever tolerating each other, while Page and Plant apparently didn't even have the decency to argue very much. I wrote about the Page-Plant pair in another fine Open Court book, *Led Zeppelin and Philosophy*, but I could add in this context that it looks to me as if almost anyone could probably get on well with Robert Plant, who seems so easygoing as to be almost otherworldly. It also appears that Roger Waters can't even manage to tolerate himself, perhaps that's why others have difficulty (and his art may well require just these problems). I don't know any of these people, so I could be very wrong. I'm just saying how it looks. But I am sure of this much: Mick and Keith both have huge personalities, big enough to fill a stadium, and when you lock something that powerful in a single room, and it doesn't blow up the whole house, *that's interesting*.

Picking a Fight

So we're talking about artistic temperaments here. That has to be a part of the story about the collaboration of the twins. But we want more than psychology from this little exploration. Let's get at something about *creativity*, when it comes from *interaction*, instead of just one person. The kind of creativity that only happens between two people, and *particular* people at that, the interdependence, is fascinating. We have a habit, in this culture, of thinking that "genius" (whatever it is) lives in *individual* artists, but I am convinced that isn't the whole truth. There are people who can only achieve genius together, and who absolutely *cannot* get at that level of creativity alone. I think Mick and Keith are like that. Don't get me wrong. They are both very good alone, and I think they might both have become famous alone, but when they work together, that's when we get into the realm of genius.

There are really two ways philosophers mull over the question of art (including music). There are those who worry mainly about the "work," such as the song or the symphony or the painting, or the sculpture. They will argue about the definition of what does or doesn't count as a "work of art," and they will discuss how we can or should interpret the work. This is the stuff most of us are on about. So, if I were like that (and I'm not), I'd try to get you wondering about certain songs or albums, or even certain concerts or videos. It's pretty natural to be curious about those things. We like to take the *product* of our creativity and use it to find the meaning and value of art in our common experience. The work itself is our guide to thinking about what artists *are*, and so forth. In this case the philosophy of art is about *things*, and what things can tell us.

Other philosophers (like me) worry more about the creative process itself, and we want to understand what happens and what *can* happen in the course of *creating* works of art. Such philosophers are often more interested in the artist than in the art, wanting to know what (if anything) makes (good, great) artists different from other folks, and inquiring into why and how they do what they do. From this viewpoint, the key to understanding the *work* is to understand how it came into existence. For folks like us, to think about works of art *without* thinking through the creative process is like building a castle in the air. So this is about processes, not about things.

In fact (and now I'm picking a fight), I would go so far as to say that there isn't a single "thing," strictly speaking, that *is* "the" work of art. Artworks *are* processes, even after they're nominally "finished." Mick's and Keith's song "Street Fighting Man" means one thing in 1968 and something different now, and you can't completely separate one from the other. To speak of that song as an artwork *in the fullest sense* is to begin when it didn't exist—was just a glimmer in the twins' eye—and bring the story up to the present day. You can cut off a slice of time at some point, if you like, and just talk about the song in that context, but don't try to claim that this half-story just *is* the song. You can't really bottle up a work of art in a single slice of time. Artworks don't really work like that.

To give another example, hearing Keith do "Gimme Shelter" with the X-Pensive Winos really transforms the song. They totally jam on that song, and I am really moved by the way Keith sings it. Prior to that new interpretation of the song, it was something less than it is now. Go to Youtube and watch it. See if you don't agree. Artworks are living processes, and the processes are connected with their origins, their creators. Sometimes an artwork awaits the right context— Michelangelo's *David* surrounded by his own unfinished works in the *Academia* in Florence instead of standing in the entrance way for which it was commissioned, or Aretha Franklin singing "You Make Me Feel (Like a Natural Woman)," instead of Carole King (who certainly did a decent job, but anyone can see she wrote it for Aretha, whether she knew it at the time or not—and I'll bet both would agree). So context is a moving target and it matters very much to thinking about works of art.

Only Rock'n'Roll

One of the best known among philosophers of the creative process was Susanne Langer (1895–1985). She believed that any philosopher who wanted to talk about art at least needed to try a hand at *making it*, first. That's the only way to prevent "empty or naive generalizations," she said. Really it takes more than that, though, since nobody can be good at all the arts, even enough to get a fair sense of them. What we have to do, if we want to say true or wise things about art, is choose the arts we are good enough at to enjoy a few real moments of successfully creating *within* the art form or medium. But even then, the real artists themselves must be our teachers. So when we later look at art *philosophically*, aiming to understand how it is created, we need to begin with what the artists *say* along with what they show us. The uncomfortable truth is that Mick and Keith are doing something you and I can't do (not at anything like their level), and that's why we have to listen to their version of what's happening.

Artists have peculiar ways of talking about what they do, however. Here is Keith, for example, on the question of rhythm:

> There's something primordial in the way we react to pulses without even knowing it. We exist on a rhythm of seventy-two beats per minute. The train, apart from getting them from the Delta to Detroit, became very important to blues players because of the rhythm of the machine, the rhythm of the tracks, and then you cross onto another track, the beat moves. It echoes something in the human body. So then when you have machinery involved, like trains, and drones, all of that is still built in as music inside us. The human body will feel rhythms even when there's not one. Listen to "Mystery Train" by Elvis Presley. One of the great rock-and-roll tracks of all time, not a drum on it. It's just a suggestion, because the body will provide the rhythm. Rhythm really only has to be suggested. Doesn't have to be pronounced. That's where they got it wrong with "this rock" and "that rock." It's got nothing to do with rock. It's to do with roll. (*Life*, p. 244)

This is all over the place. I think I know what he's getting at here, but this is a string of insights and reports and examples and assertions all tangled together. I'm sure it's all true, in its context, properly qualified, and so on, but it isn't in the artist's temper or among his purposes to explain it all. Langer says:

> The philosopher must know the arts, so to speak, "from the inside." But no one can know all the arts in this way. This entails an arduous amount of non-academic study. [In other words, you have to learn to play guitar or something.] His teachers, furthermore, are artists, and

they speak their own language, which largely resists translation into the more careful, literal vocabulary of philosophy. This is likely to arouse his impatience. But it is, in fact, impossible to talk about art without adopting to some extent the language of the artists. The reason why they talk as they do [see Keith above] is not entirely (though it is partly) because they are discursively untrained and popular in their speech; nor [are] they [simply] misled by "bad speech habits" [just the beginning of Keith's bad habits I'm sure] . . . Their vocabulary is metaphorical because it has to be plastic and powerful to let them speak their serious and often difficult thoughts. They cannot see art as "merely" this-or-that easily comprehensible phenomenon; they are too interested in it to make concessions to language. (*Feeling and Form*, p. ix)

Artists really do try to understand what they're doing, and that's because they are in constant pursuit of the end product, trying to nail down whatever it is that can pull the best stuff into concrete existence, from all the possibilities. Maybe it's only rock'n'roll, but that doesn't matter unless we all like it.

Genius

Even at that, things are still pretty mysterious in the creative process. Maybe it's better to look at a creative *collaboration* because at least you get *two* takes on what happens. That strategy also adds complexities, sure enough, but it may be easier to get at the core of the creative process by triangulating: place yourself at one angle in the triangle and watch the other two move around you. Whatever Mick and Keith may say or do, they are held together by *you* (your question "how'd you do that?") and by the fact that they did really write those songs and play those shows. The songs exist and the shows actually happened. The collaboration occurred. You've heard the results. We can get to the bottom of this, at least in a general way.

The tempting word for what they make together is genius, but I think in their case we're more likely to want to call the outcome—the song, the show, the video—a *work* of genius than pin the label on either of our twins. The word "genius" has a weird sort of history. It used to be thought of as a sort of spirit that comes from beyond and settles on certain people for a time. Then it came to be thought of like a reliable muse of some sort. People would say "he has the genius of writing" or "she has the genius of painting." But nobody said that one person or another was "a genius," in our modern sense, until the late eighteenth century. There was a dude with the unfortunate name of Immanuel Kant (which is pronounced very close to what you think—it's what Keith calls people he really holds in contempt). He made good on his name, some people think, by being one. But he's the guy who wrote about genius in a way that stuck:

> *Genius* is the talent (natural endowment) that gives the rule to art. Since talent is an innate productive ability of the artist, and as such belongs itself to nature, we could also put it this way: *Genius* is the innate mental disposition through which nature gives the rule to art. . . . For every art presupposes rules . . . [and] since a product can never be called art unless it is preceded by a rule, it must be nature in the subject (and through the attunement of his powers) that gives the rule to art. (*Critique of Judgment*, pp. 174–75)

Admittedly the guy is a little bit stuffy. Okay, he's a twit, but this really is the guy who is responsible for the way we talk about individual people being "geniuses" these days. We added scientists and mathematicians in with the artists somewhere along the way, but at first it was just artists. Something in their subjective natures allows them to produce works that give the rule to the rest of the art. To be genius, Kant goes on to say, talent procures originality, originality leads the work to be an exemplar, and "exemplarity" of the work just is *nature* in the artist. Blah, blah, blah. It's a fancy way of saying they're not supernatural, but they're not exactly like us, either.

Kant goes on to say that geniuses don't understand and can't explain their own powers, and you might as well not bother asking them because all you'll get is bullshit. (That's my summary; Kant himself, being very old-fashioned, rarely used the word "bullshit.") This all seems fine, as far as it goes, but why do some people have this genius and others don't? And also, I think he left out something really crucial, which is that sometimes genius works only when two people are at it together. So we're back to Mick and Keith, together.

Let It Bleed

To get the philosophical stuff worked out, we'll have to rehearse our facts, as far as we can know them. It's sort of like trying to guess what happens inside of a marriage. You never really know, even if you're the marriage counselor. Even if you get to hear both sides and ask any question, you still don't really know. But we do the best we can with what we have, and I'll try not to draw too many conclusions about what really happened between Mick and Keith, when they were being geniuses. (It's a little clearer what to think when they're just being assholes, since we can all pretty well pull *that* off.)

Even though Keith usually wrote the music and Mick the lyrics, there weren't any rules in their collaboration, and these guys never liked rules very much anyway (and we all know what they'd think of Kant). Some songs are all Mick's, some are all Keith's, and every variation in between, and some of those, although largely created alone, are works of genius (or at least rules through which the *nature* of rock'n'roll gives the rule to the *art* of rock'n'roll). Keith says, for example, that when Mick would bring in a song that was largely complete, like "Brown Sugar," he (Keith) would start out playing it on a six-string guitar in standard tuning, not his five-string guitar in open G tuning. The reason is that Mick plays standard and Keith didn't want to just assume the song should be crammed into his favorite nook. But often the songs would take on a wonderful new life when Keith did pick up the five-string and say to Mick, "What about this . . . ?"

I have a friend and old band mate, a well-known guitar player in Memphis, who is a Keith Richards expert and has learned to do everything Keith does. I remember him telling me about the first time "Brown Sugar" came on the radio in Memphis in 1968. "From the first chord, you just knew," he said. Knew what? "It was a number one song." I have to agree. That was certainly one that "Mick wrote," but it received some ineffable part of its life, of its nature, of its genius from the five-string tuning and from that tight sound, so different from "Honky Tonk Women" or "Start Me Up," where you can hear just a bit of the separation among the five strings, as the chord is stroked. On "Brown Sugar," not only is the guitar sound a little more like a green cherry than a ripe apple, it's also exactly the tart thing it just *has to be* to convey the song, to *make* it a work of genius. Did Mick write "Brown Sugar"? Not alone, in the important sense, because without that perfect sound, and the perfect riffs (both the three-note and the six- note riffs that punctuate that rhythm guitar), it just isn't genius.

The boundary between what Mick did and what Keith did would be impossible to draw. There were also boundary problems in their partnership, mainly because there apparently weren't any healthy ones ever established, and maybe that was a needed feature for them to succeed. The twins reversed roles of bad guy and good guy even though they always were, to their later and mutual consternation, better together than apart and thus rendered creatively (and emotionally) interdependent early in life. The things they could do only together became, at times, an open wound, so for the sake of better art they just let it bleed. At other times their interdependence was a scab they couldn't resist picking.

Keith says it's "in the DNA code" that "sooner or later the two principals will turn on each other because one of them will be driven crazy by the knowledge that to be at their best they need to perform with the other person and therefore they need that other person to be successful, or even to be heard. It makes you hate that person. Well, it didn't in my case, because I wanted us to depend on each other and carry on" (*Life*, p. 501). It doesn't appear the twins have been genuinely happy with each other since about late 1968 (the Anita Pallenberg film debacle), which is to say that there are people in this world with grandchildren, who weren't themselves even *born* the last time Mick and Keith were really "good mates," as they might put it.

Anyone can see why they "stay together," practically speaking. Each wants what he can get only with the co-operation of the other, sort of like why people stay in difficult marriages to be with their children. In this case it looks more complicated, though, because the creative side of their partnership, especially the songwriting process, requires more than a set of practical decisions concerning the kids, more than détente. It requires at least some genuine vulnerability to the judgments of the other, along with an openness to finding complementary wavelengths. There is a kind of pre-verbal communication that occurs in artistic (and any creative) collaboration, and it seems to require a kind of trust, at least if the songs have any depth (so these are *not* like those Nashville-style arranged songwriting dates).

In past years, Keith would stand at the microphone with his musical ideas and sing fragments of lines and make vowel sounds in a semi-linguistic encounter with possible language, while Mick would turn this "voweling" into lyrics. It was speaking in tongues. By the time they did *Bridges to Babylon*, their producer, Don Was, had to bounce between them so they could write the songs. Don Was would try to take notes from Keith's glossolalia, go over to Mick and toss all that nonsense out, while Mick wrote lyrics. In that fashion, if Keith has it right, they made the entire album without even speaking to one another. I'm sorry folks, but that's just strange . . . not that they aren't speaking, but that they're still writing songs without speaking.

So, in a way, it's not that Mick and Keith are staying together for practical reasons, working out the business decisions through lawyers and producers, even though that side of it certainly exists. Rather, even after they decimated and belittled one another on the world stage, to the point of no return, it's like they still agreed to have more children, so to speak, by surrogacy if necessary, and they did so for a long, long time (perhaps now they're post-menopausal, but I don't know; I wouldn't bet on it). Whatever the "genius" is here, it lives outside of the subjective existence of these boys, each taken alone. It's about how sparks fly when two powerful subjectivities clash, and mesh.

This is a classic case of what philosophers like to call "dialectic." It is a simultaneously destructive and creative encounter of standpoints, and if the "dialectical philosophers" are right, pretty much everything in cultural history gets made by means of such strife. You never get anything worth having without a fight. The master of this kind of philosophy was Georg Hegel (1770–1831), and he didn't think very highly of Kant's idea of "genius." There is a spirit of the times (a "Zeitgeist") that moves the world from one stage of history to the next, with or without the co-operation of the individuals involved. The Stones are a pretty fair example of a group of people on the edge of the Zeitgeist of the 1960s, and somehow they were able to surf that wave all the way into the second decade of the twenty-first century—and that's a long ride.

Fifteen Minutes of Fame?

It may be good to remember that Mick and Keith have been famous for almost half a century, and it's unlikely that either can remember what it's like to have anonymity. They never were easily embarrassed and they learned early on that their dirty laundry would be on public display (not that it was altogether bad for business), and even though Mick is generally thought of as being image-conscious and sensitive to criticism, I think it's pretty obvious that both of these guys were temperamentally well-suited to the limelight. If they minded at first that their quarrels ended up in the tabloids, that's all over now. These guys have leathery hides and they're tougher than we are. Ordinary folks like us can't really imagine what their lives are like—but then, they also can't imagine our lives, and surely they envy us at least a little that we can pop over to the corner for an ice cream cone whenever we take a notion.

In hindsight, we see that Mick and Keith are (and always were) serious artists, or if that goes too far, serious *about* their art. They weren't just seeking money or fame. They definitely had a sense of the history they were living. They saw their music as being grounded in a thorough understanding of the side of American culture that gave rise to the blues as an art form. Unlike the blues purists, the twins were quite willing to repackage and sell what they had gleaned; the times required it. But their sincere devotion to blues as an art form is beyond questioning. It's not just that these guys loved the blues, as fans. They also approached it with real intellectual curiosity, made themselves true students, and in time, also initiates. They recognized the enduring aesthetic and cultural value of the blues back when Americans themselves did not. The twins didn't just pore over the music because it was cool; they knew it was good art, in the sense of aesthetically and spiritually significant. They were surprised to find out that Americans didn't pay it much attention.

Hegel thought that the movement of history is given its sensuous appearance by art. To put that in clearer language, when you hear Keith's guitar sound, and you see Mick prancing down the runway, that "show" is the very clothes that history wears when it is rolling from one stage to the next. The geniuses are the ones who are a little bit ahead of the wave. They don't really know or understand what they're doing. They're actually hitting a target no one else even sees, and they are showing us what the future looks like, even before it has to be filled in with politics and religion and all sorts of other slower moving innards. Art is out ahead, giving our senses what *will be* before it really *is*. But it doesn't do that out of the pure blue, it uses all the materials that history has already made, and it taps into all the tensions that currently exist, and then it pulls off a reversal so that what was *last* is now *first* and what was on top is now dependent on what came later, up from the swamp.

The Stones used their fame and influence, both with the public and in the art world, to draw attention to the blues, the bottom rung of the cultural ladder. At the time the Rolling Stones were on the rise, pop art was also pulling down the barriers between fine art and commercial/popular imagery, the beat poets wrote seriously about how the other half lived, and all that messiness cleared the way for low culture to become an object of curiosity around the world. Eventually, "high culture" found itself begging at the banquet.

For whatever reason, American low culture seems to have fascinated everyone who had the opportunity to consider the matter. People had been writing about the plight of the poor and painting and sculpting ordinary life since the Romantic era, so it wasn't the subject matter that was new. What had changed is that the sensibilities of the lower classes, their types of expression and even their aesthetic sense was coming to the center of things, slowly crowding out the old dominance of the earlier age (when the bourgeois tried to ape the aristocrats in taste). Suddenly it had become cool to affirm that the people's art was good, nay *better* than the stuffy old crap we were told we should appreciate.

Art for Art's Sake

Even in the midst of a move across the tracks, there is still a place for what philosophers call "aestheticism." People whose moral and even religious values are drawn from the aesthetic realm are "aesthetes." The pure bluesman is a kind of low culture aesthete, *living* the blues so he can *play* the blues, and not expecting anything more from life or from death. Hank Williams is an example of how that view plays out in country music, or see Townes Van Zandt, or Steve Earle. And The Stones are aesthetes in the rock'n'roll sense, but they came at a time of transition. The worlds of high and low culture were in a dialectical tango in the 1960s. Being a rock'n'roll version of the aesthete is not enough to conquer the world (and The Stones, *and* their aesthetic, most definitely *did* prevail). The bluesmen and the hillbilly aesthetes hadn't conquered the world, they had been spit on by it. But The Stones were different.

It isn't an accident that Mick and Keith both began to associate very early with visual artists like Andy Warhol, and with mavens of art world like Robert Fraser. Painting still represented the domain of high art, like ballet and opera did, but painting was changing. While The Stones were treating blues as something to be elevated, painters were becoming curious about how to take painting down a notch. That Keith was drawn to visual art from the first, and that Ronnie Wood, also a recognized painter, would be a natural fit, seems to confirm the idea that the collective *lives* of The Stones have been and remain a generalized artistic project. Andy Warhol would have been among the first to impress upon them that the lines between fine art and pop culture were being erased, and that to be an artist *now* was to embrace many art forms at once and to cultivate celebrity itself.

The new, post-modern art form was to achieve fame *as an artist*, and so painters needed to be acting and actors should be writing musical scores and composers should take up architecture, while the architects are writing novels, and so on. The all encompassing category of "the artist" as a type of celebrated performer was being popularized. This is, in a sense, the very extreme of the idea of genius. It's genius pushed to its limit, so that no longer does the nature of the genius give the rule to art; now, the genius is a powerful subject who tells both nature and culture what art *is* and *isn't*. It's the apotheosis of celebrity as justified by the idea of genius. It was an irresistible role for anyone with the balls to claim it.

Mick has big balls. He took the bait right away. Keith was a pure musician, but he was willing to play the role, and in this I think Mick was probably his guide. Mick saw that being outrageous and re-inventing one's persona in successive spurts was *de rigueur* for the world Warhol prophesied. Mick saw how to do that. He needed Keith to remain grounded in the music, to keep him on some kind of tether and bring him back down to what he really does well, which is front The Stones, and Keith needed Mick to be out there doing that Warhol-esque thing so as to keep The Stones on top, so that everyone would listen to the new music. Keith's job was to develop and deepen himself as a serious musician, and to speak in tongues while Mick interpreted for the world. Each of them was very good at his own principal side of the collaboration, and each was nothing short of brilliant in support of the other.

So, although our twins came from the world of music, specifically the blues, there was no reason to assume that being The Stones, or more specifically, being the Glimmer Twins, was just about being good musicians. They never saw it as being only about fame, fortune, celebrity, or even just about music. There was something about what was happening and had happened to the world itself that called forth a new kind of artist. The Stones knew and intended to be artists themselves, first as bluesmen, and then as creators of songs, albums, images, shows, films, books, and all manner of other things, in an age when being an "artist" meant being perceived and received by the public as a creative person and an aesthete. The older lines were fading.

Sweet Home Chicago

Still, making excellent art always involves getting schooled by the masters. If you want to know why the great movement of Romanticism declined after the first generation, it's because being an excellent Romantic poet requires a classical education that is then (supposedly) rejected for the sake of the power of the personal will, blah, blah, blah. As soon as that first generation of Romantics was gone (Byron, Keats, Shelley), all that was running around Europe was a bunch of narcissistic idiots who thought that being cool was all it took to be a genius.

The Stones, especially the twins and Brian Jones, *did* have masters. They were Muddy Waters and Howlin' Wolf and Willie Dixon and Little Walter and a host of others who are only now recognized for their true cultural and artistic importance. So if you want to know why Nickelback sucks, all you need to do is remember that they don't know the blues. If they did, they wouldn't have to suck. Maybe they went to school on The

Stones or Zeppelin, but that's not the right school. That's like trying to learn to paint before you know how to draw. Long before ethnomusicology was a recognized discipline, with its own intellectual standing, The Stones studied everything they could find and used their hands and feet and vocal chords to profess what they knew. Anyone who wants to know how they created what they did has to go to the same school, the University of South Chicago. The Stones wasted no time, when it became possible for them, in arranging to go and sit at the feet of their heroes at Chess.

Keith remarks that if The Stones did nothing else for America, at least they introduced us to our own music. It wasn't easy to see at first, through all the bright lights and the purple haze, that The Stones were teaching us something. For example, Joe Walsh talks about how he learned the blues from The Stones, since no one knew about the blues in the various places he grew up. Many Stones fans would tell a similar story. If Joe can play now, it's because he didn't stop with The Stones, but went back and studied the blues.

The Stones themselves always said, repeatedly, and their actions proved, what they regarded as their artistic bedrock, but the truth is, *to us* their music sounded different from Chicago or Delta blues. It's like going to a distant city and overhearing some strangers have a deep conversation about the place you're from. They see things you never noticed, and if they never mentioned the name of the place, you might not even recognize that they were talking about your hometown.

Even though I come from Memphis and grew up around some of the music The Stones professed to follow (I didn't know much about the Chicago stuff), I really couldn't *hear* what the connection was supposed to be between what The Stones were playing and what I regularly heard in Memphis. I *loved* The Stones too, from the first, but it didn't sound or feel like anything I ever heard coming out of the Delta. I knew it wasn't the Beatles, but it sounded English to me, what The Stones were doing. Like many fans, I only slowly learned to recognize how the two kinds of music were connected, and as I did begin to understand it, my appreciation for (and understanding of) the blues was transformed.

It took still longer for a lot of other Stones fans (and some still haven't made the trip home) to go back and successfully "retrieve" the Chicago and Delta blues traditions, but that train ride is worth the trouble. Led Zeppelin was so much more overt in its appropriation of that music, so it was easier to see how they did what they did. But that came later. After doing some intense ear-study, and then listening to The Stones again, especially beginning with *Beggar's Banquet*, it all starts falling into place. The Stones' music has the sort of relationship to Chicago blues that Impressionist painting has to Post-impressionism. If you look at Monet's flowers next to Van Gogh's you might agree.

Doomed to Repeat It?

My point here is that the genius of the Glimmer Twins can't be separated from its historical setting. I'm not saying history made them what they are, I'm just saying that their genius depended on getting history right and being just ahead of the spirit of the times. When the future historians of art take a look at the second half of the twentieth century, in two or three hundred years, The Stones are going to be remembered as serious artists, partly because of their cultural impact, but also because they created something of their own which has lasting aesthetic value, and that was a kind of music that hadn't existed before. They may end up being mentioned second, after the Beatles, like Mozart and Beethoven, but you could do worse than *that*. Beethoven also inspired riots by breaking the rules, and he most definitely *was* a rock star, as was Mozart, in that day. There is something to the old saw "the Beatles or The Stones?" as a way of getting to know someone, but I can't personally answer the question at all.

Not that it needs defending, but I don't think anyone ought to sneer if philosophers who specialize in aesthetics take The Stones seriously *as artists*. Critics clearly do, and sociologists, and historians, and musicologists. The engine of that original contribution to culture is the Jagger-Richards collaboration, and *as* a collaboration I think it is probably more important than any other in the same time-frame, and I don't just mean in music. I'm in a good mood, so I'm willing to be argued with about this, but I can't think of a collaborative team in any medium that is clearly and obviously *more* important, although the challengers would almost all come from the world of film

(I'd put the Coen brothers on the top of that pile, but the Coen Brothers don't come close to The Stones in cultural impact). I've been wracking my brain trying to come up with any two artists whose joint achievement raises as many philosophical questions as this one does. Maybe there's an obvious pair I haven't thought of, so help me out here if I missed something.

In The Shadows

Some of the other puzzles about the Glimmer Twins include their sometimes contradictory accounts of the collaboration itself. They agree on many points, of course, but their views of what they were doing, how it happened, who did what, well, it isn't easy to decide what to believe. How can people who were both there, and who collaborated so successfully, many thousands of times, disagree so thoroughly on what was happening, and where, and when? This practical question becomes theoretically interesting, too, when we ask, to what extent is *anyone* really a good or reliable or authoritative interpreter of his or her own experience—especially *creative* experience? I think this is the key to the whole thing: how well anyone really understands his own experiences, especially the creative ones.

Hegel thinks the artists don't understand at all what they do when they give sensuous expression to the "objective spirit" moving in history. And they don't *need to*, according to him. So he thinks history made The Stones what they were and are, and it had nothing to do with what they set out to do, or took themselves to be doing. On the other hand, Langer thinks artists do understand what they're doing and how to do it, but they are discursively "untrained," and their "difficult thoughts" resist clear formulation. These two philosophers can't both be right. Or can they?

Like some of you, I am old enough to remember when everybody thought Mick *was* the Rolling Stones. Keith was quiet and a little bit menacing, but he was just "in the band" as far as most people knew. It took the world quite some time to begin to discern what was really happening within the group. Keith just wasn't the sort to draw our particular attention to himself, and back in those days people didn't think of The Stones with the sort of seriousness and questioning we now take for granted. Their importance has come partly from their stamina at the top of the heap of pop art, and partly from our growing hind-sight. We have enough distance now to see how very important this music was. We thought it was just the soundtrack of our lives, but now we're in a position to see that the music, and these artists, were also changing our consciousness, our ideas about value, about social acceptability, about art.

So The Stones were great, but until Keith stepped out of the shadows (the last ten years or so) they weren't a puzzle that needed a solution or an enigma that demanded a theory. All we *saw* was an unusually good English rock band with an image of being rough around the edges, with a prancing, leaping fool in the front; and what we *heard* was pop songs that were edgy and irreverent. The mediator of all we saw and heard was Mick's twitchy, big-lipped, strained, in-your-faceness. Keith was, at most, a brooding, dangerous, semi-animal, whose black eyes flashed in a challenge to any and all. He didn't seem much different from the rest of the band, and he certainly didn't fit our preconceived notion of a creative force in pop culture. His name went second behind Mick's. That's what we knew.

Saviors of Rock'n'Roll

Things have really changed, nowadays. We didn't get tired of Mick, but slowly we also became more fascinated by Keith. We knew Mick was an intellectual, that he aspired to elite circles, that he navigated the full range of possible social domains from dope dealers to Knight of the Realm. (Can you believe that shit? The guy with his hand down his pants, licking Ronnie Wood on live network TV, that dude is "Sir Michael Jagger"?) He got away with it all, the court jester who is smarter than the court. Meanwhile, Keith was and is mysterious and dangerous, and he had a talent for suffering, for taking into his body all of our sins and somehow rising from the dead every night at show time, not redeemed, but certainly ready to party. Both Mick and Keith actually lived the sort of life we could barely imagine— and they survived when we were all certain they'd never grow old. Keith's talent for suffering, and for rejecting the very society Mick courted, was every bit as important as Mick's public climbing. It kept things grounded and kept them real. The saviors of rock'n'roll have to be real and they also have to be able to get behind the gilded doors in order to rip the joint.

I'm not saying we quite have the needed historical distance to begin drawing conclusions, but we wouldn't have been wondering about the Glimmer Twins twenty years ago like we do now, because so much of Keith's personality has begun bubbling to the surface. And there is something about the way that Johnny Depp, an artist everyone takes seriously, captured what we hadn't quite managed to put our fingers on. He modeled the character of Jack Sparrow—the look, the physical movements and gestures, even the accent—on Keith Richards. How could we have missed this? Keith is a sort of pirate, and that's what we had always responded to in his Stones persona. Having been shown Keith in a two-dimensional form, by Johnny Depp, we began to become more aware that this guy really had to be something else, even to have survived. It dawned on us how smart he must be, too, in spite of his earthy vocabulary. I've never met a truly good artist who was anything less than killer smart, and Mick and Keith both have that.

Keith is now pretty much out of Mick's shadow these days. His autobiography has surprised the world. We didn't really expect something so insightful, even intellectual. It is so well written that I have to wonder how much is Keith and how much is James Fox. On the other hand, I now realize I should have been wondering about the Jagger-Richards pair long ago, and I can see that I never tended to think of Keith as a creative force until Johnny Depp drew my attention in that direction. I was told by those wiser than I to pay attention to Keith, long ago, and I tried, but I now see how far behind the curve I was. It's a good thing I don't agree with Hegel about history. If he was right, I'd be totally screwed. I can't even figure out what has already happened, let alone what's going on now or coming next.

Anyhow, it's now pretty clear that the shadow Mick was casting, which was large, was also part of the total package. It wasn't important that the public know how the art was being made, and in a way, it was actually more important that we *not* know. Some of The Stones' mystique would disappear if we knew too much about the nuts and bolts. That Stones mystique is like the secret of the varnish on a Stradivarius violin. It may or may not really make the thing good, but it makes us wonder, and that's more important. I had the strange fortune to learn from my college roommate, who later became one of the sound crew for The Stones for the Steel Wheels tour, how very *un*-mysterious it all is. "All business," he reported to me some twenty years ago. "It's a show and these guys are businessmen." That sort of burst the bubble, but what did I expect? It's art, and this art is about creating illusions—that's what Langer says—and in this case, where the artist is an all-pervading public persona, it's about creating *that* illusion, a public perception, while disguising the mundane realities is as much a part of the arts as is the finish on a violin.

The Songs

But there has to be something real in the illusion, and in the case of The Stones, it's the songs that are real, which is to say, the songs are the primary illusions that give life to the rest of it. Your life is not a song, and neither is anyone else's. Rather, the songs symbolize in an artistic work, how it *feels* to be living our lives in our times. In another essay for this volume I talked about how the rhythm section contributes to the aesthetic value of The Stones' music, and I avoided talking about songwriting there because it is a very different art. Writing a song doesn't even have to involve learning how to *play* the song. Any songwriter will tell you that after a song is written, it still has to be *learned*. It's like the difference between successfully creating perfect pigments and learning to paint with them. Certain kinds of changes will occur in the learning process that are finishing the work of writing the song, but the collaborative process between the Twins, as it originates in songwriting, is a different process.

Beginning with *Aftermath*, we began to see the credit Jagger-Richards after nearly all the songs, and The Stones stepped into the company of the Beatles at that point as creative forces, more than just glitzy personas. That was a huge step into history. It made it obvious then, as now, that these guys intended to say something of their own. If they hadn't made the move into being songwriters, The Stones would have faded after two or three years, along with many other groups whose names now only show up in trivia questions.

Andrew Oldham, their "producer" is credited with putting Mick and Keith together and insisting they write songs. I would guess that he had an eye for talent, and he had scoped out the situation and saw where the creative energy in the band was. Long before we could tell which of The Stones was Keith, and point him out, Oldham had worked out that the pairing of Mick and Keith was his own personal retirement plan. And maybe he saw even more than that. Who knows? What people saw on stage was a presentation, in highly organized space and for very limited time, of something quite real that was happening in a complex and interesting way back behind the scenes.

But the outcome wasn't just forty or fifty songs that were works of cultural genius—and with the self-destruction of the fine arts, these songs became works of cultural genius, historically contextualized, since that is all the genius that was left. There were, in addition to the songs, a dozen albums that were works of genius. And there were shows and tours of cultural genius. In the latter category, it is really hard to imagine cultural events that would or could ever top the great tours between Steel Wheels and A Bigger Bang. The Rolling Stones perfected the "tour" as an art form, which wouldn't even have occurred to me as a *possibility*, frankly.

Beyond that, we have the personas of Mick and Keith as art forms. Unlike so many of today's pop icons, who have to re-invent their personas every three years or so (Marilyn to Cher to Madonna, or Michael Jackson, et al.), Mick and Keith each worked on perfecting the one persona they had initiated in 1962, and have found that plumbing the depths of what they *really are* is better than trying to make up something superficial and new. That "something real" is the way they write the songs, which is the basic building block of the whole shebang. Keith describes this process at the time the band was working on *Exile on Main Street*, where the twins were writing the material as they were recording it, which they have done many times. People would be coming to the studio, expecting to record, but the songs didn't exist yet. Mick or Keith might be tempted to panic when they realized they had nothing to offer the other studio performers, who might be expecting ready-made material straight from the gods, when in reality it could come only from Mick and Keith. But the twins knew they could come up with something new every day or two—even if it was just the bare bones of a riff, it would be something to go on. And as the band tried to shape this elemental idea, the song would just fall into place:

Once you're on a roll with the first few chords, the first idea of the rhythm, you can figure out other things, like does it need a bridge in the middle, later. It was living on a knife edge as far as that's concerned. There was no preparation. . . . The idea is to make the bare bones of a riff, *snap the drums in and see what happens*. It was the immediacy of it that in retrospect made it even more interesting. There was no time for too much reflection, for plowing the field twice. It was "It goes like this" and see what comes out. And this is when you realize that with a good band, you only really need a little spark of an idea, and before the evening's over, it will be a beautiful thing. (*Life*, pp. 305–06, my italics)

The secret, then, to the creative power of the Glimmer Twins is that the dialectic between Mick and Keith just builds in its tension until Charlie kicks in. I don't mean to pull a cheap one on you, but the twins aren't enough by themselves to pull off what The Stones did. It would be cheating to end the chapter this way, except that you can keep reading and I'll try to explain in another chapter how this rhythm section of The Stones channels the creative energy to ground and makes it rock. The works of art in question originate with Keith and Mick, but their genius lies beyond the dialectic and in the group. What Mick is to Keith, or what Keith is to Mick, is the left and right ventricles of the heart of rock'n'roll, exchanging blood between sixty and 160 times a minute, but the body that dances to that beat is the band.

2
My Dinner with Mick

JERE SURBER

When the Stones played Denver in the early 1980s, a local
Moroccan restaurant hosted an after-hours post-concert dinner
for the band. I knew the owner of the restaurant and he invited
me. Completely buying into the public image of the Stones as
rock's original 'bad boys,' I expected that there would be an
orgy of fawning groupies, raucous and rude behavior, alcohol
and drugs in abundance maybe a fight or two. It turned out
that my expectations could not have been more off-base.

Of The Stones, only Keith and Mick attended. Keith sat at
the other end of the table, and he seemed to mumble a lot in his
heavy accent. He just seemed tired. But both Mick and Keith
were very polite (in a rather 'British' sort of way, it struck me)
and dinner came off entirely without incident (and as for
groupies, Keith and Mick were accompanied only by a few managers, road staff, and local promoters). Now I don't remember
all the details of the conversation I had with Mick, but it struck
me that offstage he was exactly what you would expect of a
middle-class lad who had attended good English schools and
studied at the prestigious London School of Economics. He was
slightly reserved, thoughtful, considerate, witty, and seemed
quite interested in my work as a philosophy teacher. He had
interesting things to say about various types of music, both as
art and, especially, as business. And, of course, he had some
entertaining 'stories from the road' to share.

Ever since, I've been trying to wrap my mind around these
different Mick Jaggers—the one I met and talked to at this dinner, the rooster-like frontman for the world's greatest rock

band and all that they symbolically represent (groupies and drugs, again), and the "Mr. Jagger" (as the local concert promoters called him) revered as one of the must successful businessmen in rock. Some of the puzzle pieces fit, since money, drugs, and groupies often go hand in hand. But I remain puzzled about the violence that had long become associated with rock and, through Altamont, with The Stones themselves. How could a 'nice bloke' like Mick be at home in a rock'n'roll culture that was so often black, blue, and bloody?

The Death of the Woodstock Nation

Altamont, of course, was a bad scene. On December 6th, 1969, only four months after the birth of the Woodstock Nation with its credo of Peace and Love, the Rolling Stones played the closing set of the Altamont Speedway Free Festival. Originally planned to be "Woodstock West," the concert was a fiasco from the beginning. It was moved from San Francisco's Golden Gate Park to the Sears Point Raceway, and then again, at the last minute, to the Altamont Speedway, a venue that lacked most of the basic amenities required for 300,000 festivarians, including trained security personnel, enough toilets, and adequate water supplies. Concertgoers remembered the vibe as being 'ugly,' with crushes at the front of the stage, fights in the crowd, bad drugs circulating, and projectiles flying overhead and occasionally onto the stage. To make matters worse, the Hell's Angels, over the protest of the Grateful Dead's Jerry Garcia, had been 'paid' $500 worth of beer to provide security for the area around the stage. Things subsequently became so violent that the Dead refused to play their set, scheduled just before that of the Stones, and left the scene. By the end of the concert, four young concert-goers had died and uncounted others had been injured. (Much of this, by the way, was documented in the Albert Maysles film *Gimme Shelter*.)

It's probably not fair to blame The Stones for this. They were only a group of musicians playing a gig and most of the bad decisions were made by their management team. But they were the main force behind it, its major attraction, and their reputation suffered most of the consequences. By most accounts, the final crescendo of violence commenced about the time the Stones launched into "Sympathy for the Devil" (their third number), which they had to interrupt more than once, admonish the crowd to "cool it" and stop shoving, and then restart. Then, soon after they started "Under My Thumb," the eighteen-year-old Meredith Hunter pulled a gun and was quickly beaten and stabbed to death by a contingent of Hell's Angels. The Stones themselves were unaware of the Hunter's death and continued their set. You can see them first viewing the footage of all this in *Gimme Shelter*. By the looks on Mick's and Charlie Watts's faces, it's clear that they never wanted anything like this to have happened. But the popular imagination (fed by songs like Don McLean's "American Pie" and *Rolling Stone* magazine's coverage[1]) came to see Altamont as an orgy of drug-driven violence presided over and egged on by a band that 'sympathized' with 'his satanic majesty' and glorified aggression, domination, and violence.

Before and After Altamont

Before Altamont, rock'n'roll had enjoyed a certain innocence when it came to matters of overt physical violence. While rock had its detractors from the beginning, the only violence usually attributed to it was a sort of cultural affront to the dominant 'happy days' sensibilities of the American 1950s. Not only were its predominant themes teenage love, longing, and loss, together with the beach, school, and soda fountain, but viewers could tune in every Saturday to view well-dressed teens (even representing various races) mingling, dancing, and enjoying themselves on Dick Clark's *American Bandstand*. Changes in society at large, especially the ever-escalating war in Southeast Asia, the Civil Rights Movement, and the assassination of several public figures, confronted rock with a 'culture of violence' that initially helped to solidify its own role and self-image as a principal agent of the 'Counterculture'. Woodstock, with its message of Peace and Love, represented the zenith of rock's own self-image as intrinsically innocent and non-violent. As Joni Mitchell's anthem proclaimed, "We are stardust / we are golden / and we've got to get ourselves back to the Garden."

---

[1] "The Rolling Stones Altamont Disaster: Let it Bleed," by Lester Bangs and others, *Rolling Stone* (January 30th, 1970).

Altamont shattered this undoubtedly naive self-image once and for all. No longer could such former countercultural heroes as the Hell's Angels be viewed as our 'barbarian brothers'; no longer could rock bands be regarded as "jus' singin' and playin' our guitars"; no longer could rock concerts be seen as safe, innocent occasions for young people to blow off some libidinal steam. Rather, it became clear to most that the idea of a peaceful and non-violent Counterculture was "just a dream some of us had," that the Counterculture, and rock music itself, harbored in its own midst the same potentials for violence that it had previously attributed to the 'violent other', the culture that it had earlier rejected. After Altamont, the door opened for rock not only to realize its own implication in violence-infested institutions and practices but to adopt its own increasingly violent themes and ways of expressing them. Punk, death metal, racist forms of Southern rock, and gangsta rap were some of the more notorious offspring ultimately spawned at Altamont.

Violence and Philosophy

When philosophers of the past have discussed violence, their approaches may seem naïve, faced with events like those at Altamont. Plato held that violence is one among many results of the failure of human reason to control passion. Viewed in this way, violence is exceptional, a sort of sporadic aberration that can, in principle at least, be remedied by more determined exertions on the part of reason. Directly opposed to this is an older attitude, already present in Greek mythology, Homer, and some pre-Socratic philosophers and revived in modern times by such figures as Goethe, Hegel, and Nietzsche. This line of thought takes violence to be a fundamental and ineliminable aspect of the universe or, for later thinkers, of the unfolding of human history. A third view, characteristic of Enlightenment thought, is that nature's violence is an 'inconvenience' (to borrow Locke's term) which can be controlled and perhaps even eliminated through a combination of political legislation, the institutions of civil society (especially 'moral education'), and economic progress.

Do any of these approaches help to make sense of Altamont and my puzzle about Mick Jagger? It's pretty clear, I think, that they don't. But in more recent times, beginning with Marx and

Freud, and throughout the (itself very violent!) twentieth century, violence has emerged as a central philosophical theme. Especially valuable is the work of Slavoj Žižek, himself something like a rock star in philosophy who draws crowds wherever he goes (see the movie *Žižek!* from 2005, and Žižek's book *Violence* from 2010).

In *Violence*, Žižek borrows a fundamental idea from the French philosopher Jacques Lacan that our experience of the world and the relationships in it can be organized into three "orders." First, there is "the imaginary" order, which has to be understood literally: it is that dimension of our experience that involves *images* that picture or represent things, qualities of things, other people, and even ourselves. It includes sensations, perceptions, memories, and thoughts (which may equally be 'true' or 'false,' 'actual' or 'imagined' in the more ordinary senses of these terms) such as my memories of Mick as the person with whom I had dinner and conversation. It follows from this that the Imaginary is, in a sense, always subjective, private, and personal, since only I have full and direct access to my own impressions, perceptions, and memories.

Then there is the "Symbolic" order of language, symbols, and the culture in which they circulate. Unlike the "imaginary," the Symbolic order is public, shared, and 'intersubjective'. For instance, my preconceived idea of 'Mick Jagger the Rock Star' was a product of intersecting symbols I had seen in magazine articles, album covers, concert films, and conversations I'd had about Mick and The Stones.

The Imaginary and Symbolic interact and work with each other. Most of my story about meeting Mick, even though I was describing my personal experience, is a complex product of my subjective images and the public, intersubjective codes that you and I have learned to employ beginning in early childhood. This combination of the Imaginary and the Symbolic orders is what makes it possible for me to tell my story in terms that you and I understand.

Equally important, what you and I understand in the Imaginary and Symbolic realms, whether we're talking about Mick or anything else, is never 'the full story'. This is where Lacan's third order, "the Real," comes in. The Real is literally the 'unthinkable' and 'unsayable'—that which is excluded by the Symbolic order and its codes. It might seem strange to call what we *don't* know and talk about more "real" than what we do, but as we'll see this is how Žižek's explanation of violence, which is very "real," is going to work. The idea is that although 'the Real' can never present itself directly, either in experience or language, we sometimes encounter it and feel its force, especially at those traumatic points at which our usual cultural codes break down or rupture. Zizek cites 9/11 as an example. Prior to its occurrence, such an event was, for most Americans, unthinkable. Žižek says that, prior to the attacks, it fell into Donald Rumsfeld's notorious category of 'unknown unknowns'.

For a Marxist philosopher like Žižek, it's not surprising that most of what belongs to the Real, or what is most interesting about it, is economic. For most of us, Žižek would say, the actual operation of the global capitalist economic system that shapes our world of experience is something that lies outside the scope of what we ordinarily think about or are able to understand or articulate. Nor, typically, do we think about the broader consequences of global capitalism such as poverty, homelessness, and malnutrition. Still, without the steady operation of this economic 'Real', none of us would be who or where we are today. Without the machinery of record companies, for example, Mick Jagger would likely have given up rock long ago and would now be retired and playing with his grandchildren in a nondescript middle-class London suburb, like countless others his age.

Violence, Rock, and the Rolling Stones

Žižek says that violence can occur in each of the three orders, and to understand it fully in any specific case we have to distinguish its different manifestations and see whether and how they interact. In the Imaginary realm of private experience, there are all kinds of violence and disruption, most of which are connected to our desires. If Žižek had written the song, it would have been "You can't *ever* get what you want . . ." and when you can't get what you need, the resulting frustration can lead to overt physical violence. When the Stones sing, "Don't play with me, 'cause you're playin' with fire," they directly evoke this psychic link between desire and potential violence. Or if "Little Susie" continues to send "dead flowers" (refuses to satisfy the desire of the song's author), the singer vows, in an unnervingly threatening final line, that he "won't forget to put roses on your grave."

The Stones fast became familiar with one kind of violence in the early 1960s. In his memoir *Life*, Keith devotes a lot of time to "the power of teenage females of thirteen, fourteen, fifteen, when they're in a gang. . . They nearly killed me" (p. 139). "If you got caught in a frenzied crowed of them," he explained, "it's hard to express how frightening they could be . . . this unstoppable, killer wave of lust and desire, or whatever it is" (p. 140).

Purely symbolic violence, on the other hand, remains within this realm of symbols and codes, but can still be destructive and hurtful. It can be deployments of words or other sorts of signs that tend to harm, injure, or degrade persons either by further reinforcing the social distinctions already operative in the Symbolic order or, sometimes, by creating new ones. This can take many forms, including overt 'hate speech' (for instance, the 'N-word' Mick quotes in "Sweet Black Angel" on *Exile*); more or less explicit stereotyping in terms of race, ethnicity, gender, or objectification like "babe" or "bitch."

Looked at in this way, the Stones have consistently employed Symbolic violence in their lyrics. The two general types are the objectification of women and racial stereotyping, especially of African Americans (in, for example, "Under My Thumb" and "Brown Sugar"). But these lyrics, you could say, are "only rock'n'roll" and do nothing to explain the kind of violence witnessed at Altamont.

Both these Imaginary and Symbolic kinds of violence, however, remain ever connected to, and enabled by, the Real, whose operations are usually cloaked by the Imaginary and the Symbolic. While we think that a rock star's getting mauled on a street by violent fans is just an aspect, however unfortunate, of relations between musicians and their fans, you can't understand this violence apart from the underlying economics of popular culture. Girls weren't attacking Keith and Mick when they were just members of an obscure blues band trying to make a go of it in London, but once they were on the charts, being promoted by Decca, everything had changed. Suddenly, Keith Richards himself became a spectacle within the Symbolic order—"Look, that's Keith Richards!!!"—that obscures the 'Real' source of violence and renders it, under 'normal' conditions, 'unimaginable' and 'inexpressible'. I'm guessing that few of us have ever thought, in the middle of a rock concert, that, in the end, it's really all about transferring the small bits of cash from millions of fans to the accounts of a few people who run a large record corporation and thereby become fabulously wealthy.

So, Back to Altamont . . .

At Altamont, each of these kinds of violence seems to have been present. The concert itself was free and would not itself generate revenue for The Stones or the owner of Altamont Speedway. But, according to Ian Inglis (in *Performance and Popular Music*), that does not mean they did not hope to profit from the festival. The Stones, who did not play Woodstock, would get credit and counter-cultural prestige for their generosity by playing a free concert near San Francisco, the acknowledged spiritual home of the counterculture. Dick Carter, the owner of the Altamont Speedway, was eager to make a deal with The Stones' attorney Melvin Belli (much of these negotiations are filmed in *Gimme Shelter*) and bring the festival to Altamont. That way he would get worldwide publicity for his speedway, usually in the shadow of the better-known Sears Point Raceway (who backed out of the concert over a dispute about the rights to the Maysles brothers' film and the revenues it was likely to generate.)

If those collective desires for profits of various kinds made the ill-suited Altamont Speedway the venue for the concert, there are also the desires—the frustrated desires—of the three hundred thousand music fans. They endured the lack of facilities, the cold night air as The Stones waited hours to take the stage (because Bill Wyman had missed the band's helicopter ride to the speedway), and a hilly geography that encouraged fans to gravitate down toward the stage and into the Hell's Angels that were guarding it. Judging from *Gimme Shelter*, one of the most striking acts of violence resulting from this was purely symbolic: a Hell's Angel's motorcycle that was parked in the middle of the crowd was toppled (inadvertently, it seems) and that seemed to make the Angels more abusive and agitated as the night wore on (there are few greater insults to a motorcycle owner than to 'mess with his bike'). To this day, observers dispute the symbolic politics between the Angels and the crowd, the Angels and The Stones (who had Hell's Angels present for their concert in Hyde Park in the days after Brian

Jones's death), and, of course, the symbolism of race. Meredith Hunter was one of the few black men in the audience and, according to his girlfriend, was growing more agitated and angry about the Angels before the fatal encounter.

Judging from the framework that Lacan and Žižek provide, there is no one simple explanation for the violence at Altamont or the bad-rap that The Stones got in its wake. But that very complexity does help solve the puzzle of having such a peaceful, civilized meal with two very nice guys who supposedly killed "the Sixties" at Altamont. Obviously the Stones neither wished nor intended the violence to occur or to continue— "People!" Mick implored multiple times from the stage "What war are we fighting?" and "Please, just chill out." But that does not mean as artists trying to make a living they were not "playing with fire" by crafting music that made them high priests of excessive desire that, if the conditions were right, could flame higher than they ever expected.

In fact, that could be what we like most about The Stones. By obsessively and maybe even consciously highlighting some of the more excessive and neurotic elements already present in our Symbolic order, they took rock (and countless of its fans) in directions that they might not otherwise have gone. But we wanted to go there. It's only rock'n'roll, and "we like it" because it skirts limits and plays with fire. If The Stones and rock'n'roll only sang us "love songs so divine," they wouldn't have either the appeal or the financial success that they have enjoyed— and we wouldn't "like it" nearly as much. But we also can't forget that, in indulging our transgressive desires, we're "playin' with fire."

Who really killed the Sixties? It may just have been you and me.

3
The Beggar's Genius

KEEGAN GOODMAN

The sexiest song on The Rolling Stones' 1968 album *Beggars Banquet* has got to be "Parachute Woman." The song opens with Keith Richards delivering a standard blues lick on the acoustic guitar. Two bars later the snare, electric guitar (also played by Keith, at least on the album), and bass have joined in. Then Jagger's vocals, mumbled, coarse. Its allure is its indecipherability, its attitude of refusal to be clear, its license to be an instrument or sound among the others. The song was recorded on cassette and double tracked. The thin tape does what it can to hold all this sprawling roughness. The result is a track that is not merely unpolished—it's dirty and flagrant.

That immediacy fits the content, too. Our pleasure is wrapped up in the familiarity of the standard blues rhythm, in the almost immaterial electric guitars haunting the edge of the tape and the understated percussion. Jagger's pleasure is likewise wrapped up in the ease of song, as he tells us that his "heavy throbber's itching just to lay a solid rhythm down." The song has a job to do.

The job, of course, is getting the singer laid. "Parachute Woman," the singer pleads, "won't you land on me tonight?" Keith's guitar, Charlie Watts's drum, Wyman's faint upright bass, Brian's harmonica—all this music also wants to "lay a solid rhythm down," but not because any of The Stones are particularly concerned about Mick's sex life. Maybe it's as simple as this: they are making a rock'n'roll song, and a rock'n'roll song does not need ornament or innovation.

This is why "Parachute Woman" speaks against a popular view of art, that it works by adding something new to the tradition that it comes from. Is the pleasure we experience in "Parachute Woman" explained by the newness of the song or its elements? It's an original song, in the commonplace sense of the word. The credits name Keith Richards and Mick Jagger as the authors, and the musical parts, however homespun, were thought up by the rest of the band. But can we really call it new without trivializing our sense of newness? The rhythm guitar, the harmonica parts—these do not diverge in any important way from what a music historian would recognize as the song's lineage. In the chord progression, there is no fooling around with clever harmonic surprises that The Beatles, the anti-Stones, liked so much (think: "Good Day Sunshine").

There's nothing unexpected in "Parachute Woman." Even the lyrics, which are so wonderfully debauched, are just Mick Jagger's take on generic blues and not some innovation or new style of music. The image of the parachute woman landing is a little strange, but compared to The Beatles' trim little tunes about colorful submarines and fields of fruit, it's earthbound and ordinary. So "Parachute Woman" is an original song in only the most superficial sense. We would have a hard time saying what it adds to its own past. I like it for other reasons. In fact, I like it because it doesn't even try to add anything new.

As I Watch You Leaving Me, You Pack My Peace of Mind

Repeating the past is not as simple as it seems. The boys running the rock'n'roll circus knew this, and I think this knowledge stirs some of the feeling in another song on *Beggars Banquet,* "No Expectations." In this song, the singer asks to be taken to the station and put on a train. Things have ended badly, and he "has no expectations to pass through here again." Fortunes—both in love and money—have been gained and lost, and never in his "sweet short life," has he felt this bad. The subtle reminder of the singer's youth seems almost prescient:

Our love was like the water
that splashes on a stone.
Our love is like our music:
it's here and then it's gone.

It's difficult to listen to these words and not hear, just beneath the surface, what would become a self-referential observation. *Beggars Banquet* will be Brian Jones's last contribution to a studio recording, and in this song he is masterly with the slide guitar. In the televised version of the Rock and Roll Circus, we can see a glimmer of his mania. The image of water and a stone will become more bizarre when, a year later, Brian Jones drowns in a swimming pool. More broadly, the Sixties were nearing their pinnacle, and all the idealism and benevolence that had arisen in the youth of that generation would be forfeited at Altamont in December 1969. The Rolling Stones were at the height of their powers then, and it's easy to imagine that their fate was bound up with the larger movements of their generation. History—whether art history, political history or personal history—is such that no one will "pass through here again." You could even argue that history rewards those who don't expect to do so.

Certainly The Stones had to abandon their original expectation that they would remain a rhythm and blues band playing covers of Chuck Berry and Bo Diddley tunes. It was inevitable that they would have to write their own songs if they wanted to make it big. One afternoon, when The Stones were rehearsing at Studio 51 Club, in walked John Lennon and Paul McCartney. They'd heard from Andrew Oldham that The Stones were having trouble coming up with a song. Being the serious creative types, Lennon and Paul—"who are by that time very much into hustling songs"—sat down to the piano and played a bit of something they'd been working on. Mick and Keith liked it, and so Lennon and McCartney wrote the middle eight bars, finishing what would be the Rolling Stones' first hit "I Wanna Be Your Man." As their popularity increased, the issue of writing an original song became more urgent. Shortly after recording their first LP, which consisted of all covers of American rhythm and blues tunes and rock'n'roll hits, Mick Jagger was quoted in a newspaper as saying "Can you imagine

a British-composed R&B number?—it just wouldn't make it."
Shortly after this their manager Andrew Oldham locked Keith
and Mick in the kitchen and refused to let them out until they
had written a song.[1]

This complicates our depiction of rock'n'roll as a thing that
gets better the more it stays the same. "No Expectations" seems
to say that the past is not always a given. It's not just that the
music gets boring; it becomes irrelevant, left behind by the
march of time. "No Expectations" seems to suggest that the
dominant view of art is right, that a musician strives to make
meaningful variations on the material that preceded him—just
enough to keep his stuff sounding new—but at the same time
remains true to his origins.

The problem is that this view leaves us entirely in the dark
about what constitutes meaningful variation. How are we to
know whether a song matters? What exactly allows us to recognize a new, innovative arrangement of chords in a very finite
schema (there're only twelve notes, after all)? Does the slight
shift in emphasis when Jagger sings the line "pain in my heart,
won't let me sleep," really differ from Otis Redding's singing
those same lines? Does such a slight alteration justify our calling it new or just an imitation?

What's Puzzling You Is the Nature of My Game

The eighteenth-century philosopher Immanuel Kant faced a
closely related problem in thinking about aesthetics. In his
Critique of Judgment, he argues that works of art can and do
in fact come into the world that are at once genuinely new and
intelligible to audiences by virtue of their relationship to the
past. This might seem obvious, but let me explain the problem
Kant is trying to solve, since it is directly applicable to the
problem of originality and newness in rock'n'roll.

For something to be genuinely new, Kant explained, it must
be related to what has come before it in a special way. A new
work must have some foundation, some context in order to be
understood. There are certain rules of composition, for

---

[1] Stanley Booth, *The True Adventures of the Rolling Stones* (A Cappella, 2000), pp. 139, 147.

instance. A song may be made of verse and chorus, comprised of melodies and harmonies, structured according to the key signature. While the rules for art-making change radically over the next two centuries of music history since the time of Kant, the requirement always remains. In other words, while the rules themselves are changing and historical, the need for something to guide and regulate art is written into art making. Kant sees this as the "foundation by means of which a product that is to be called artistic is first represented as possible." The noise that comes from tuning a guitar, for instance, we would not call a song because it isn't being made with any of the rules of composition in mind. Its material, its notes, might be identical with the material of a song, but it is not properly a song since it was not meant to be understood against a context of song-making. A musical composition, then, relies on some fixed standard established by tradition, by previous endeavors of songwriters. That doesn't mean it has to submit wholly to those patterns, only that it must be understood in reference to them.

An artwork that follows the rules too well is no good. This is especially true in rock'n'roll. Think of the innumerable covers of "Bouncing Ball," of the lackluster bands Keith was thinking of when he imagined those pathetic boys standing on stage in their "shitty little suits." Sure, they may have varied the song to fit the demands of the occasion, whether it was a night club or a debutante ball, but it would be a mistake to call these variations constitutive of a new thing. Nor does the work of the studio musicians, who might be able to execute a song perfectly and add their own little charm to it, deserve to be called new. We're looking for a more robust meaning of newness, and so was Kant, one that is something other than the "predisposition of skill for that which can be learned in accordance with some rule."

To solve his problem, Kant calls "genius" to the stage. Now in contemporary usage, this word is vague and over-used. It's sometimes meant as a term of praise. Other times it refers to a person who has achieved some high score on an intelligence test. In Kant's day, too, the word had all kinds of connotations that he didn't care about. He invoked the term 'genius' for the specific reason of explaining how a meaningful artwork can come into being.

For his theory to be coherent, two conditions must be upheld. The first is that the new work of art must be made according to some rule. The second is that the work must not be determined simply in accordance with some rule. Kant's solution is that, in the person of the genius, the rule comes from nature and is given to art. "Nature," as Kant means it here, is what I have been calling "the past" that determines what sort of thing rock'n'roll is. Nature, then, can be understood as the raw material there at the start, before anyone adds anything to it. Kant believes that the artist has an "inborn productive faculty" that itself "belongs to nature." So when the artist uses this faculty to make a work of art, the rule that makes the work of art intelligible has come from nature.

Many artists would agree (even if they've never read Kant). We often hear artists, in describing their creative process, speak of some point in the process at which the work starts to make its *own* demands, starts to direct the hand of the painter, for instance, or starts to tell the songwriter what the middle-eight needs to be, or can *only* be. This is what artists mean when they say, "and then the thing just wrote itself."

For Kant, it amounts to saying that there is some talent that the artist can summon but can't fully explain or control. The source of this talent lies beyond the reach of the artist's intellect. This talent "cannot itself describe or indicate scientifically how it brings its products into being," he writes. And, "the author of a product that he owed to his genius does not know himself how the ideas for it came to him."[2] The artist might be able to give poetic or impressionistic explanations of how he works, but he cannot say anything substantial or scientific about his process. If he were able to, then the art would fail its concept, since its concept is to be produced free from a determining rule.

This is Kant's answer to what we value most about art, what sets it apart from other kinds of creations. The engineer might say, "Here's the plan, here's what works," and whether or not he succeeds depends on how well he sticks to the plan. You could say the same for the businessman, who understands products that will satisfy the market's demands. Both the product of the engineer and of the businessman are products of creativity. But they are determined by a design that can be fully

---

[2] *Critique of the Power of Judgment* (Cambridge University Press, 2002), p. 187.

articulated in a systematic way. Their form that they take in the world is already decided by the idea they are supposed to fulfill. This is not so with art. Art, in the hands of the genius, is free from such determining constraints.

The Beggars at the Banquet

It may seem now that the Kant hasn't solved anything at all regarding The Rolling Stones or "Parachute Woman." The genius for Kant is, if nothing else, an artist who generates (hence the name). "Originality," he says, "must be a primary characteristic" of the genius (p. 186). But The Rolling Stones, from their inception, were decidedly unoriginal. The R&B tunes Keith and Brian dug up to perform in front of those audiences of febrile teeny-boppers may have been obscure, but they were not new. The Rolling Stones are famous, or infamous, for stealing what other people have made, songs that others have written, singing styles that others had invented, lyrics and melodies and guitar licks that were solidly ingrained in the rock'n'roll mythic past. The Rolling Stones seem like beggars at the banquet table of music history.

What is it that a beggar brings to the table? He brings a mouth, an appetite. He has nothing of his own to bring. His blue jeans have holes in them, his "shirt's all torn." The reason the Rolling Stones are the greatest rock'n'roll band is precisely because of what they have brought to the table: their bodies, themselves.

The genius of The Stones, in Kant's sense of the word, is that they have altered the aesthetic object in question, music, in an important way by becoming a constitutive part of that object. We can't think about the music of The Stones and, at the same time, think about the individual members, their bodies, Mick's maniacal dancing, Keith's trademark slouching, Bill's statuesque motionlessness, and so on. This is one reason why they so transfixed their teenage fans and made their parents very, very nervous. "Would you let your daughter go with a Rolling Stone?" the papers famously asked.

Kant's conception of genius explains how the Rolling Stones themselves, their bodies, entered the frame of their music and merged with it. It is not a coincidence that we think of the rock-'n'roll spirit as natural to the boys in the band. Keith Richards fascinates me because he's so natural—not merely a natural at guitar (we can say that about a lot of studio musicians, or even the charmless Eric Clapton), but that he's got a natural rock-'n'roll essence. It gets to the heart of the matter that we can see this: we look to his person, his character, his body and how he acts on the stage, in the studio, and at home after a tour when he starts drinking because he gets bored, waiting for the next time he and his telecaster can take the stage.

You might say that any rock band merge themselves with their work in this way, but that's not true. What comes to mind when you think "Strawberry Fields Forever"? It's probably not John Lennon himself, in the same way that Keith and Mick flash before your eyes the moment someone says "Brown Sugar" or "Jumpin' Jack Flash." A self-styled artist like Lennon wanted his art to have a life of its own, as if it were bigger and more important than him. He was sincere about this. But The Stones aren't sincere. They know that sincerity is the real enemy of rock'n'roll. It's appropriate for bloodshed: the violence of Altamont, of Charlie Manson's girls, of Vietnam—these are things a person can be sincere about. The Rolling Stones know, in a way that Lennon never did, that it's only rock'n'roll, there to be liked, to be loved, here and then gone.

The Rolling Stones are not sincere. But that doesn't mean they don't mean what they say. They're forced to mean what they say, because they have brought themselves to the banquet with nothing but their bodies. An interviewer once famously asked Mick whether or not he had gotten any satisfaction. I want to assume the answer and put the question like this: Why can't Mick get any satisfaction? It's not because he has a legion of erotic needs, nor because he lacks money or material things. No, Mick Jagger is barred from getting any satisfaction so long as he is telling us in his song that he "can't get no satisfaction." We are forced to take his word for it, and so is he. The work, what has always been thought of as the song, is now partly the person who sings it. Mick can't get satisfaction not because the world has refused to conform to his idea of satisfaction but because his body, his identity has conformed to the demand of the song: he will not be able to get satisfaction so long as he's singing that song, no matter what the world gives him.

This is not a psychological claim; it's a philosophical claim, meaning there's some necessity that comes from the ideas themselves: to say that Mick and Keith and company are the greatest rock'n'roll band is to say that rock'n'roll is the kind of thing whose art-objectivity has expanded to include the Rolling Stones themselves.

What Can a Poor Boy Do?

I think this is why we love The Stones and their music so much. But it also might be what puts them out of our reach. I recently saw a tape of The Stones, in the early days, 1965, on *Ready, Steady, Go!* just months after "I Can't Get No (Satisfaction)" had hit the charts. Their set began with some covers from earlier albums, and they played them well, with verve and with a little irony. It was striking how close the audience was to the stage, to The Stones themselves. The teenagers swooned beneath Jagger, some screaming, some chuckling self-consciously when the camera was on them. The Stones went through "Good Thing Going," and "That's How Strong My Love Is." Then Keith struck the first note of "Satisfaction" and a visible change came over both the crowd. Whatever distance had previously separated them from The Stones had to be overcome. But none of the kids in the audience knew exactly how to do this. And so the song was played. Mick toyed with the camera and girls. Brian Jones luxuriated in the attention. There was a shot of Watts, rocking slightly back and forth as he beat out the quarter-note snare, focused, classy, poised. The television camera panned out and the credits appeared on the screen, over the action, over the face of Mick Jagger and over the transfixed audience.

Those credits, I could easily imagine, pointed to the genius of this band in a way that would have frustrated and enthralled any teenager sitting in a 1960s living room watching this. They broke the link between the viewer who wanted to be there, in the audience, near to the band and the growing frenzy of "(I Can't Get No) Satisfaction" and returned him or her to their own domesticity, their own ordinariness there in some humdrum living room, with no cameras, no money, no screaming girls, only the glowing black and white screen, and the unreality and utter attraction of the figures framed there.

4

You Probably Think This Chapter's about You

CHARLES TALIAFERRO AND THERESE COTTER

When is a person vain? Here's one possibility: How about when he promotes himself as a sexed-up, crazed, macho-chauvinistic, street-fighting, Satanic, sometimes sadistic and sometimes seducing (and sometimes both, and for both genders), spoiled rock'n'roll star, who wants a girl to be under his (sticky) thumb? And he wants cameras rolling the whole time.

You know who we're talking about because nearly everyone recognizes the persona Mick Jagger has created. This was how he looked to Sonny Barger, the Hell's Angels' lifelong spokesman, who saw Jagger and the band up close at the Altamont Free Concert. Barger said,

> The crowd had waited all day to see the Stones perform, and they were sitting in their trailers acting like prima donnas. The crowd was getting angry; there was a lot of drinking and drugging going on. It was starting to get dark.
>
> After sundown the Stones still wouldn't come out to play. Mick and the band's egos seemed to want the crowd agitated and frenzied. They wanted them to beg, I guess. Then their instruments were set up. It took close to another hour before the band finally agreed to come out.[1]

According to Stanley Booth, in *The True Adventures of the Rolling Stones* (A Cappella, 2000), one reason The Stones took the stage at Altamont so late was that Bill Wyman had missed

---

[1] Barger cited in John Strausbaugh, *Rock 'Til You Drop* (Verso, 2003), p. 77.

his helicopter ride to the raceway. But whether or not that's true, Altamont only added to Jagger's reputation as a guy who mainlines egomania. Don McLean's blockbuster "American Pie," for example, popularized the image of Jagger on stage at Altamont as the devil himself, basking in the spotlight, and even "laughing with delight" at that concert's tragedies:

> no angel born in hell could break that Satan's spell
> And as the flames climbed high into the night
> To light the sacrificial rite,
> I saw Satan laughing with delight
> The day the music died.

Those who've seen Jagger perform live know that he seems possessed by the goal of keeping all eyes on him. Mike Doughty recalled seeing Jagger at Shea Stadium in 1990, running back and forth across the stage "for no reason that I could see, other than to say, 'Look at me! I can still run!' And yet he sold out Shea Stadium, what, eight nights in a row?"[2]

Many believe that Jagger is the target of Carly Simon's 1972 hit "You're So Vain," a conclusion that seems initially plausible because Jagger can be heard singing vocals during the chorus. (Who better to announce Mick's over-the-top vanity than Mick himself?). But Simon to this day keeps the secret about who was behind her lyrical laceration of a self-indulgent ex-lover (according to Wikipedia, the odds-on favorite seems to be Warren Beatty).

Two Jaggers

But are these and countless other reports and legends really the signs of vanity? There's another way to see and appreciate Mick Jagger if you think about him from the perspective of the great nineteenth-century philosopher Friedrich Nietzsche. The key idea is that Jagger may be treating his life and himself as a work of art.

He certainly wasn't born "Mick Jagger" as we think of him now, so it had to come from somewhere. Early in his career, he

---

[2] *Rock 'Til You Drop*, p. 238.

even seemed to downplay any heroic or romantic conception of his musicianship and talent. In the 1960s, this former student at the London School of Economics said he saw the Rolling Stones as a "business": "I came into music just because I wanted the bread. . . . I looked around and this seemed to be the only way to make the kind of bread I wanted. It worked, and I don't treat it as a joke. It's my business."[3] Decades later, in 1992, Jagger recalled his early days in music and said, "I wasn't trying to be rebellious in those days; I was just being me. I wasn't trying to push the edge of anything. I'm being me and ordinary, the guy from suburbia who sings in this band . . ."[4]

From the beginning, though, Jagger understood his stage persona as quite different from this ordinary suburban guy:

> I feel all this energy coming from an audience. I often want to smash the microphone up or something because I don't feel the same person on stage as I am normally. . . .[5]

In an interview with *Rolling Stone*'s Jan Wenner, Jagger recalled learning how he could use this other person on stage to affect, especially, his female fans:

> **WENNER**: It was the attention of the girls that made you realize you were doing something onstage that was special?
>
> **JAGGER**: You realize that these girls are going, either quietly or loudly, sort of crazy. And you're going, "Well, this is good. You know, this is something else." At that age you're just so impressed, especially if you've been rather shy before. There's two parts of all this, at least. There's this great fascination for music and this love of playing blues—not only blues, just rock'n'roll generally. There's this great love of that. But there's this other thing that's performing. . . .

When Wenner asked how Jagger came to be such a performer, he answered:

---

[3] Tim Dowley, *The Rolling Stones* (Hippocrene, 1983), p. 49.

[4] Lynn Ashton, *Mick Jagger: Close To 70 and Still Rocking. Daily News Pulse* (2011).

[5] *The Rolling Stones*, p. 41.

I didn't have any inhibitions. I saw Elvis and Gene Vincent, and I thought, "Well, I can do this." And I liked doing it. It's a real buzz, even in front of twenty people, to make a complete fool of yourself. But people seemed to like it. And the thing is, if people started throwing tomatoes at me, I wouldn't have gone on with it. But they all liked it, and it always seemed to be a success, and people were shocked. I could see it in their faces.[6]

Since the late 1960s, when his mature style of performing took shape, Jagger's reputation as an actor, for becoming a different person on stage, is unequaled. Truman Capote described him as "one of the most total actors I've ever seen. He has this remarkable ability to be absolutely totally extroverted."[7]

Perhaps the most vivid illustration of the two Jaggers is in the documentary *Gimme Shelter*. We see the classic Jagger strutting and dancing onstage, but behind the scenes, as Jonathan Vogel puts it, "he frequently reins in and manages his image in an almost workmanlike manner offstage."[8] When Meredith Hunter was knifed by Hell's Angels—the moment when, according to Don McLean, Jagger was onstage laughing diabolically at all the mayhem—we can see that Jagger had actually taken a more business-like tone as he repeatedly tried to calm the crowd ("Whose war are we fighting, people?"). When Jagger and Charlie Watts are first shown the frame-by-frame footage that revealed Hunter brandishing a gun just before being set upon, there is no face in the room more focused, concerned, and dismayed than Jagger's.

A Little Help from Nietzsche

Nietzsche ideas about life and art help make sense of the relationship between these two Jaggers. As a philosopher, Nietzsche believed in the centrality not of ideas, but of life itself and the importance of vitality, strength, and power. He is not

---

[6] Jan Wenner, *Being Interviewed Is One of Mick Jagger's Least Favorite Pastimes* (1995) <www.mickjagger.com/interviews/jagger-remembers-the-rolling-stone-interview>.

[7] *The Rolling Stones*, p. 87.

[8] Jonathan B. Vogels, *The Direct Cinema of David and Albert Maysles* (Southern Illinois University Press, 2005).

unlike the popular author Ayn Rand (whom our colleague Gordon Marino describes as "Nietzsche without the fun") in valorizing the strong and showing little empathy for weakness. Jagger does not seem to us to be very Nietzschian or Randian in contempt for the weak and slavish (we do not think that Nietzsche and Rand would join Richards and Jagger in the uncharacteristically quasi-Christian song "The Salt of the Earth"). But the two Jaggers can be seen as an illustration or application of Nietzsche's idea that the meaning of art is life itself.

In *The Twilight of the Idols* he asks:

> what does all art do? does it not praise? does it not glorify? does it not select? does it not highlight? By doing all this it *strengthens* or *weakens* certain valuations. . . . Is this no more than an incidental? an accident? Something in which the instinct of the artist has no part whatever? Or is it not rather the prerequisite for the artist's being an artist at all . . . ? Is his basic instinct directed towards art, or is it not rather directed towards the meaning of art, which is *life*?[9]

Could the meaning of art really be life itself? Nietzsche would say that what Mick Jagger has become is praiseworthy. Adding more aesthetic appeal to your own life is the best kind of artistic creation because it invents something new and beautiful, and covers up any ugliness that is ordinarily present.

But more than beauty is at stake in Nietzsche's reasoning. Unlike many philosophers who take the purpose and highest goal of life to be understanding, Nietzsche belittled understanding when it presupposes that the world is merely and entirely an object of knowledge, something to be known. Instead, Nietzsche praised vital, living experience—aesthetic experience—as a more worthy goal: "We have our highest dignity in our significance as works of art," Nietzsche wrote in his *Birth of Tragedy*, "for only as an aesthetic phenomenon is existence and the world eternally justified" (*Birth of Tragedy*, Allen and Unwin, p. 50). "It is necessary to raise ourselves with a dar-

---

[9] Friedrich Nietzsche, *Twilight of the Idols* (London: Penguin, 1968), p. 24.

ing bound into a metaphysics of Art" (p. 183), he claimed, in order to truly live and experience the world. Art and aesthetic experience is simply more real and more valuable for us, Nietzsche says, than knowledge.

That's why, he suggested, we should treat our own lives and selves as works of art:

> *One thing is needful.* —To "give style" to one's character—a great and rare art! It is practiced by those who survey all the strengths and weaknesses of their nature and then fix them into an artistic plan. . . . For one thing is needful: that a human being should *attain* satisfaction with himself, whether it be by means of this or that poetry and art.[10]

Satisfaction? Nietzsche thinks we can find it by molding and shaping ourselves, even if it means fighting or ravishing ourselves: "This secret self-ravishment, this artists' cruelty, this delight in imposing a form upon oneself as a hard, recalcitrant, suffering material and in burning a will . . . into it."[11]

Nietzsche's proposal is puzzling. Normally one has to step back from a painting, sculpture, photograph, stage play to really see it as art. Sure, there are "happenings" when the difference between the performer and the performance can get blurred. But how might one step back from *oneself* to see the work of art Nietzsche urges us to be?

That's why there are two Jaggers. By creating and becoming a character beyond himself, Mick was able to create a rare and celebrated art form. He was able to remove his own inhibitions and characteristics and become something that people wanted to watch. People came to rock concerts not only to hear The Stones play but to see the legendary craziness in the lead singer of the world's greatest rock'n'roll band.

Jagger's whole life—on *and* off stage—can be seen as a complex work of art that encompasses the two Jaggers. Mick certainly distinguishes his on stage and off stage personae, as he does in this BBC interview:

---

[10] *Twilight of the Idols*, p. 81.

[11] *On The Geneology of Morals* (New York: Vintage, 1969), pp. 87–88.

Q: I'd like to know if the Mick Jagger one sees on stage is the real persona or a caricature developed over time and influenced by what you think the public expect. Ian James, Aylesbury, England.

A: What a cynical question! A character perhaps. Or different characters within characters because you've got to do the sad, the happy, the cynical—whatever song you're doing. It's a bit like acting. Obviously I think the on-stage character when you're in front of fifty thousand people is slightly different from the character that would be talking to you today, one-on-one, or making the kids' breakfast. You don't want to be making the kids' breakfast going [puts on stadium voice] 'Are you alright?' Obviously it's different being on stage than being at home.[12]

There has to be a difference if Mick is to be artist and work of art at the same time.

You're So Not Vain

Of course, thinking of and treating one's life aesthetically or as a work of art, can be vain and self-indulgent. You wouldn't want to be like Carly Simon's ex, always keeping "one eye in the mirror" to make sure your performance is going well. But the mere fact that Jagger is a legend that inspires and captivates so many people suggests a larger role for his (and Nietzsche's) project. The kind of self-ravishment involved can create glory that energizes others to follow this guiding light of aesthetics, in the Nietzschean spirit.

Jagger's aesthetic sense that a life well lived should be sublime and ravishing, a great and dangerous light, unhampered by convention, is unmistakable at the concert in 1969 in London's Hyde Park, during which the band paid tribute to Brian Jones who had died shortly before. Jagger read stanza 39 of Shelley's poem *Adonais*.

Peace, Peace! He is not dead, he doth not sleep—
He has awakened from the dream of life—

---

[12] BBC, *Mick Answers Your Questions* (2010),
<www.mickjagger.com/interviews/bbc-mick-jagger-answers-your-questions>.

'Tis we, who lost in stormy visions, keep
With phantoms an unprofitable strife,
And in mad trance, strike with our spirit's knife
Invulnerable nothings.—We decay
Like corpses in a charnel; fear and grief
Convulse us and consume us day by day,
    And cold hopes swarm like warms within our living clay.

Jagger then skipped to Stanza 52:

The one remains, the many change and pass;
Heaven's light forever shines, Earth's shadows fly;
Life, like a dome of many-coloured glass,
Stains the white radiance of Eternity,
Until Death tramples it to fragments.—Die,
If thou wouldst be that which thou dost seek![13]

Unless we strive to make something of ourselves, Jagger, Shelley, and Nietzsche seem to be agreeing, we will be nothing more than "corpses," consumed by our "fear and grief." We must instead seek sublime beauty in a mortal life that shines brilliantly as something made, a work of art, like a "dome of many-coloured glass."

Appreciating those among us who can give themselves over to such a vision, making art out of their lives, seems more a matter of wild exuberance rather than a matter of the self-absorbed vanity. They deserve to have a chapter about them.

---

[1] Bill Wyman, *Stone Alone* (Viking Penguin, 1990), p. 537.

II

A Rolling Stone Gathers No Illusions

5
The Head and the Groin of Rock

JOHN HUSS

Keith Richards once quipped: "the minute rock'n'roll reaches the head, forget it. Rock'n'roll starts from the neck down." He could just as well have said "from the waist down." Keith clearly meant to keep rock'n'roll's primal and visceral appeal from being contaminated by—or even co-opted by—headier, brainier sensibilities.

After all, it's only rock'n'roll. No matter how much we like it, it's not going to come to our notional rescue. Rock'n'roll, especially in a live setting, is to be felt, not pondered. And from the context of Keith's remark (he was justifying his opposition to The Stones' playing the 1985 benefit concert *Live Aid*, where by the way he and Ron Wood eventually did perform, backing up Bob Dylan), he clearly sought to go beyond merely exalting rock's corporeality. He wanted to stake out a noncognitive, morality-free zone for rock'n'roll music far away from entangling alliances with the likes of "No Nukes" and "Rock Against Racism."

"Nukes may obsess your brain," he explained, "but they don't obsess your crotch. Rock'n'roll, it's a few moments when you can forget about nukes and racism and all the other evils God's kindly thrown upon us" (Victor Bokris, *Keith Richards: The Biography*, Da Capo, p. 344).

To Riff or Not to Riff

Richards's remark calls to mind the famous distinction between "higher" and "lower" pleasures, with rock'n'roll ranked among the lower, alongside other mindless animal appetites such as eating and sex (let's not get started on drugs). The distinction was famously drawn by British philosopher John Stuart Mill (1806–1873) in his 1861 essay "Utilitarianism." Mill was taking issue with English philosopher and social reformer Jeremy Bentham (1748–1832), whose views he otherwise endorsed and defended.

Considering different sources of pleasure, Bentham had claimed that "Prejudice apart, the game of push-pin [a simple parlor game] is of equal value with the arts and sciences of music and poetry." In doing so, Bentham meant to do away with centuries of philosophical wrangling over the role of pleasure in human life. Is pleasure, as Bentham believed, the only state valuable in and of itself? Is its opposite, pain, the only intrinsic bad? Is pleasure more of an activity, as in "name your pleasure"? Is pleasure simply the by-product of a life whose sources of happiness lay elsewhere? Or is it just one among many components—including pain—of a rich, full life? The biggest philosophical question had always been whether pleasure is the ultimate intrinsic good to which all other good things in human life could be reduced.

Bentham's take on all this was simple. When all preconceptions are stripped away—including any biases that stem from one's station in life, any moralizing as to what "should" be preferred to what else—the fact of the matter is that pleasure is pleasure and pain is pain, and the balance of one over the other is a *quantitative*, not a qualitative issue. Some people get pleasure from playing chess, while others like hanging out at the Checkerboard Lounge. What ultimately matters is the net amount of pleasure these things provide, not how respectable they may be.

To judge the pleasures of a Hamlet soliloquy as a somehow higher pleasure than a Keith Richards riff is without foundation if Keith's riff provides *more* pleasure than the good old "To be or not to be." Any notion that some pleasures are higher and others lower must be rooted in prejudice. Hell, even animals experience pleasure and pain and, as Bentham well knew, if right and wrong, good and evil, happiness and unhappiness can be boiled down to pleasure and pain, then the moral community would expand not only to include marginalized members of society, but animals and as well.

Monkey Man

So what about rock'n'roll? Does it really start from the neck down, as Keith said? Or is it a higher pleasure? I think there is something inherently cool about Mill's disagreement with Bentham on the very possibility of a distinction. Mill was responding to centuries of criticism against a doctrine given perhaps its fullest formulation by the Greek philosopher Epicurus (341–270 B.C.). That doctrine is hedonism—the view that what's ultimately of intrinsic value is pleasure—whose chief twentieth-century proponents were—coincidentally—The Rolling Stones.

Throughout history, hedonism has always been tagged "the doctrine of the swine." Mill thought this unfair. To downgrade pleasure simply because the swine and other beasts of burpin' are capable of it is to misunderstand human beings. Many pleasures derive from the exercise of various mental capacities, sensitivities, and capabilities—in a word "faculties"—some of which only humans possess. These are what Mill called the higher faculties, and their use and satisfaction create what Mill called the higher pleasures.

Mill ranked music among the higher pleasures, apparently taking it for granted that the brute beasts were incapable of taking pleasure in music. Mill was writing this at just around the time of Darwin's *On the Origin of Species* (1859), but the questions evolution raises here have really been addressed only recently. Here are some of the big ones: do the evolutionary continuities between humans and other animals have any bearing at all on the alleged divide between higher and lower pleasures? Is pleasure the missing link between survival value and aesthetic value? Do the pleasures of listening to music rely more on our animal or on our uniquely human faculties? Obviously, as human beings evolved from other primates, we not only developed the capacity for thought, language, and cave painting, but for rock'n'roll itself. In fact, evolution is probably key to understanding what Mill's supposedly "higher" pleasures are all about.

Only Rock'n'Roll?

Have you ever listened to "It's Only Rock'n'Roll (But I Like It)" through headphones? Do it. This song perfectly illustrates the

way that your musical expectations, built up through a lifetime—of being introduced to language through motherese and
nursery rhymes, of listening to music (live, on AM radio, then
FM, vinyl, cassettes, CDs, mp3s), going to parties and concerts,
playing in bands—give rise to the partly shared, partly private
emotional experience of listening to The Stones.

There's a moment about forty-four seconds in when the first
chorus and a new rhythm guitar part kick in (I'm hearing it
just behind my forehead), which sounds a hell of a lot like a
horn section (at least I can imagine it being played by a horn
section, and in fact, always thought it had been till I recently
listened more carefully). I'm not sure exactly what leads me to
expect a horn section there, but there's something very
Memphis about it. Then a strange thing happens: that horn
part that isn't a horn part morphs into a Chuck Berry riff—a
riff that Keith reprises later in his solo. Following that solo and
the next chorus, the electric guitars all drop out for an
(un)expected bridge, leaving acoustic guitars (the backbone of
the song throughout), bass and drums to support Mick as he
whispers, sings, teases, and tokes "I like it."

In other words, what the song sounds like and how you hear
it depends on one's familiarity with music, with rock'n'roll as a
tradition, with The Stones, and with particular songs and performances of theirs and of other bands. Obviously certain elements of a song that were once surprising cease to be
surprising on repeated listening, as Mill tells us:

> the pleasure of music . . . fades with familiarity, and requires either to
> be revived by intermittence, or fed by continual novelty. (Mill,
> *Autobiography,* Holt, 1873, p. 145)

But here's a little grist for Mill: a listener is a dynamic being,
changing in ways that make it possible to be surprised by com-
positions heard a zillion times. Contra Mill, sometimes elements *emerge* as novel and surprising upon repeated listening
due to subjective, learned changes in the receptivity and the
expectations of the individual listener.

Tell Me, Sister Dopamine

You cannot understand the pleasures of The Stones, nor the
channels of the human brain through which they work their

emotional magic, without directing your attention to what have been called life's four F's: feeding ("The Spider and the Fly"), fighting ("Street Fighting Man"), fleeing ("Before They Make Me Run"), and fornicating (too many to count). To survive and perpetuate their kind, humans and all other animal species require adaptations for each of these functions. The human brain has evolved to derive pleasure from rock'n'roll—and drugs—by hijacking the basic brain mechanisms associated with these fundamentals of survival. For a readable account of the neuroscience of music, read Daniel Levitin's *This Is Your Brain on Music* (Dutton, 2006).

From a neurological standpoint, the higher pleasures are inextricably linked with the lower. They share a motivation and reward system that produces a two-phase rush associated with the release of the neurotransmitter dopamine, a feel-good chemical. The first phase occurs in anticipation of a pleasing stimulus, such as the part of a song that sends shivers down your spine. Research by Valorie Salimpoor's lab at McGill University has shown that the music listener's brain releases a mild dose of dopamine in the period *just before* the chill-inducing segment of a song. The second, larger dose accompanies the spine-tingling sensation itself. We can think of these two hits of dopamine as positive reinforcement for *anticipation* and *fulfilled prediction* of the pleasing stimulus. This two-hit high relies on exactly the same brain chemistry as the animal appetites. Take feeding. The brain does not simply reward eating a meal. There is also the thrill of the hunt. Or sex. Before orgasm comes foreplay. In each case, the first, anticipatory dose of dopamine correlates with *motivation* (for seeking the pleasure), and the second is involved in *reward* (for having succeeded). Drug addiction exploits the same pathway—the heroin addict feels an anticipatory rush upon seeing his blood enter the needle, well before the dope enters his veins and reaches his brain.

What about the pleasures of listening to a piece of music one has never heard before, such as the first time Keith heard Chuck Berry? How does one *anticipate* a pleasing stimulus one has never experienced? The answer lies in the expectancy structures of the listener. Perception and sensation are *active* processes, even when we're not consciously attending to sensory inputs. Neural networks constantly feed back with stimuli from the environment to develop a working model of the outside world, on the basis of learning, experience, and innate elements of brain architecture.

The brain is constantly anticipating what the next sensory input will be, generating predictions which are at times satisfied, at other times close enough for rock'n'roll, and at other times completely frustrated. The brain has a reward system for correct predictions, sometimes even for predictions that are close enough, and registers surprise when predictions are unmet. In the wild, unmet predictions (a predator's yowl when we were expecting dead silence) kick the nervous system into alertness: hair stands on end, goose bumps form, and so forth. Our conscious and unconscious expectations help us navigate our world, and the satisfaction or frustration of those expectations feeds back into the neural network and updates our working model of reality.

We depend upon these mental models far more than we realize. When it comes to processing each and every stimulus from the real world, time is literally not on our side. There's not enough time for all of these stimuli to pass through our nervous system, into our brains, and for another nervous impulse to be sent back out from the brain to move our muscles. Our mental models, reinforced by correct predictions, and updated by encounters with the unexpected, serve as a surrogate for external reality, so much so that for us, they usually pass for reality (Bo Digg was only half wrong when he sang, "reality is a parody of my fantasy"). If you've ever texted while driving, you're allowing a mental model of the road to pass for reality until you look up again to update the model.

Some Things Just Stick in Your Mind

All Western music (including honky tonk blues) is composed of the same basic elements of melody, harmony, and rhythm. In most rock'n'roll, this has been simplified to the basic elements of the blues: four beats to the measure (or bar), a repeating pattern (often, but not always, twelve bars long), and a chord progression that often goes from the tonic (or *I* [one], which corresponds to the key the song is in), to the subdominant (or *IV*, corresponding to the fourth note of the scale in that key), then the dominant (or *V*, corresponding to the fifth note of the scale in that key), before returning to the *I*.

If you're not up on your music theory, you must already be convinced that anything this complicated has got to qualify as a higher pleasure (although Levitin's primer to music theory in *This Is Your Brain on Music* makes it all seem easy). Not so fast. The fact is, as with much learning, a lifetime (or even a short time) of listening suffices for the brain to forge enough neural connections that, even lacking the vocabulary to talk about it, the casual listener can intuitively feel the moment when a song should come slamming back into the *I*, and likewise can sense the tension when a song lingers on the *IV* or the *V* without resolving to the *I*. Western music theory has simply developed terminology to capture these intuitively felt phenomena. But much of the tension and release that *is* rock-'n'roll involves the delay, frustration, and eventual satisfaction of our learned expectation that eventually the melody with return to the *I*.

This kind of expectation is so crucial to the experience of listening to music that David Huron aptly called his book on the psychology of music *Sweet Anticipation*. If Huron and other neurorockologists are right, this manipulation, frustration, postponement, and fulfillment of expectations is precisely what allows rock'n'roll to tap into the animal-pleasure pathways of life's four F's.

In his engrossing autobiography, *Life*, Keith returns periodically to something he calls "Keef's Guitar Workshop" and it is clear that, coming at it from the performer's end, rock'n'roll is about as high a higher pleasure as you can imagine. I mean, Keith, Mick, and especially Brian Jones before he checked out, really paid their dues with careful study of the blues. Keith is especially clear in his dissection of the guitar technique of bluesman Jimmy Reed. What he soon figured out from listening to a lot of vinyl was that Jimmy seldom played exactly the chord that was expected—he'd leave notes out or allow open strings to drone on partly because it was easier—*especially when fingering the V chord*. What this implies is that Reed was a master at throwing off expectations just at the point of maximum unresolved tension, before taking it on home to the *I*. It was from listening to Jimmy Reed that Keith arrived at his distinctive style, junking up chords with colorful extra notes on songs like "Jumpin' Jack Flash" and "Gimme Shelter." And it was from Chuck Berry that Keith learned the economical trick (when The Stones were a more stripped-down act) of forgoing a horn section by adding extra notes to chords to simulate the horn part, triggering just the right unconscious musical associations in the listener. I'm sure I'm not the only one who's fallen for it in "Only Rock'n'Roll."

Satisfaction

The neurorockology of pleasure is in its infancy, but based on our current best understanding, can we say with any confidence whether (listening to) rock'n'roll is a higher or lower pleasure? Although we've looked at it scientifically, this is more fundamentally a philosophical question. At the core of the higher-lower debate there is an ambiguity about the terms "higher" and "lower" that, once resolved, may make the debate . . . well, perhaps not fade away but at least reach a rapprochement. Look at it this way: Keith's cause is to preserve for rock'n'roll its connection with sex and, presumably, the other animal pleasures, that make it a distinctive musical form.

When placed in the service of "higher causes" such as "No Nukes" and "Rock Against Racism," rock'n'roll ceases to be valued solely for its intrinsic, visceral pleasures, but instead as a means to achieving some "higher" cause. The hedonist and purist in Richards seem to bristle at this distortion. Conceiving of "higher" and "lower" as polar opposites in a scale of moral, social, or even religious values, Richards seems to be saying that rock'n'roll can do just fine without dragging any of that into it, thank you very much.

Bentham thought that pleasure-pain could serve as a common currency for what's of intrinsic value (or disvalue) across all human beings and even other animal species. Ranking the pleasures of the aristocracy or the industrialists as "higher" than those of artisans, farmers, and factory workers, or the pleasures of animals as "lower" than those of humans reflected, as far as Bentham was concerned, nothing other than unjustified societal prejudices. So from a moral point of view, we can think of pleasure and pain as the great levelers, collapsing any distinction between "high" and "low."

Mill resisted this. By introducing the distinction between pleasures high and low, Mill sought to rescue hedonism from its reputation as the "doctrine of the swine." Higher pleasures rely on "higher" faculties, such as the ability to think abstractly, to reflect on our own psychological states (including states of pleasure and pain), and to contextualize our pleasures and pains. Although Mill argued that higher pleasures were preferable to lower pleasures (according to any competent judge who had experienced both kinds), "higher" and "lower" as he used them mark a neurobiological or perhaps an evolutionary distinction that is based on the distinctive cognitive capacities of humans (as opposed to swine and other animals). Mill's insistence on the importance of the higher pleasures, as Martha Nussbaum suggested in her article "Mill between Aristotle and Bentham,"[1] may simply reflect his hard-won belief that greater levels of pleasure—and satisfaction—would come to those who flourished most fully and tasted the many different pleasures the world offered.

If Mill, Bentham, and Richards were to spend the night together hashing this all out (with Brian Jones and Anita Pallenberg as competent judges), neurorockology would shine a light on the source of the disagreement, and, I think, could help contribute to its resolution to the satisfaction of all involved. For Keith rock'n'roll exploits (albeit in an open G tuning) the same neurochemical pathways as life's four F's and thus takes its place among the animal pleasures. Surely, Bentham would agree. This leaves Mill, who may seem to be the odd man out here. But I don't think he would be bothered by the discovery that "higher" music produces pleasure using the same "lower" neurochemical pathways as the animal appetites, for this does not exclude the possibility that the "higher," or more evolutionarily derived cognitive capacities, of human beings are also involved.

Keith and Bentham wouldn't be bothered by the idea that some things require thought to produce pleasure, so long as such pleasures are not accorded a higher moral value than animal pleasures. Did Mill think that those uniquely human pleasures were of higher *value* than the animal pleasures? It

---

[1] <www.utilitarian.net/jsmill/about/20040322.htm>.

certainly seems so, but this may have simply been the prudish Victorian in Mill speaking. For the Victorians, sex was a moral duty, and a place "in between the sheets" meant a bookmarked book page.

Telecast Mill some 110 years into the future, with those preconceptions stripped away, stick him on the tour bus, and I'm sure Mick, Keith, and the boys would demonstrate to his satisfaction that rock'n'roll is both a higher and a lower pleasure.[2]

---

[2] For sound checking and suggestions, I thank Travis Hreno, Tom McBride, and Joanna Trzeciak.

6
Paint the Flowers Black

RICK MAYOCK

While the Beatles are singing "Good Day Sunshine," Mick Jagger is screaming "I want to see the sun blotted out from the sky." In the midst of the sunny optimism of the mid-1960s pop music explosion, The Rolling Stones' songs were dark and out of step with the times.

Innocent and carefree lyrics, The Stones seemed to be saying, do not always reflect the culture or the times, especially a decade torn by poverty, war, racial prejudice, and segregation. The times, as Bob Dylan said, were "a-changin'," and the music of The Rolling Stones began to reflect some of those changes.

Unlike The Beatles, with their sanitized pop idol image, The Stones preferred to see themselves as outcasts and misfits, as beggars at a banquet. From Keith Richards's perspective, they were blues artists, not pop stars. "We're anti-pop, we're anti-ballroom, all we want to do is be the best blues band in London" (*Life*, p. 109). Their rebellious image set them apart from The Beatles and other British Invasion groups, and their focus on the blues made them advocates of the music of the oppressed.

Philosophy also has its sunny and optimistic periods that reflect an attitude of hopefulness and progress. This kind of optimism found expression in the Enlightenment, an intellectual movement of the seventeenth and eighteenth centuries that celebrated reason as a way of attaining knowledge, freedom, and happiness. It was an optimism based on the belief that we can discover truth, in its purest form, that reason will enable us to reveal the secrets of the universe, help us to solve our social and political problems, and show us how to live good, virtuous lives.

But it came under attack by critics in the post-Enlightenment, or post-modern movement, beginning with Friedrich Nietzsche (1844–1900) and continuing in the twentieth century with Jacques Derrida (1930–2004) and others. Suspicions arose about the motives that drive this philosophical optimism, suspicions that revealed an underlying set of unexamined assumptions about the origins of philosophical concepts. This optimism in philosophy is an expression of what Derrida calls "white mythology."[1]

Philosophical thinking that relies on abstract concepts and reason becomes a kind of mythology, according to Derrida. Like all mythological thinking, it requires an attitude of faith, an unwillingness to question its beliefs and practices, and a denial of the sources and origins from which it arises—all in the attempt to see its teachings as universally true. It can also propagate and sustain a sense of privilege and superiority by its adherents and marginalize those who are excluded and oppressed.

White mythology is not exclusively an intellectual movement. It is also a cultural phenomenon, which includes attitudes about music. As The Rolling Stones attune themselves to the blues, they reject the optimism of white pop music and return to the musical roots of rock'n'roll. The Stones are the Nietzsche and Derrida of rock—by taking pop music to a new territory, colored by darker images and textures, and to an emotional and psychological landscape that had previously been explored only by blues artists, they are a musical repudiation of white mythology, of a cultural landscape that turns its back on the downtrodden and marginalized and facilitates an exploitation and denial of its cultural roots. They take the white mythology of pop and paint it black.

Flowers

In the midst of the "flower power" era, The Rolling Stones presented an unusual arrangement. In July of 1967 they released

---

[1] *Margins of Philosophy* (University of Chicago Press, 1982), p. 213.

the album *Flowers*, which appears, on the surface, to be a collection of bright, colorful images. But these flowers evoke darkness and uncertainty, and leave us "standing in the shadows" with nothing but questions. They remind us that sunlight is followed by darkness: "while the sun is bright, or in the darkest night," optimistic feelings can be overshadowed by darker emotions and loss. Some flowers must turn away from the sun, for they "can't be chained, to a life where nothing's gained and nothing's lost, at such a cost" ("Ruby Tuesday"). Philosophers traditionally celebrate what is stable and unchanging, if only because it then becomes knowable if not more real. But this lyric moves us to wonder about the importance of change. If nothing is gained and nothing is lost, what is the cost? According to Nietzsche and Derrida, the cost may be the death of the living idea, which leaves us with conceptual stagnancy and dead flowers.

The heliotrope is a flower that always faces the sun. In popular music the sun usually represents happiness and hopefulness; flowers signify affection, friendship or romantic love. Visual images of color and light are complemented by melodies that inspire joyous celebration: "she shoots her colors all around, like a sunset going down" ("She's a Rainbow"). Darkness, night, rain and clouds, on the other hand, point to loneliness, heartache, pain, and despair.

While flowers, sunlight, clouds, darkness, and rainbows can be symbols in popular music, they can also give birth to concepts in philosophy. The heliotrope, then, has a double meaning. It can literally mean a flower that continually turns itself to face the sun, or it can mean a figure of speech or way of writing and thinking that orients toward a conceptual "sun." Derrida sees traditional philosophy as a heliotrope that continually turns its attention to a particular sun, whether that sun is "truth," "knowledge," or "enlightenment." The problem is that this creates what Derrida and other philosophers call the "metaphysics of presence." This is the idea that philosophy privileges that which *is*, or that which appears as present. But it does so at the cost of neglecting or forgetting the conditions by which that which *is* or that which is present comes to be. In doing so, presence is itself privileged, and the absence of presence is taken to be a lack or privation and has no metaphysical reality.

For example, St. Augustine (354–430 C.E.) makes the case that evil is not something that has any metaphysical reality, but is merely a privation or absence of good.[2] Just as darkness is not a thing in itself, but a privation or absence of light, evil is the absence of good, so it has no metaphysical reality. As the heliotrope always seeks the sun and turns away from the darkness, heliotropic philosophy seeks its conceptual sun (for example, the good) and turns away from and ignores its opposite—the shadows. For Nietzsche, this could not be more wrong. In his critique of what he calls "slave morality," he argued that the very opposition of "good" and "evil" derives from the same source, and an investigation of the origins of these concepts will lead us "beyond good and evil."[3]

Heliotropic music also turns away from its shadowy past and tries to deny its origins. Some early songs of The Stones can be seen as a critique of this musical "white mythology." As they began their recording career, the Stones promoted traditional blues as part of their repertoire and as an alternative to the pop music that was heard on American radio in the early 1960s. After Elvis was drafted into the Army in 1958 and Buddy Holly died in 1959, the segregated American airwaves were dominated by sentimental romantic idealism. The music heard on the radio that most resembled rock'n'roll was about hot rods and surfing in the sunshine by The Beach Boys.

Standing in the Shadow

For Keith, the band's mission was to reawaken white America to the blues. "We turned white America's brains and ears around," he writes. The Beatles broke the door down, "and then they got stuck inside their own cage, 'The Fab Four'" (*Life*, p. 159). Black music was marginalized to regional radio audiences, and blues artists in America were struggling to get by. Keith even remembers Muddy Waters doing menial labor at the Chess Records studio in Chicago in order to stay on the payroll.

---

[2] Augustine, *The Confessions of St. Augustine* (New American Library, 1963), p. 60.

[3] Nietzsche, *On the Genealogy of Morals* (Random House, 1967), p. 44.

The plan worked. While The Stones became popular as a blues band, they discovered that they are also songwriters capable of producing top-forty hits that question the reigning white mythology of pop. Yes, they created occasional ballads of arresting beauty and aristocratic imagery, as in "Lady Jane" and "Back Street Girl." Yet even in their ballads the lyrics express a shadowy darkness that turns away the metaphysics of presence. The first song Mick and Keith write together is a picture of sadness evoked by children playing in the evening, "Smiling faces I can see, but not for me, I sit and watch as tears go by."[4] Mick and Keith unveil the dark side by turning to the shadows where your mother may be standing: "live in the shadow, see through the shadow, live through the shadow, tear at the shadow, hate in the shadow, and *love in your shadowy life*" (Have You Seen Your Mother Baby Standing in the Shadow?").

Out of the Cave

The heliotropic tradition in philosophy began with Plato (429–347 B.C.E.) who used the image of the sun as the symbol of enlightenment, contrasted with the ignorance and darkness of the cave. Plato's story about prisoners condemned to live in a dark cave is an allegory about life in the absence of philosophical reflection—what Socrates (470–399 B.C.E.) called the "unexamined life." Medieval philosophers continued the tradition by referring to the presence of divine ideas in the mind as "illumination." Historians refer to the long period when much science and learning was at a standstill as the "Dark Ages," and the great flowering of human knowledge that culminates in the eighteenth century as the "Enlightenment." These are all examples of a rich metaphoric tradition that collects truth, knowledge, beauty—all things that are good—into images of light and the opposite into images of darkness.

God is in the spotlight of this tradition, too, represented in theological texts as the light or the sun. Jesus declared himself the "light of the world" and in his conversion St. Paul was

---

4 According to Keith Richards, "The first one we wrote was 'As Tears Go By'." Mick Jagger, Keith Richards, Charlie Watts, and Ronnie Wood, *According to the Rolling Stones* (Chronicle, 2003), p. 82.

blinded by the light of Christ's divinity. St. Paul says we see the divine presence "through a glass darkly," and only later face to face (1 Corinthians 13:12). The Stones' retrospective album *Big Hits, Volume 2* is a journey "Through the Past, Darkly." The songs on it continue to provide a darker alternative to sunny pop imagery and, on subsequent album covers, The Stones themselves project an image of a darker, brooding defiance.

A philosophical tradition that ignores the shadows, Nietzsche believed, is in danger of marginalization and distortion. Nietzsche recognizes that "shadow is as needful as light" and acknowledges the necessity of opposites in philosophical thinking. Derrida's method of deconstructing the metaphysics of presence similarly aims to overturn the classical oppositions of presence-absence, positive-negative, good-evil, light-shadow, in order to reveal the less obvious, less "present" underside of philosophical thinking. The process of philosophical writing, says Derrida, exposes that which has been suppressed or repressed, and covers over that which has been disclosed.

The Rolling Stones' music also celebrates the dark side by overturning opposites and revealing what's beneath, as in: "Just as every cop is a criminal, and all the sinners saints, As heads is tails, Just call me Lucifer, 'Cause I'm in need of some restraint" ("Sympathy for the Devil"). The Stones' early music had the effect of deconstructing the pop music of the day by celebrating the R&B roots of rock'n'roll, revealing that which had been oppressed and suppressed by radio programming and had fallen under the influence of white mythology. Pop music had covered over the roots of its origins, just as the abstract philosophical language of concepts had attempted to cover over its hidden roots, found in poetic and metaphoric language. The Beatles-Stones oppositions take on philosophical meaning in this context. "I'll Follow the Sun" and "Here Comes the Sun" are overturned by the darkness of "Paint It Black," and "Let It Be" is overturned by "Let It Bleed."

Dandelions on My Cloud

"Dandelion don't tell no lies, dandelion will make you wise." This song presents us with an image of a bright yellow flower, a metaphor for truth and wisdom that many philosophers of the seventeenth and eighteenth centuries might have appreciated. Rationalists and empiricists may have debated whether reason or the senses were the best avenues to truth, but they agreed that truth, like a bright yellow flower in bloom, was available and plain to see. But in the late 1960s, The Stones' dandelion and the truth is represents came to an end: "Blow away dandelion." Under the influence of Derrida and other deconstructionists, the hopeful, optimistic ideals of the Enlightenment began to wither and blow away as doubts arose about the possibility of attaining truth and certainty at all.

But that doesn't mean truth is altogether blotted out from the sky. The sun, as we have seen, can represent *the* truth, but a cloud can be *my* truth. As the Danish philosopher Søren Kierkegaard (1813–1855) put it, "Truth is subjectivity."[5] For Kierkegaard, truth must be apprehended subjectively and personally in order to be "clearly" understood. Otherwise we see, as St. Paul says, through a glass, darkly. Objective truth must be made subjective and appropriated as a real part of our own experience. As a result, that truth may not be transmitted or shared in a direct way from another person ("Hey, you, get off of my cloud")—only indirectly in a private and enigmatic way ("Don't hang around 'cause two's a crowd").

Nietzsche tooks things a step further than Kierkegaard by claiming that truth is not merely subjective but impossible. We artistically create our "truth" but then deceive ourselves into believing we have discovered it. What we want, says Nietzsche, is to discover truth, but there is no fixed, objective truth to be found, only various "wills to power" that make these truths. If you want to discover truth, "You can't always get what you want." But if you are willing to invent it, and you try, "you just might find you get what you need."

Back to the Roots (Again)

The Beatles created mythological alter-egos for themselves with the release of *Sgt. Pepper's Lonely Hearts Club Band* in 1967. They did so, perhaps, to escape from the confines of their public image as "The Mop Tops" and "The Fab Four." The Stones responded with their own mythological misadventure, *Their*

---

[5] *Concluding Unscientific Postscript to the Philosophical Fragments* (Princeton University Press, 1992), Vol. II, p. 45.

Satanic Majesties Request. But doing so took them further out of their element. Although some of the songs from that era, like "She's a Rainbow" and "Dandelion," reflect the ethos of the summer of love and the influence of LSD, the Stones had wandered into psychedelia and away from their roots.[6] The departure of their manager Andrew Oldham, who had carefully steered their public image away from copying Brian Epstein's Beatles, left them a bit unfocused and *Satanic Majesties* turned out to be less than a great success. They needed to get back to where they once belonged.

Beggars Banquet included some driving rock'n'roll, like "Street Fighting Man," and a return to traditional blues and acoustic guitars with Rev. Wilkins's "Prodigal Son." Having gone back to the source of their inspiration, they discarded their mythic robes and costumes, and returned, like prodigal sons, to their home in the blues, with "no expectation . . . to pass through here again."

Dead Flowers and Concepts

One feature of philosophical tradition Derrida and Nietzsche sought to undo was Plato's conception of art and poetry. According to Plato, poetry nourishes laughter, anger, love and joy, and sex and dreams, and all the human desires that just might leave you in tatters. So philosophers need to be on their guard against the damaging effects of poetry and music. Since they can corrupt the soul, and drive us to a state of emotional crisis, they need to be kept in check and controlled by our sun-seeking rationality.

Plato's masterpiece *The Republic* includes a quarrel between philosophy and poetry. Plato argues in favor of censoring poets because they endanger our souls by stimulating our emotions at the expense of our reason. Plato takes the side of philosophy and non-poetic, non-metaphoric, literal truth (which is ironic, given that his allegory of the cave is itself a metaphor). Poetry can only provide us with illusions or appear-

---

[6] Mick Jagger: "There's a lot of rubbish on *Satanic Majesties*. Just too much time on our hands, too many drugs, no producer to tell us 'Enough already, thank you very much, now can we just get on with this song?'" *According to the Rolling Stones*, p. 107.

ances, he says, just as a painter can only present approximate representations. Just as the rational part of the soul corrects the errors of optical illusions, such as the unequal angles of a bed in a painting, reason must correct the emotional errors that are fostered by poetry. In other words, Plato prefers the dead flowers of philosophical abstraction to the living flowers of poetry.

Derrida and Nietzsche disagree and take the side of poetry. Abstract thinking, according to Derrida, distorts philosophy by leaving us with a conceptual graveyard of ideas that have been effaced of their original life and meaning. The process of abstracting metaphors into concepts strips them of their color, and causes them to wither like dead flowers. It is, in effect, a process of "abstraction without extraction," of focusing on the dead flower and ignoring its life source derived from its metaphoric roots. Derrida claims that philosophers wish to escape the world of appearance expressed in poetry, and to concentrate their focus on what is real. But in doing so, they, in effect, become poets by creating a new world of appearances.[7]

For Nietzsche, Plato's attempt to strip philosophy of its poetic content leaves us with empty, abstract concepts because in our attempts to "purify" reason we have forgotten its origins in metaphors and poetry. Poetry, the language of the emotions, is more immediate, less abstract, and closer to the source of what is signified. Consequently, metaphoric language is more real. Philosophy should embrace it, and not fade away into lifeless concepts.

Philosophy's Bad Boys

Nietzsche and Derrida are misfits and outcasts within a long philosophical tradition. Western philosophers, they believed, elevated reason to new heights and worshipped it falsely in its purified state. But they remind us that while the heliotrope may seek the rays of the sun, it is nourished by the soil from which it originates. White mythology leaves us with concepts

---

[7] "The very metaphysicians who think to escape the world of appearances are constrained to live perpetually in allegory. A sorry lot of poets, they dim the colors of the ancient fables, and are themselves but gatherers of fables. They produce a white mythology," *Margins of Philosophy*, p. 213.

that are colorless, blanched and anemic, lacking in the life blood which gives them their richest meaning.

The Stones similarly took pop back to the soil and the roots from which it is nurtured and earned their image as outcasts, misfits. They helped integrate Black American blues in White America, which had stripped and effaced its music of its African and slave origins and had presented itself as a white mythology. White rock'n'roll, like philosophy, had attempted to purify itself, stripping itself of its roots and the pathos from which it originated. It had become, to use Derrida's phrasing, an "abstraction without extraction." It needed to find its roots in its emotional pathos and white musicians needed to learn to "let it bleed." And it needed some color—it needed to be painted black. The heliotrope of rock'n'roll cannot always face the sun. White music, like white mythology, was beginning to fade in significance and needed to reconnect to its original and concrete meanings. The Rolling Stones and their music rebelled against a prevailing white mythology by painting it black.

7
Zen and the Art of Being a Stones Fan

Philip Merklinger

I'm a serious man with serious lusts.

—"Summer Romance," *Emotional Rescue*

Recent reports say that The Rolling Stones are planning once again to go on tour. News like that automatically evokes in me memories of Stones concerts past, and a serious lust for Stones concerts future.

For me, The Stones truly shine live! I would even argue that on their *worst* days, their live concerts are far better than those of any other band. I have so enjoyed Stones concerts that I divide my life into periods: the *Tour of The Americas* (1975) signifies my movement from high school and being a teenager into my early twenties; the *Some Girls Tour* (1978) signifies my movement from ordinary undergraduate university student into passionate lover of philosophy; the *Keith Richards Concert for the Blind* (1979) signifies only itself, a *moment* of sheer *ecstasy*.

This is familiar terrain for most people. We always use concerts, weddings, graduations and so on to mark time. But mapping out my life by Stones concerts prompts me to remember not only what I was doing at various times in my life but also what it felt like 'from the inside' doing those things. 'From the inside'? The subjective *'feel'* or, *'feeling-tone'*, of what it was like being me. From the inside, the songs of the Rolling Stones are a soundtrack to my life.

If you've seen The Stones in concert, you know that going to a Stones concert has it own set of *concerns*, such as:

Anxiety over tickets

Getting *good* tickets is usually the least of my concerns. Invariably I have to be concerned about getting tickets, period. Fortunately, I am fanatical enough to feel blessed just to be able to be in the building.

I remember getting tickets for the Voodoo Lounge Tour concert in Toronto. Since I live a couple of thousand miles from Toronto, my father, at the time seventy-six years old, drove to Toronto and stood in line for six hours in order to purchase them for me. Not surprisingly, others in line were very curious about Dad. He said that he responded: "Oh, because Keith is my favorite." This response is tremendously funny if you knew my Dad. He is straight (in all ways possible), conservative, and deeply religious. He would never dream of smoking a cigarette let alone smoking a joint, but he always supported my love of music. I played The Stones (and other favourite bands)—loud— while he read the paper.

Exponentially growing anticipation

Waiting for the day of the concert to arrive seems to never end. Time stretches out for infinity and as each new pre-concert day arrives. I feel that I simply cannot take it. It has to happen *now*! So, I immerse myself in live recordings of The Stones. That eases the pain somewhat. Then, concert day arrives, and suddenly I don't yet feel ready for it. But off I go, my normal life completely disrupted, caught up in the frenetic swirl of getting to the concert on time.

Opening notes of the concert

This is *the moment* that makes the expense, the anxiety, and the disruption worth it. Any Stones fan will know the mystical magic of the opening notes. Usually it's Keith's guitar sounding those notes (although on the Voodoo Lounge Tour it was Charlie's drums, kick-starting all of us in the audience, to rise up as if one and ascending into sonic heaven, laughing, dancing, singing, weeping, yelping, and in general giving thanks all at the same time. Sheer ecstasy! Then *we know* that once again our gods are defying divine protocol so that we can be graced by their presence. In the words of Sam Cutler, circa 1969:

> Ladies and Gentlemen, the Greatest Rock'n'Roll Band in the World,
> . . . The Rolling Stones!

It there a more holy invocation of the divine than this?

The concert itself

Once it starts, it goes quickly, so I try to imprint every moment on my memory banks, as well as each and every detail: the songs played, how they were played, the surprise selections ("You Can't Rock Me/Get Off of My Cloud" blew me out of the water in 1975; Keith and Ronnie's magical 'ancient art of weaving' their guitars together; Mick's divine mastery of the stage; and, Charlie's bass drum and snare pounding a savage rock-'n'roll AR (artifical respiration) on heart and soul. Then, horror of horrors, the concert is over and it all seems like a dreamworld evaporating upon waking. And *I want more*!

Unfortunately, this news of an upcoming Stones tour also carries a touch of grey, that this is a *farewell* tour! They have got to be kidding. After all these years of The Stones denying that this is 'the last time' they are now saying 'yes'? Unbelievable.

Of course, we diehard Stones fans refuse to believe such nonsense. We always wait for the official announcement from The Rolling Stones office. (This is an unspoken Stones-fan maxim: do not believe any media reports which has not been officially confirmed.) We *believe* deep down inside that they have to play until they 'drop' (dead), perhaps even on stage. Their blues idols—Muddy Waters, Willie Dixon, Howling Wolf, and the others—didn't retire. Well, we diehard Stones fans know that at least Keith Richards will not give up so easily. Keith has said right from the beginning that "it is not about the money, it's about the music." So I can only conclude that it's *not* about the money and that it is *not* 'all over now.' The true fans will get both what we need and what we want.

For sure, gossip and rumors can distract us from what we seek. I imagine that most Stones fans, like me, cringe at hearing the well-worn clichés being regurgitated once again in the recent farewell tour reports. For example, from the original report of the 2011 tour in *The Sun* (a British daily tabloid): "The Stones have sold more than 200 million albums and recorded a string of classic hits including *Satisfaction, Paint It*

Black and *Brown Sugar."* This reads as if it was borrowed from the paper's obituary file. It displays no signs of life—its own or anyone else's. Close runners-up in the well-worn cliché department: "Time is no longer on their side," or "Taking it easy. Stone me, it's Mick Flagger. SIR Mick Jagger is having to pace himself and take breaks during live shows now he's sixty-six, etc." These lame, 'age-ist' word-plays and puns make me cringe. They trivialize The Stones and their fifty-year achievement when their longevity is no joke. I can't think of any other musical unit, regardless of genre, that has lasted so long. Yet the media gossip machine gives us nothing more than *celebrity profiling.*

Hey Paparazzi, Get Off of My Cloud

This is a term I invented. As we all know, 'racial profiling' is the practice of stereotyping persons according to their *ethnic* or *racial* background—alone. It has been used since 9/11 by American police and security forces to help them determine whether a person is likely to be involved in criminal or terrorist activity. This type of profiling, must of us would agree, is totally unacceptable. Racial profiling sacrifices *real* security for the *apparent security* of fighting the war against crime or terrorism merely by hassling people because of their race or ethnicity. This doesn't help stop either crime or terrorism. In fact, it may inspire crime or terrorism that grows out of the sheer frustation of being so unfairly labeled.

Celebrity profiling is equally unacceptable. It describes *famous* people according to stereotypical categories of contemporary vices (sex, drugs, alcohol, gambler) in order to entice the public to buy various products, such as magazines, newspapers or TV channel subscriptions. It takes some aspect of a celebrity's life, such as Keith Richards's drug use, and exaggerates it to the point of utter stupidity. Nobody could live the life of drug taking that the media says that Richards has lived. Keith himself has noted this.

Nevertheless, stereotypes of The Stones are plentiful. You know them:

'Indestructible Keith', the 'heart or soul of The Stones'

'Womanizer' Mick, the 'cold hard-nosed businessman'

'Homebody' Charlie, the 'stoical drummer' (well, maybe this one is true)

'Bum note' Ronnie, the 'chronic boozer' whose marriage and home life is in a shambles

'Creative' Brian, his genius destroyed by drugs and Mick and Keith's lock on songwriting in The Stones

'Innocent' Mick Taylor, lucky to have left The Stones alive

'Sex-obsessed' Bill Wyman, the quiet, frustrated bass player who is also lucky to have left The Stones alive

The trouble with celebrity profiling like this is that it's false. A name, label, or stereotype can never capture the essence of a person. In my experience, human beings simply overflow any and all stereotyping. Yet, in the popular mind, stereotypes stick like glue and they're permanent. Once a celebrity has been slotted into a stereotype, it's virtually impossible for that celebrity to lose it. Conversion to an ultraconservative religion might make some difference, but not necessarily.

True, The Stones have profited greatly from 'celebrity profiling' over the years. Andrew Loog Oldham's simple maxim, "there is no such thing as bad press" has served them well. Near the beginning, there was the 'urinating in public' incident; then, the various drug busts, the 'sex scandals' (Marianne Faithfull and the Mars bar) and deaths (especially those of Brian Jones and Gram Parsons), marriage breakups and affairs, the falling out of trees and the defying anti-smoking laws while playing on stage (Ron and Keith). These 'rebels' are master manipulators of 'celebrity profiling'. They always manage to keep their names in the news. Remember the hubbub created a few years ago when Keith casually mentioned to a reporter that he had snorted his father's cremated ashes?

But celebrity profiling diminishes our understanding of The Stones, especially from a philosophical point of view. Even some academic philosophers are among those who believe the conclusions of 'celebrity profiling' and dismiss The Stones and their music out of hand as mere entertainment and nothing more. Upon learning that I was writing about The Rolling Stones one of my colleagues said to me, "Don't you think it's about time those old druggies just gave up? They haven't done anything worth listening to for years." Clearly, my colleague hadn't actually listened to a recent Stones album, like *Voodoo Lounge, Bridges to Babylon,* or *A Bigger Bang.* And, I suspect, all the celebrity profiling of The Stones obscured for him the fact that The Stones are not just a studio band. For me and most Stones fans, their true excellence comes in their *live performance.*

The Stones, more than another band of which I am aware, use studio recordings only as *templates* for playing live. They never play a song exactly the same way twice. They revel in a loose, improvisional style which flesh out a song's framework in new, sometimes unexpected ways. Even old warhorses like "(I Can't Get No) Satisfaction" or "Brown Sugar" are like gifts from the band to their fans who open them up by listening closely and being surprised by what they find inside. Their songs have plenty of creative space for further fine tuning and variation. Consequently, live performances of songs by The Stones are usually very exciting, their loose improvisational style often teetering between total disaster and rock'n'roll perfection. Keith once said that if he was jumping around on stage, either things were going extremely well or they weren't going well at all. The beauty of it all is that it's hard to tell the difference.

My Philosophical Experiment

Ball of Fire is a 1941 *comedy* starring Barbara Stanwyck and Gary Cooper. The main action takes place in the home of a group of professors researching and updating an encyclopedia. Gary Cooper plays a professor studying contemporary slang. Barbara Stanwyck plays a gangster's moll, who knows too much and ends up hiding out from both the police and the gangsters in the home of the professors.

One day, Stanwyck walks in on a group of the professors researching the *conga,* a Latin American dance of African origin popular at the time. They have worked out its basic pattern: three step forwards followed by a kick. They have diagrammed it on the floor, and when Stanwyck walks in they are trying to understand the conga by following the steps marked on the floor. But with little success.

Stanwyck shakes her head in amazement and takes over by taking off the record playing in the background and putting on some conga music. Stanwyck's point, in effect, is that these scholars should ignore their objective formulas and diagrams and instead feel the conga 'from the inside.' Once they start dancing, the professors learn quickly what the conga's all about.

It's the same with The Stones. The celebrity profiling I've been describing obscures not only the fact that The Stones are essentially a live band, but also the history of what a live performance means in human experience and human history. To recover some of that, I want to go back in time, before The Stones, before the conga, all the way back to ancient Greece. I'm not too concerned with historical accuracy. We will never know the objective truth about the past, but our lack of objective certainty is not necessary a bad thing. It frees us to experiment and see if any new perspectives and ideas emerge that may be valuable.

Live at Epidaurus

For the ancient Greeks, everything that exists was called the *kosmos* ('order', 'world', 'universe') and was understood to be *aesthetikos*—the Greek word from which our word 'aesthetic' is derived. *'Aesthetikos'* meant 'perceive' and 'perceptions'. There is a sense therefore that, for the ancient Greeks, the universe is made up of 'perceptions.' Think of some of the Olympian 'smaller' spiritual forces, such as *nymphs* (river spirits), *Naiads* (spring-dwellers), *Nereids* (sea-dwellers), and *Dryads* (tree spirits). They are alive and active and perceive the regions and things they inhabit. In a sense, they *are* those perceptions, much as the Olympian gods, like Athena (the goddess of wisdom and war) and Aphrodite (the goddess of love), exists as wisdom, anger, or love in nature. In some cases, the ancient Greeks perceived each powerful emotion—like anger, hate, or erotic love—to be an active 'mass' or 'cloud' moving according to its own inner logic across the landscape. When a cloud strikes us, it envelops us, alters our perception of the world and then draws us forward, following its own logic and negating any plans we mere humans might have had.

For the Greeks, therefore, the phenomenological world they experienced was aesthetic, with physical and non-physical things alike being understood to exist *in the world*. There was no transcendent God, above and beyond His creation, as would become hallmarks of Jewish, Christian and Islamic religions. Everything that exists was in the world and everything that exists was an artistic, aesthetic expression of the world. Understanding and aesthetic experience, therefore, were not two different kinds of things. Thinking itself was understood to creatively shape meaning out of experience and bestow that meaning back into the world.

This is what makes The Rolling Stones *theorists* from my experimental point of view. The ancient Greek concept of *theoria* means a technique (*techne* means 'to bring forth') through which the aesthetic can *perceive itself*. *Theoria* should seem familiar to anyone who has seen The Stones play, given the two meanings it took in the ancient Greek world-view.

First, *theoria* meant the collective ritualistic dancing that took place in the large open-air Dionysian festivals every spring. (Dionysius was the god of wine and intoxication). Second, these festivals often produced a state of *ek-stasis*, or 'standing outside oneself'—ecstasy—which bestowed participants with an ability 'to look on' the world with the clarity of a God's eye point of view. In *theoria* ('to look on '), a clear head seems like a divine smile—a moment of grace.

The eruption of the '*ek-stasis*' of 'theoria' disrupted routine ways of thinking and acting—at least for awhile. Yet as a routine feature of early western civilization it cultivated what we now call our own "self-consciousness," and our ability to think reflectively about ourselves and our perceptions, to *think about thinking*. This comes easily to us. You can see what the ancient Greeks meant by *theoria* simply by looking at something, even continuing to look at this page, and then looking at yourself looking at this page. The ancient Greeks, on the other hand, were just discovering, identifying, and naming this human *techne*.

Music clearly played a central role in these festivals and in the evolution of *theoria*. *Theoria* was thought to arise spontaneously from the music played by the festival musicians who were themselves considered to be 'priests' and 'holy theorists'. The ancient Greeks found *theoria* to be so crucial to their own lives that they even developed professional 'theorists' whose job was to attend the festivals of other city-states in order 'to look on' their *theoria* and report back home.

After a few hundred years, *theoria* developed into the *theatron* ('looking place' or what we call the 'theatre'). Finally, it evolved into the concept of 'theory' as used in Plato's theory of ideas (or 'forms') and other philosophical theories. This concept of 'theory' is very close to ours, a 'theory' being a set of ideas, usually systematically ordered and arranged, designed to explain some thing or phenomena.

Zen and the Art of Being a Stones Fan

You can draw a direct line from the ancient Greek Dionysian festivals to a Stones concert of the twentieth or twenty-first century. I have no doubt that ancient Greeks, planning to go to a festival, got as anxious and flustered as I do when I hear about an upcoming tour (only that they didn't need to worry about tickets. Everyone was welcome!)

Rolling Stones fans too have been known to become intoxicated at these large open air concerts, drinking wine or engaging in the use of some other intoxicant. I am willing to bet that Stones fans have also experienced the *theoria* of collective ritualistic dancing. I have many times transcended myself in a moment of ecstasy, suddenly able 'to look on' my life and what I had done with it up to that time. This is why it is so easy and natural to organize my life and my history around The Stones concerts I've been to.

So, are The Stones 'theorists'? Yes—*in the ancient Greek sense of the word*. As an essentially live band, they play the same role as the festival musicians played in ancient Greek Dionysian festivals—festivals have never disappeared but merely have taken on different forms over the centuries. Their music incites us to collectively, ritualistically dance and offers us the opportunity to disrupt everyday patterns and routines of thinking and behaving and just possibly create seeds for new ways of thinking, understanding, and living in the future.

They do this, of course, through their music and the spectacles (like The Stones' famous stages and props) they invite us 'to look on' or theorize about at their concerts. Their songs articulate the realities of being human, perhaps most famously: 'Let's spend the night together'; 'I can't get no satisfaction'; 'look at that stupid girl'; 'I'm shattered'; 'I have to walk before they make me run' and so on. Their songs draw attention to important aspects of life that we seem to systematically over-look or are reluctant to admit. The *theoria* of The Rolling Stones has also expanded our musical vocabularies. Many Stones fans were introduced to the blues through the music of The Stones. Think of the ways in which they have 'spun' old genres in new ways, in some cases, creating songs archetypal of a complete genre.

As well, The Stones' musical theoria helps us to recognize self-transcendence and the importance of 'looking on' for living a good life. Their songs remind us to 'look on' our very being in the world, with its moods and feelings, cares and concerns, anx-ieties and fear, as well as hopes and aspirations, all of which fill our being at each and every moment. We often don't acknowl-edge what is really going inside and live in a state of optimal ignorance, telling ourselves: 'If ignorance is not bliss, then I don't know what is'.

But The Stones shove all that in our face and shatter it. And we should thank them for it. The Rolling Stones have played a valuable role involving nothing less than the ongoing develop-ment of human self-understanding for the last fifty years. Their music has aided many millions of people in our time to recognize their own capacity to look on life and negotiate their way through it in a quest for the good life. Like ancient Greek 'theorists,' the Rolling Stones have shown the way to philoso-phy, whose *'theoria'* too arises out of the spirit of music.

I can even claim that The Stones have shown me a way to religion (of a kind). I discovered it as I was travelling across Canada in 1974. It was on a washroom wall in a youth hostel on Prince Edward Island. One evening I was sitting around a campfire with other people staying at the hostel, playing gui-tars and singing songs. My contribution to the songfest were various songs from The Stones' catalogue.

After everyone called it a night, I went to the washroom where, totally exhausted, I sat down and looked up to read:

Zen is like the mind which understands The Rolling Stones.

I was enlightened.

8
Epicurean Satisfaction

RUTH TALLMAN

The Rolling Stones have long embodied the quintessential rock'n'roll lifestyle. If asked what moral code The Stones and their music endorse, many people would say that they don't have any morality, or that they embody an immoral lifestyle.

As it turns out, however, there is an important difference between morality, immorality, and amorality. Morality is the willful and considered adherence to a particular set of actions in the belief that those actions are right, and opposing actions are wrong. Immorality is just the opposite—the willful and considered deviation from a particular set of actions that are believed to be right. Both morality and immorality require that the agent recognize a moral code, and either choose to follow it, or choose to violate it. Amorality, on the other hand, involves acting without consideration for morality at all. Amoral people do not choose to follow or to break a moral code, but simply act with no thought to morality.

Although we tend to see the world in terms of polar opposites—there is moral, and then there is immoral—in reality there are many different, conflicting moral belief systems. If I accept moral code A, and you accept moral code B, it might be that I call some action moral while you call it immoral. Yet we're both accepting a moral system, and we could each live faithfully according to our accepted system, even though the two systems might prescribe different courses of action.

Why do people choose to live by particular moral codes? Although many of us follow a moral system without giving it much thought, simply because our parents, church, or society tell us to, when people adopt a moral system after thinking about it carefully, their reasons usually boil down to one simple answer: living according to that moral system is good, and will lead to happiness. This answer can help us see why there are so many different moral codes, for there is a great deal of disagreement regarding what kind of behavior leads to happiness. Regardless of how you think happiness is achieved, if you make decisions about how to behave based on those beliefs, you are living according to a moral code.

Though the music of The Rolling Stones may seem either immoral or amoral, an underlying moral system is there, if you know where to look. There's even a name for it: hedonism. Hedonism is a moral theory that tells us happiness is to be found through the fulfillment of desire and indulgence in pleasures. This might sound like immorality to you—or just a really good time!—but if you make the conscious decision to live in this way so as to achieve happiness, you are following the moral system called hedonism. This should come as good news to some of you, as you can now tell your parents, teachers, and bosses that your wild nights of indulgent partying are actually your way of behaving morally. You simply accept a different moral code than they do!

Out of Control

Our oldest record of people choosing to live according to a hedonistic moral code dates to the fourth century B.C. The people were called the Cyrenaics because their leader, Aristippus (around 435–356 B.C.), was from a place called Cyrene, in Greece. Although historians believe that the Cyrenaics were the first to systematize the moral code of hedonism, they lived so long ago we no longer have any of their writings. So, we have to rely on a biographer named Diogenes Laertius (third century A.D.), who was kind enough to write a book called *Lives of Eminent Philosophers*, in which he explains the belief systems of the many philosophers of his time, including Aristippus and the Cyrenaics.

Diogenes tells us that the Cyrenaics' version of hedonism was the first and most basic form of hedonism. It is sometimes called simple hedonism. The Cyrenaics believed that all pleasures are equally good, differing only to the extent that more intense, frequent, and long-lasting pleasures are better than more subtle, rare, and short pleasures. Basically, for the Cyrenaics, it was the more pleasure the better, and get it any way you can. Does this sound like anyone we know? Let's take a look at a few lyrical examples. "Shake Your Hips," a song from *Exile on Main St.*, urges us to focus on moving our bodies in pleasant ways. "Don't move your head / Don't move your hands / Don't move your lips / Just shake your hips / Do the hip shake, babe." The hips are the crux of many of life's pleasures. Of course, rock'n'roll was always about more than just the pleasures of dance form, and the pleasure from one gyration often hopes to lead to another. The lives of the Stones seems to make that clear.

In addition to just pursuing pleasure, we see an example of a "no holds barred" attitude to pleasure conveyed in the song, "Brown Sugar," from *Sticky Fingers*. Here, rough, bondage and discipline-type sex with sixteen-year-old black girls is endorsed. "Ah, brown sugar, how come you taste so good? / Ah, brown sugar, just like a young girl should." "Out of Control" from the 1998 album, *Bridges to Babylon*, sends a dual message: not only is it okay to pursue pleasure with untamed abandon, it's better to grab all the pleasure you can in the moment. There is an urgency, a sense that the best pleasures are fleeting and so must be seized before they are gone, that is clear example of Cyrenaic hedonism. "Now I'm out / Oh out of control / Now I'm out / Oh out of control /Oh help me now / In the hotel I'm excited / By the smile on her face."

The Stones' emphasis on bodily pleasures—sex and drugs—is in keeping with the Cyrenaic views on pleasure. What's more, the Cyrenaics tell us that, "pleasure is a good, even if it arises from the most unbecoming causes . . . for even if an action be ever so absurd, still the pleasure which arises out of it is desirable, and a good." (Diogenes Laertius, *Lives of Eminent Philosophers*). This type of thinking serves to justify the sorts of limit-pushing behavior described in "Brown Sugar," as well as "Rip This Joint," from *Exile*. "Mama says yes, Papa says no /Make up you mind 'cause I gotta go / Gonna raise hell at the Union Hall / Drive myself right over the wall."

Cyrenaic hedonism is about attaining particular instances of pleasure. Diogenes Laertius explains:

> Happiness is a state consisting of a number of particular pleasures, among which, those which are past, and those which are future, are both enumerated. And they consider that particular pleasure is desirable for its own sake; but that happiness is desirable not for its own sake, but for that of the particular pleasure. (*Lives of Eminent Philosophers*)

Rather than believing that we seek pleasure in order to be happy, the Cyrenaics think that happiness simply is a life of successive pleasures. They also believe that pleasures of the flesh will always trump pleasures of the mind. Unlike most moral theories, and even other forms of hedonism, Cyrenaic hedonism insists that the road to happiness lies not in our rational natures, but in our most base animal instincts. The Stones' 1969 song from *Let It Bleed*, "Monkey Man," could serve as a theme song for the entire Cyrenaic movement. The song not only acknowledges our animal nature, but embraces it. "I'm a fleabit peanut monkey /All my friends are junkies. . . . Well, I am just a monkey man / I'm glad you're a monkey woman too."

A Rolling Stone Gathers . . . Happiness?

Cyrenaic hedonism thrived in Greece for about a hundred years. Even after it died out, core hedonistic principles remained in the air. After about fifty years, another Greek philosophical school, led by Epicurus, decided to give hedonism another shot. The Epicureans followed the Cyrenaics in understanding pleasure as basic, but they argued that pursuing pleasure on the basis of sensation alone was inadequate. Cicero (106–43 B.C.), a Roman Epicurean, and one of the movement's most well-written spokesmen, explains that running headlong after pleasure in the manner of the Cyrenaics is flawed because, "great pains result for those who do not know how to pursue pleasure rationally."[1]

Where the Cyranaic recommendation was to grab hold of as many pleasures as quickly as you can, Epicurus recommends a careful study of the pleasure that awaits you before you decide

---

[1] Cicero, "On Ends," in *The Hellenistic Philosophers: Translations of the Principal Sources, with Philosophical Commentary*, Volume 1 (Cambridge University Press, 1987), p. 113.

to indulge. This is because, Epicurus points out, sometimes pleasures, though good in the moment, carry with them negative consequences as well. If a pleasure will lead to a future pain that is worse than the original pleasure was good, it makes sense to avoid it. Since the goal is to net as much pleasure as possible, it's foolish to reach for pleasures that bring along a negative balance of pain by the time all is said and done. What's more, sometimes it makes sense, according to Epicurus, for a hedonist to choose to engage in a painful action.

While this point would have been inexplicable for the Cyranaic hedonist, it has a clear logic. Some pleasant activities have negative consequences later, such as the small fortune Keef has spent on his drug-related legal woes. Conversely, some painful activities have pleasant consequences later, such as the cold-turkey aches, pains and messes, of kicking a junk habit that later enable the pleasure of raising children. Epicurus says, "We sometimes pass over many pleasures in cases where their outcome for us is a greater quality of discomfort; and we regard many pains as better than pleasures in cases when our endurance of pains is followed by a greater and long-lasting pleasure."[2]

The Epicureans differ from the Cyrenaics in other ways too. The Epicureans recommend learning to live very simply, as they believe that those who are unaccustomed to luxuries will derive the greatest pleasure when they do attain them. This is, of course, antithetical to the high-flying rock'n'roll lifestyle epitomized by the Stones, and exemplified in their songs.

Why would the Epicureans think that a life of quiet simplicity is to be preferred to the life of a rock star? Working from the belief that the intense pleasure of high luxury carries with it an unacceptable amount of pains as well, they advise us to find pleasure in simple, easy-to-attain goods, arguing that humbler joys actually end up amounting to more pleasure once you subtract all the pain that results in harder-to-get goods. The simple life is better, according to the Epicurean, because it removes the hassle and anxiety that always follows the thrill-seeker who has no time to rest before he is compelled to continue the hunt for his next pleasurable experience.

---

[2] Epicurus. Letter to Menoeceus, in *The Hellenistic Philosophers*, p. 114.

   Again, Keef is a prime example. The pleasure obtained from heroin is followed by incessant search for more fixes. Once a hedonist becomes accustomed to the intensity of the hard-to-attain pleasures, his taste for simple pleasures will be dulled, and he will no longer be able to derive satisfaction from those things. This is the desperation of 1971's "Sister Morphine" from *Sticky Fingers*: "Tell me, sister morphine /When are you coming round again? / Oh, I don't think I can wait that long / Oh, you see I'm not that strong." Keith Richards complained in a 2006 interview that he is no longer able to achieve a high off of drugs.[3] Rather than worry about all that, Epicurus advises avoiding hard-to-attain pleasures altogether, thus sparing the pain that comes when those pleasures are not available.

   While the Cyrenaics make it clear that they think one pleasurable activity is as good as any other, and that each should be judged merely in terms of the amount of pleasure it provides the person who engages in it, the Epicureans thought that pleasures exist in a hierarchy. Epicurus is very explicit about what he means in holding pleasure as the ultimate good, and he decidedly does not mean unbridled bodily indulgence. He says:

> We do not mean . . . those that consist in having a good time . . . but freedom from pain in the body and disturbance in the soul. For what produces the pleasant life is not continuous drinking and parties or pederasty or womanizing or the enjoyment of . . . dishes of the expensive table, but sober reasoning which tracks down the causes of every choice and avoidance, and which banishes the options that beset souls with the greatest confusion." (*The Hellenistic Philosophers*, p. 114)

For Epicureans, prudence is the greatest virtue, for it is the key that allows us to live happy lives. Although not a particularly common word today, the concept of prudence, or *phronesis*, in Greek, is an idea that is readily recognizable. Prudence is the ability to foresee the results of our actions, to recognize the implications for tomorrow of what we do today. Prudence was extremely important to the Epicureans because the ability to predict the consequences of our actions was integral to choos-

---

   [3] <www.dailymail.co.uk/tvshowbiz/article-406075/Rolling-Stones-star-gives-drug—theyre-weak.html>.

ing those actions that would lead to the most pleasure, all things considered, rather than the most pleasure right now. So you see, their goal of pleasure, pleasure, and more pleasure really isn't essentially different from the Cyrenaics, or the Stoics. The difference is their reliance on prudence to help them achieve more lifetime pleasure over pain. Unlike the Cyrenaics, they would not be continually subtracting from their pleasure score to account for the pains that inevitably follow the unconsidered pursuit of pleasure.

This doesn't mean the Epicureans had anything against physical pleasures, either. Cicero says, "I cannot conceive of anything as the good if I remove the pleasures perceived by means of taste and sex and listening to music. . . . Certainly it is impossible to say that mental delight is the only good."[4] What's more, the Epicureans are not categorically opposed to any particular pleasures. Epicurus says, "No pleasure is something bad per se: but the causes of some pleasures produce stresses many times greater than the pleasures."[5]

Rather than rule out certain kinds of pleasure altogether, then, the Epicureans merely rule out pleasures that result in greater pain than pleasure at the end of the day. This means that, though a particular pleasure, such as drug use, is still permissible, it must be indulged in a way that avoids the negative consequences that often follow it. A life free of addiction will have more pleasures than the life of an addict, so the Epicureans will advise responsible drug use that avoids the perils of addiction. Likewise, a life free of disease will have more pleasures open to it than a life cut short by AIDS, so sexual pleasures should be pursued in ways that minimize disease. In other words, if you ran into some Epicureans at a rock festival today, they'd be the ones passing out free condoms and running the needle exchange programs.

What Can a Poor Boy Do?

Since the purpose for adopting a moral code is the belief that it will lead to happiness, which form of hedonism—Cyrenaic or

---

[4] Cicero, "Tusculan Disputations," in *The Hellenistic Philosophers*, p. 117.
[5] Epicurus, "Key Doctrines," in *The Hellenistic Philosophers*, p. 115.

Epicurean—is more likely to do that? Is it better to live in the moment and fully enjoy each fleeting pleasure as it presents itself, or should we take a more considered and choosy approach to the pleasures we encounter, turning some pleasures down when it seems all things considered most reasonable to do so? A careful study of some of The Rolling Stones' lyrics can give us some insight into these questions.

At first glance, it looks as if the answer is clear. The music of The Rolling Stones reflects Cyrenaic hedonism. Time and again, The Stones seem to celebrate the unbridled indulgence of physical pleasures. One would think, since the songs tell us to be Cyrenaics, that The Stones' music could be understood as reflecting Cyrenaic hedonism as the moral path most likely to lead to happiness. But a closer look suggests that The Stones' most hedonistic songs are more about agonizing desire and unfulfilled pleasures, rather than the achievement of happiness through pleasurable indulgence. If this is the case, it could turn out that it's a mistake to understand The Stones as recommending Cyrenaic hedonism as the road to happiness.

Now I Need You More than Ever

The Stones' lyrics tell us that, sometimes, seeking pleasure can cause physical pain. In "Let's Spend the Night Together," from the 1967 album *Between the Buttons*, Jagger describes his bodily sufferings as he attempts to convince a woman to consent to the sexual pleasure he desires. "I'm going red and my tongue's getting tied / I'm off my head and my mouth's getting dry." While the physical manifestations of sexual desire are familiar not only to hedonists, if one's sole interest in a particular person is sexual satisfaction, pain at the denial of that satisfaction would be keenly felt.

More dramatically, "Sister Morphine" on *Sticky Fingers* describes the physical state of someone who has long enjoyed the intense pleasure of morphine and cocaine. Nearing death, he (or she, as the song was first written and recorded by Marianne Faithfull) is so weak he cannot even drag himself across the floor in pursuit of one last hit of the drugs that are killing him. If these two songs are representative, it seems the Epicureans are correct: pleasures can sometime bring serious pain along with them—pain so bad, it can end up being worse than the goodness of the pleasure that is initially sought.

I'm Shattered

The Stones' lyrics also point to psychological pain and trauma resulting from continually grappling for pleasures. Take *Flashpoint*'s 1991 song, "Sex Drive." "I got this sex drive / Driving me mad." Rather than experiencing pleasure, it looks as if the pursuit of pleasure is leading to pain, as it does in "Shattered" on *Some Girls*: "Laughter, joy and loneliness and sex and sex and sex and sex /Look at me, I'm in tatters!"

One of the songs in which the desperation and the failure to reach happiness through pleasure is most evident is "Undercover of the Night," where descriptions of various horrors—street violence, forced prostitution, unjustified, racially-motivated imprisonments by corrupt governments—are juxtaposed against an anguished pleading chorus begging for a hedonistic escape from these horrors, "Cuddle up, baby / Keep it all out of sight." But the plan doesn't work. At the end of the song we learn that the attempt to keep the desperation "undercover" fails: "All these things I can't keep inside" (*Undercover*, 1983).

Can You Always Get What You Want?

The Stones' muse is often the pain that results from the unbridled pursuit of pleasure, just as Epicurus warned. But, has this given us enough reason to reject Cyrenaic hedonism? One reason why someone might experience pain at the headlong pursuit of pleasure that would not count against Cyrenaic skepticism is that the pain is simply the result of failing to achieve the pleasure. If the pain described by The Stones is pain caused by the inability to attain a particular pleasure, rather than pain stemming from the pleasure itself, then the problem is not with the Cyrenaics' method, but simply with the individual who doesn't achieve the pleasure he seeks. In this case, the Epicurean recommendation to focus on simple, easy to achieve pleasures looks like a good one. The question is, can inability to attain the pleasure really be the problem The Stones seem to be having?

Here we are stepping into rather complicated territory, for we know that songwriters do not always speak with their own voices in songs. Songs are a form of art, and many, in fact probably most, songs contain elements of fiction. So we must not suppose that everything Mick claims to have done in a song is in fact something he had done in real life. So, Mick and Keef could write a song from the perspective of a person who is thwarted in love, or torn up by drugs, without actually having had that experience.

However, we also know that art is often autobiographical, and that The Stones have made it their business to project a public persona of decadent rock'n'rollers. The public face of a celebrity is not always a mirror of the way that individual actually lives, but there are certain readily available facts about the Rolling Stones, particularly Mick and Keith, which offer strong evidence to support the belief that they have in fact lived quite hedonistic lives. Jagger has seven children with four women, and is well known for his many high-profile dalliances with bombshells. Richards has been tried five times on drug charges, from marijuana to amphetamines to heroin. Additionally, both men are multi-millionaires and, despite being more than a little crusty, remain the objects of sexual desire for hundreds of thousands of women.

These facts about Mick and Keef, while not giving us any conclusive information regarding the extent to which their songs are autobiographical, do give us very good reason to believe that, if they experience unhappiness in the face of a pleasure, that unhappiness is not the result of a thwarted attempt to attain that pleasure. If they want to experience a pleasure, they have the money, celebrity, and raw sex appeal to make that happen. This is one reason why the morality of The Stones is so interesting. They have, over a period of many years, presented the case for Cyrenaic hedonism. Yet, their songs persistently reveal a nagging unhappiness and frustrating search for satisfaction.

Satisfaction?

Given what we have learned, we are now in a position to offer a suggestion. Cyreanic hedonism has been well tried by The Rolling Stones, and it clearly is not an effective road to happiness. Rather than give up hedonism altogether, though, the Epicurean modifications to the theory ought to be given a shot.

What would Epicurean Rolling Stones look like? Would the Stones themselves find the Epicurean lifestyle acceptable? The Epicureans agree with the Cyrenaics that bodily pleasures are good, and to be embraced, so the Stones can maintain their dedication to physical indulgence. However, rather than grabbing every opportunity for pleasure, they will need to pause and consider the consequences of their pleasurable activities, choosing only those pleasures that prudence tells them will result in more pleasure than pain.

There's some evidence that Epicurean-style hedonism would hold some appeal for The Stones. Consider "Waiting on a Friend," from 1981's *Tattoo You*: "Making love and breaking hearts / It is a game for youth / But I'm not waiting on a lady / I'm waiting on a friend." Or, *Exile's* "Happy" explains pretty clearly that Keith sees love, instead of money or a career, as the road to happiness. This lends more credence to the argument that tempered hedonism beats unbridled hedonism. The Epicurean version of pleasure fulfillment just might be the path to contentment and, finally, some real satisfaction.

III

Time Is on Rock's Side

9
From Main Street to Guyville

George A. Reisch

In the summer of 1971, The Stones were living in the south of France. They left England after splitting with their manager, Allen Klein, and finding themselves broke and potentially in big trouble. Klein had purchased the publishing rights to their songs from Decca, their former English label, leaving The Stones with little income to pay the enormous tax bills they faced. Mick and Keith had already been arrested on drug charges in 1967, and they probably weren't looking forward to another round of legal problems over unpaid taxes. So they headed for the Riviera.

Their new home base was a mansion named Nellecôte. Keith, Anita Pallenberg, and their son Marlon lived upstairs, while downstairs became a kind of daily headquarters for the rest of the band and their friends. With the famous mobile recording truck parked just outside, the mansion's basement became a recording studio and the sessions were going well. New songs, some of The Stones' best, were born nightly.

Yet Nellecôte was not home. The Stones were still rolling, their eyes now set on the United States. Their original musical love, American blues, had by now moved over to make room for American country music, a new interest fed by Keith's friendship with Gram Parsons, the former Byrd and country-music purist who visited Nellecôte that summer and taught Keith how to play and sing country classics. The band's financial problems also pointed them to the United States, for they knew that only by creating a great album and following it with a successful tour of America could they get their financial problems solved.

Even the title of that future album, *Exile on Main Street*, pointed to America. There are no "main streets" in England or France, after all. And its artwork featured an unmistakable collage of photos from Robert Frank's *The Americans*—a book that portrayed Americans in such a freakish, carnevalesque light that it only found a publisher in the United States after it had become a hit in (of all places) France. With snaps from *The Americans* on the cover, the new album seemed to say that Americans were just as freakish, out-of-place, and dangerous as England's long-haired bad boys of rock'n'roll. If The Stones belonged anywhere, it was the cultural and ethnic circus of America.

The View from Guyville

Some twenty years later, Liz Phair was living in Chicago, writing songs, and listening routinely to one of her longtime favorite albums, *Exile on Main Street*. Her self-produced "girlysound" cassettes were a hit with those who knew them, and at least two local producers were eager to producer her album. When it was finished, Phair shocked almost everyone by calling it *Exile in Guyville* and saying that it was as a "song by song response" to *Exile on Main Street*.

Ever since, critics, journalists, and fans have wondered what this means and whether it's true. There seem to be two camps—those who *accept* Phair's album as a genuine response to *Main Street*, and take it to be about gender and the sexual politics of a woman in the largely male world of rock and pop. The second, larger camp is skeptical about whether or how *Guyville* has any relationship to *Main Street*. The album's blurb at Amazon.com, for example, calls the claim "unlikely." Rock critic Jim DeRogatis tends to agree, though he admits that he might just be missing something. "I'm still not sure whether or not I believe her," he wrote.[1]

Even the liner notes to the fifteen-year anniversary edition of *Guyville* hold Phair's claim at arm's length. The writer takes a pass on the issue to say "I was never able to actually connect all the dots myself."[2] In the video included with the anniver-

---

[1] <www.jimdero.com/News2002/GreatPhair.htm>.
[2] *Exile in Guyville* (ATO, 2008, CD with bonus DVD).

sary edition, Phair reminisces with friends and producers who were there as the album was being born, yet still remain at-sea about her "song-by-song response" claim. The co-president of Matador records recalls the hype about it and stops himself to ask her skeptically, "Is that true?" "Yes!" Phair insists. Her one-time producer, John Henderson, scoffs at the idea that Phair really "spent months assembling this song-by-song response to the Rolling Stones. . . ." Again, Phair interrupts. "John! I *did*! Cross my heart and hope to die. Why would I lie now?"

Good question. Phair does not need to lie about *Guyville* now, for if she were trying to promote it by spreading rumors about its kinship with *Main Street* that effort seems pointless. Her album long ago took its place alongside *Main Street* itself in critics' best-of lists and in praise from other artists. Given that so many still find the idea puzzling and unclear, it probably was never a good marketing tool.

Why not take Phair at her word, assume she consciously created *Guyville* as a song-by-song response to *Main Street,* and figure out what her claim means?

Along the way, there's a good philosophical explanation for why it is that fans, critics, and even her friends and producers have found her claim so enigmatic. What her song-by-song response *doesn't* mean is that her songs *sound like* their counterparts on *Main Street.* The assumption that they should goes back well beyond *Exile on Main Street* to certain ideas popularized in Plato's Academy, where Plato taught his thought-by-thought responses to *his* predecessors (though, it seems to me, his responses weren't always improvements and they did nothing to help us understand the two *Exiles*).

Répondez S'il Vous Plaît

With eighteen songs a piece, there is automatically a one-to-one relationship between each pair of songs. But what kinds of relationships are they? First, they could be merely formal, with Phair deciding that each song on her album would have some structural or musical qualities in common with its counterpart on *Main Street*—a similar (or opposite) tempo? The same key? The same or a similar lyrical structure? I say "merely formal" because these relationships come easy. *Any* album with eighteen songs can be said to have a "song-by-song" relationship with *Main Street* as long as the relationships include things like "being very different" and "not sounding half as good."

Phair obviously had other kinds of relationships in mind, too. Is each song on *Guyville* some kind of *psychological or emotional response* to the corresponding song on *Main Street*? Phair may have regarded Mick and Keith's songs as Rorschach inkblots, listened to them and thought about them, and then said to herself, "Okay, now I'll write a song like that, but do it in my own way." Like an association test—tell me what comes to mind when you hear *this* guitar riff or *this* lyric?—*Guyville* might be Phair's attempt to personalize the feelings and emotions she hears in *Main Street*. Finally the relationships might be *critical* or *theoretical*, meaning that Phair's songs respond to *Main Street*'s ideas about life, people, romance, relationships, exile, and the rest of the human circus depicted on the album's cover. From this angle, the song-by-song response sets up something like a debate or discussion about things that go beyond the craft of songwriting and musical aesthetics.

If you make a playlist that puts Phair's responses next to each song on *Main Street*, you'll hear all three kinds of relationships.

In part, *Guyville* is a sonic response to the world's greatest rock'n'roll band and its macho, masculine sound. Phair's "girlysound" tapes, containing demos for some of the songs on *Guyville*, point directly to her unmistakeably light, nimble guitar playing. Compared to Keith's crunchy Les Pauls and Telecasters, her Fender Duo-Sonic sounds clean and fast. And her voice has none of Mick's bark and shout.

Emotional relationships abound, too, in so far as Phair's songs, like Mick's and Keith's, often look at romance, sex, and relationships, though they emerge through a different prism and sensibility.

Yet the most interesting responses, at least to me, are the ideas Phair puts on the table alongside these formal and emotional or affective relations. Yes, Mick and Keith know a thing or two about exile and the human condition, but they don't know everything. And they're not twenty-two, female, and trying to launch a music career in Chicago in the early 1990s.

Bloody Hermeneutics

Phair's "song-by-song response" is real, complicated, and not usually obvious. You have to compare each pair of songs deliberately and analyze them in terms of these three kinds of relationship and follow the clues, usually lyrical, that show Phair's mind at work in response to what Mick and Keith originally wrote. In no cases is her "song-by-song response" rule-bound or automatic—as if she had said, 'when Keith plays it like *this*, I'm going to play it like *that*; when Mick sings slowly, I'll sing slowly'. In each case, you have to do some thinking and interpreting, some hermeneutics, to solve the puzzle and see the relationships in play.

The good news is that you don't have to learn anything new about hermeneutics because you're already doing it. Start with this very page and the little squiggles on it. You assemble them into larger and larger chunks—words, sentences, paragraphs, sections—and extract from all them the meanings and ideas I, as a writer, am trying to convey. The essential point of philosophical hermeneutics is that you are an active participant in this transfer. You are not a passive receptacle, like a DVD reader or a scanner that just takes in the information and meanings that are specified and final. Instead, what you take away from the squiggles on this page is jointly created by my words and intentions and the way you read and understand them—a way that is shaped by your own history, your experiences, your knowledge and expectations.

Because author and reader are both involved, everything gets more complicated when viewed through hermeneutic lenses. We tend to think that meanings and ideas in works of art are objective and simply *there* to be understood. But that's not so. Most hermeneutic theories accept that things like

the meaning of the song "Rocks Off"

are not really "things" at all. That is, they are not objective and unchanging, as are things like tables and stones and guitars. Different listeners will find different meanings in the words and in their delivery. Take the famous first lyric, the "yeeaaahhh" that Mick sings off-mic as Keith's and Mick Taylor's guitars start churning: It's like Mona Lisa's smile. Is Mick being sarcastic? Ironic? Winking at the listener? Just clearing his throat? A bit tired from all the smoke and drink at Nellecôte? Mick himself, I bet, hears and appreciates these possibilities when he listens to the track now, almost forty years later.

If you take this ambiguity and plurality seriously, it affects the very idea of what works of art like *Exile on Main Street* and *Exile in Guyville* really *are*. Instead of being fixed in all their attributes and significance, they become more fluid and multivalent and complicated. This is not to say that meanings are whatever you want them to be, but it does remind us that artists like The Stones interpret and evaluate their own work not after it's sprung from their heads in final form but as its being created. They listen to vague musical ideas, demo tapes, and countless recordings and make decisions about what's good and bad, what works and what doesn't, in the same way that their fans listen to the recordings that became the 'official' album-versions.[3]

The fact that fans and critics come later to this arena of interpretation doesn't change the fact that it's always been, and will remain, an arena of interpretation. Over time, artists and fans will revise their understandings and decide, for example, that some obscure, unsuccessful album is in fact an underappreciated gem, or that an elaborately produced album that once made a splash is not a "real" album for the band—like *Their Satanic Majesties' Request*, which fits both descriptions depending on your hermeneutic stance. With hermeneutics, then, meaning flows into metaphysics and reveals it as shifting, growing, or even dying away. More let it bleed than let it be.

Testing One Two Three

How do you know whether an interpretation of a lyric, a song, or (in our case) a relationship between a pair of songs is a good and trustworthy?

One yardstick is coherence. A good interpretation must hang together internally with other accepted facts and ideas about the work in question. The German philosopher Martin Heidegger,

---

[3] Check out Jean-Luc Godard's film *Sympathy for the Devil* which documents some of the in-studio development of this Stones classic from dull and plodding to the frenetic up-tempo classic.

usually credited as the founder of modern hermeneutics, articulated how this process takes place within a "hermeneutic circle." It's circular because interpretation never advances linearly in one direction from, say, ignorance to understanding. To even begin to analyze a book or an album, you've got to start with a stockpile of knowledge and assumptions about it. But as you build up an interpretation, you will inevitably revisit and perhaps revise these initial assumptions and beliefs as new information and ideas are added into the mix.

A word or phrase may seem to mean that Mick is angry. But something in the next verse might suggest that, in fact, the phrase is ironic or satirical. The coherence test requires that the more you interpret, the more you circle back and revise various parts of your understanding, your work must converge toward a coherent, unified idea or set of ideas. What should *not* happen, as philosopher Martin Eger puts it, is that we "go drastically astray or oscillate forever between opposing poles—we converge."[4] Without convergence, it's time to retool and start over.

Really? You Guys Are into Music?

As for Phair's song-by-song response, start with is Guyville itself, a place Phair described as

> a specific scene in Chicago—predominately male, indie-rock—and they had their little establishment of, like, who was cool, who was in it, who played in what band. Each one wore their record collection, so to speak, like a badge of honor. Like, 'This is my identity, this is what I'm into, and I know a lot about it.'

This was Bucktown and Wicker Park, neighborhoods in Chicago that were informal home bases for the "alternative" bands getting attention at the time, such as Urge Overkill, Smashing Pumpkins, and Material Issue. When Phair arrived after graduating from Oberlin in the 1980s, she met the guys there head-on. "Really? Okay, so you guys are into music. Watch—I can make music."[5]

---

[4] Martin Eger, *Science, Understanding, and Justice* (Open Court, 2006), p. 9.
[5] <www.villagevoice.com/2008-06-17/music/liz-in-the-afternoon-the-oral-history>.

But *Guyville* is not just eighteen different takes on what it means to be a woman in a (predominantly) male musical world. That's part of it, but Phair goes down *Main Street* and is most interested in what exile really means, and the different forms it can take. On *Main Street* there are at least three kinds of exile in play—sexual or romantic exile in regard to the opposite sex; exile in the geographical sense that involves ideas about other places, travel, and searching for a literal (or sometimes metaphorical) home; and a kind of exile or alienation from one's self, or the self one wants to be or has been, that I call existential exile.

Romantic Exile

An example of romantic or sexual exile are the tenth songs on each album, Keith's "Happy" and Phair's "Fuck and Run." They have similar tempos and describe life from a first person perpective. Keith sings "I need a love to keep me happy" and he's got two—Anita and his son Marlon. Phair wants to be happy, too. Phair "woke up alarmed," so it's clear right away that she's not so happy. But she's just like Keith. She's wishing for the kind of relationships he's got. Instead, she keeps finding herself with guys who, unlike Keith, don't need a love to be happy. They get up out of bed and say they've got "a lot of work to do." "Whatever happened to a boyfriend," Phair asks—"the kind of guy who makes love cause he's in it?"

In other songs, Phair's not so much identifying with the Stones as playing and flirting with them. In "Loving Cup," Mick is intoxicated with desire for a woman who won't give in to him. "Give me a little drink from our loving cup," he pleads in every chorus. But in "Mesmerizing," Phair's response, she wants to be the hypnotist who can put such a spell on her beloved: "I want to be mesmerizing too . . . to you."

Geographic Exile

An example of geographic or spatial exile is *Main Street*'s "Shine a Light," track 17. It's a lament and a prayer for someone down and out in an alley and someone stuck in hospital room "10-0-9." Phair's "Stratford-on-Guy" puts herself in a similar kind of limbo, on a airplane in seat "27D." Sonically, Phair's guitar and the flanged drums echo the phasey organ of "Shine a Light," but most of the connections between the songs are substantive. The light Mick calls to shine down on his downtrodden friends appears in Phair's song as the setting sun. It sets "to the left of the plane" and fills the cabin "with an unearthly glow" that adds to the disorientation her "movie-sized" situation. In Phair's song, at least, Mick's prayer is answered: "It took an hour, maybe a day," she sings. "But once I really listened, the noise just went a way."

Existential Exile

As for existential exile, take "Sweet Black Angel," track 8 in which Mick sings about Angela Davis, the philosophy professor imprisoned in 1970 and charged (but found innocent) in the murder of a judge by black panthers. She's "a pin up girl," known in the Seventies for her hair and her good looks—but "she ain't no singer, and she ain't no star." Mick and Keith sing for her freedom as she's "counting up the minutes" and "counting up the days." In calling her "a sweet black slave," they compare the "chains" of her imprisonment and the larger shadow of slavery in America.

Phair's response, the eerie and beautiful "Canary," sounds entirely different. She plays piano quietly and simplistically, suggesting a very different sonic landscape (compared to the uptempo country of "Sweet Black Angel") in which to make a very different point about exile and imprisonment. Putting herself in a cage "like a good canary," Phair transforms the chains of Davis's prison cell into the chains of the formal education of a proper young girl in tony Winnetka, Illinois:

> I learn my name
> I write with a number two pencil
> I work up to my potential
> I earn my meat
> I come when called.

Different scenarios follow in later verses, all of which lead Phair to contemplate her own act of domestic terrorism: "Send it up on fire, death before dawn."

Mick and Liz: Partners in Crime?

These are only a few examples, but they illustrate how nearly all of Phair's songs can be compared with their counterparts on

Main Street and seen as a "response." (Phair's responses to the other songs are described briefly at the end of this chapter.) At the same time, though, Phair's *Guyville* is no hermeneutical exercise or game, like a musical sudoku or crossword puzzle. On top of all this song-by-song dialogue and clever conversation she creates with *Main Street*, there is an undeniable personal and emotional investment. There are clues, scattered across *Guyville*, that Phair is not just a songwriting woman walking down Main Street with Mick and Keith and comparing notes about exile. Instead, she *is* the woman, or all of the women, whom they praise, seduce, and argue with over the course of their album.

In "Tumbling Dice," Mick says he's "playing the field every night" but being worn down by the women who are "always trying to waste" him. They demand too much of him, he complains. And they are always "bitchin'" about his behavior. Not Phair, whose "Never Said" responds by taking the high, quiet road about some secret rendezvous. If she and Mick had ever been "partners in crime"—or if, in the language of "Loving Cup," she had been the one Mick wanted to "spill the beans with" all night—Phair never spilled the beans about spilling the beans. Or, in her words, "I didn't let the cat out."

As for what might have transpired, listen to Phair's declaration of lust, "Flower," itself a response to Mick's ode to "the bedroom blues" in "Let It Loose." Phair's methodical description of her lover's anatomy lingers on his lips. They are, she says, "a perfect suck-me size." His lips, of course, go with his tongue, and that's what takes the spotlight in her song "Glory," Phair's response to "Shake your Hips." Where Mick focuses on a woman's hips (and not "your head," "your hands," or "your lips"—"just your hips"), Phair is enthralled by some guy with a "really big tongue." "It rolls way out" and sends her into a glorious reverie.

Now this rings a hermeneutic bell, because Jagger's are the most famous lips and tongue in rock. They became a logo for the band in 1971 when he commissioned artist Jim Pasche to design some artwork. Meeting with Jagger made the job easy: "Face to face with him," Pasche said, "the first thing you were aware of was the size of his lips and his mouth."[6] It's hard to

---

[6] Quoted by Peter Walker, "Wealth and Taste: V&A Buys Original Rolling Stones Logo," *Guardian* (September 2nd, 2008).

believe, therefore, that Phair's songs about a lover's lips, and another about his tongue, the third and fourteenth songs in an album that explicitly nods to The Rolling Stones, are not evidence that Phair was in the midst of some obsession with Jagger himself.

For me, the clincher came when I went back over Phair's lyrics a second and third time looking for additional clues. And there it is, in the very first song, "6'1''", Phair's opening response to *Main Street*'s "Rocks Off." Mick complains that his life has become a narcotized blur. He's "zipping through the days at lightning speed," and his sex life is *on* the rocks. He's so frazzled and out of touch, he says, "I can only get my rocks off while I'm sleeping."

In reply, Phair sings as an observer, perhaps even a therapist, who is trying to diagnose the underlying logic and emotion behind this over-the-top, rock-star lifestyle:

> I bet you fall in bed too easily
> with all the beautiful girls who are shyly brave
> And you sell yourself as a man to save
> But all the money in the world is not enough.

She's looking at a guy who once knew a thing or two about *satisfaction*—and who might that be?—yet has "long since passed understanding what it takes to be satisfied." Like "a vine that keeps climbing higher," he's got no goal, resting point, or hope for satisfaction in sight. Even the "yeah" she sings before the last chorus, seems to poke at Mick's famous "yeah" in the opening bars of "Rocks Off."

With You It's Always Take, Take, Take

Now Phair has discussed the origins of "6' 1"." She says that the guy in her song is not Jagger. But that doesn't disprove my interpretation. In fact, it's about both Jagger and someone else:

> **LIZ PHAIR:** I had this huge crush on this guy in the scene. He and I had like a couple interactions but nothing really serious, and I invented in my crazy-ass mind, the idea [that on] *Exile on Main Street*, Mick's character was

this guy. And so whenever I listened to *Exile on Main Street*, I felt like I was listening to what this guy. . . .

NPR: This guy who shall remain nameless . . .

LIZ PHAIR: Except if you buy the [anniversary] DVD. [I]t was totally a picture of his life. It was a perfect portrait of his life.

NPR: So you superimposed The Stones on your life.

LIZ PHAIR: On my crazy-ass crush. And then I sort of wrote back to him. Because if you think about the first song on *Exile on Main Street*, he's coming home from this one-night stand and he runs into some girl he knows who's sort of like "Where you been?" And he's still fucked up from the night before staring at her like, "Look." And he kind of alludes to this dancer chick he was just fucking before and he's like, "Look man, I can't deal with you right now," and walks off. So I put myself in the shoes of that girl he meets on the street, and that's how I write "6'1"." . . . [I]t was my answer to this guy vis-à-vis The Stones.

NPR: Did he look like Mick Jagger in any way?

LIZ PHAIR: Yeah. He didn't look like him, but he sure as hell acted like him.[7]

The guy in question, the Anniversary DVD reveals, is Nash Kato of Urge Overkill. And the reviewer's question, "Did he look like Mick Jagger?" goes to the hermeneutic jugular. No, Phair says, "he didn't look like him." But, of course, in another way he did. Phair already said that Jagger's performance was "a perfect portrait" of Kato.

These shifting grounds of interpretation—what do you *mean* by "look like"?—point to the layers of interpretations that surround any work of art. Martin Eger calls this the "cascade of interpretations" and in this case it begins with Mick who describes (and thus interprets) a character that's probably a lot like himself at the time (or quite possibly Keith, who seems to

---

[7] Jacob Ganz, "A Guy in Guyville," National Public Radio (June 4th, 2008).

be the inspiration for "Torn and Frayed"). Then Phair steps in, adds another layer by reading the song not only in terms of Mick's character in the song and the song's lyrics, but also her real-life fascination with Kato. By the time she describes her account to NPR, however, Phair's obsession with Kato seems to have transformed the interpretation she took from Mick. For in "Rock's Off," there's really no brush-off of the kind Phair describes. Jagger never says "look I can't deal with you," for he's too busy saying he can't deal with anything or anyone. The only satisfaction he's finding is in "dreaming," or "sleeping" . . . alone.

My point is not that Phair misread the song, but rather that Phair is actively *reading* the song (as anyone does) and constructing an interpretation that is true to her situation and interests. *Guyville* opens a window on this cascade of interpretations: There's Mick's take on the self-abusive rock-star life in "Rocks Off," Phair's take on Mick's take (which is doubly informed by her crush on Nash Kato), my take on Phair's take on Mick's take. It's interpretations—impressionistic, malleable, and reviseable—all down the line.

Exile from Ancient Greece—Yeah!

An obvious objection is the familiar cry of anti-relativist fundamentalists who put albums like *Main Street* in a pantheon of absolute, unchanging greatness. They scoff at the very idea that its meaning or importance has something to do with what Liz Phair thinks, or what I think. *Exile on Main Street* doesn't need to be interpreted, they'll say, because its greatness and importance is self-explanatory. Just *listen* to it!

But the self-explanatory claim is self-defeating: if the meanings and ideas in *Exile on Main Street* having nothing to do with what Liz Phair thinks, they don't have anything to do with what anti-relativist fundamentalists think, either. And I doubt any serious Stones fan wants to go there. If *Main Street* speaks to you, that means you're listening to it and you are involved in determining what you are hearing.

Neither The Rolling Stones, nor their fans, nor Liz Phair's fans were looking for some kind of philosophical enlightenment on this, but that's part of what *Guyville* offers. For while most commentators and critics were making light of Phair's claim, as if she had no idea what she was talking about, her song-by-song claim turns out to be no mere gimmick: it speaks volumes about how we listen to and think about music that, so far as I can see, are correct and important.

Look again at the near-universal bewilderment over her claim. When they heard that Phair's great new album was a "song-by-song response" to *Exile on Main Street*, what do you suppose was the hermeneutical starting point of all these skeptics? What did they suppose that claim meant? Most likely, they presumed that *Guyville*'s songs were going to *sound like* the songs on *Main Street*. When they didn't, the indie rock world shrugged its shoulders and figured the confusion was Phair's, not theirs.

The mistake is not new. Since Plato and Aristotle, we've tended to assume that artistic or intellectual inspiration inevitably involves some kind of *imitation*. What it means to understand the beauty of a statue, Aristotle would say, involves your mind actually containing a copy or representation of its shape and contours; what it means to study astronomy—among the most exalted human activities for Plato—is to establish mathematically precise and elegant harmonies in your thoughts that mirror those of the celestial bodies overhead. So, when Phair announced that her new album was an answer to *Exile on Main Street*, listeners probably assumed that *Guyville* would be some kind of imitation of that classic album.

Yet to understand her song-by-song response, you have to jettison this prejudice that inspiration means imitation as well as the non-hermeneutical metaphysics of art that goes along with it. This is no small maneuver, for the history of pop music has been in large part a celebration of imitation and pretense. When The Stones first started playing, their goal was to imitate the sounds and words that blew them away on records by Muddy Waters, Chuck Berry, and other blues artists. But they became the world's greatest rock'n'roll band by later cultivating a sound and sensibility that was all their own.

It's a long way from the sockhop of "Around and Around," which Mick and Keith did not write, to the social commentary of "Nineteenth Nervous Breakdown," which they did. Still, it doesn't stretch the imagination too much to understand even The Stones' recent work as a kind of "response" to the blues that originally inspired them. A response, that is, need not be an imitation. But until Phair woke us up and made us think about this, we tended to assume that's what it had to be.

One clue that Phair knew exactly what she was doing, philosophically speaking, is *Guyville*'s closer "Strange Loop." As the song and album end, her guitar riff morphs gradually into the opening chords of "6' 1"." She's pointed us back to the beginning, to the start of her album. But since she's also pointed to *Exile on Main Street* with her "song-by-song" claim, why not go back to that album and revisit, if not revise, our knowledge and appreciation of that album? It is a great album, obviously. But that doesn't mean it's finished and done, that it's the last word on exile, on America, on alienation and the rest of the human circus. Since she wrote *Guyville* in Chicago, home to Chess Studios and the legendary Checkerboard Lounge—Mick and Keith's unofficial musical mecca of Chicago blues—*Guyville* traced a hermeneutic circle in more ways than one.

Phair's Song-by-Song Responses to *Exile on Main Street*

Songs about Romantic or Sexual Exile

TRACK 1: "Rocks Off" and "6' 1"." Mick's take on life in the sexual fastlane, and Phair's observations about a similarly oversexed, unhappy guy who's searching for satisfaction.

TRACK 9: "Loving Cup" and "Mesmerizing." Unrequited lust from a male and then a female perspective. Mick wants to be intoxicated; Phair wants to do the intoxicating and nods to the middle-eight in "Rocks Off"—"It's all mesmerized all that inside me."

TRACK 10: "Happy" and "Fuck and Run." Keith's loves stick around, and that's all he needs to keep him happy. Phair's never do. She's not happy.

TRACK 11: "Turd on the Run" and "Girls! Girls! Girls!" Mick gets dumped and he's angry about it. Phair toys with her guys all the time and gets away "with what the girls call murder."

TRACK 12: "Ventilator Blues" and "Divorce Song." There are tense times when that "your gun in hand" becomes your code of living and "everybody's going to need a ventilator." Phair needs air, too, and she pulls the trigger on a relationship. "You put in my hands a loaded gun," she sings, "and asked me not to fire it."

TRACK 16: "Stop Breaking Down" and "Gunshy." Mick's "Mama got a pistol" and "laid it down on me." Phair takes "rifle in hand" to steel herself against the routine of being someone's "wife."

TRACK 18: "Soul Survivor" and "Strange Loop." Mick sees himself drowning in a shipwrecked relationship (probably with Bianca). Phair needs to end a relationship because she's "tired of fighting" and must be "adamantly free." Mick would "rather drink seawater" than stay on this ship, but Phair thinks her guy will be back: "nothing feeds a hunger like a thirst."

Songs about Geographical Exile or Place

TRACK 2: "Rip this Joint" and "Help Me Mary." Mick and Co. bounce from city to city in America, while Phair "locks [her] doors at night" to keep out the hordes of guys who invade her apartment and "leave suspicious things in the sink."

TRACK 6: "Sweet Virginia" and "Soap Star Joe." The Stones praise California's wine and sand, but they sing for Virginia. Phair sings about a wandering "hero" who rode into town and believes he is the embodiment of America—"you're looking at it, Babe."

TRACK 15: "All Down the Line" and "Johnny Sunshine." Mick's train is moving through town quickly, so won't you be his "little baby for a while"? Phair's been dumped and taken for "everything" she owns. He stole her car and her horse. He didn't take a train.

TRACK 17: "Shine a Light" and "Stratford on Guy." Two laments for struggling individuals—a dear friend of Mick's away from home in hospital room "10-0-9" and the "movie-sized" drama of Phair's own life that she observes in the glittering lights below her seat "27D."

Songs about Existential Exile or Self-Alienation:

TRACK 7: "Torn and Frayed" and "Explain it to Me." Mick pays tribute to the guitar player who's becoming a pharmaceutical wreck, but can "steal your heart away" with his guitar playing. Phair puzzles over "medicine" and the "fame injection" that allow someone "jump higher" and "run farther" than they should.

TRACK 8: "Sweet Black Angel" and "Canary." Mick's anthem for Angela Davis, the philosopher and political activist imprisoned in 1970. Phair knows why the caged girlfriend sings.

TRACK 13: "I just Wanna See His Face" and "Shatter." Mick sings about Jesus (sometimes you don't "want to walk and talk about Jesus / You just want to see his face"), while Phair finds her world shattered by a guy who makes her see herself in a profoundly different light ("something about being with you/slapped me right in the face").

10
When the Whip Comes Down

RANDALL E. AUXIER

> One thing drives another in a band. It all has to melt together.
> Basically it's all liquid.
>
> —Keith Richards, *Life*

Rock'n'roll music isn't supposed to be healthy or wholesome, but it's got its own satisfaction(s). It's all about energy and what to do with it. To organize energies you have to constrain them for a moment, to store up some excess, to hold that excess (against its natural tendency to flow out and diffuse itself into moments of pure enduring), and then release it again in little bursts of suffering life. To rock'n'roll is to release that pent-up power in tiny explosions, between sixty and a hundred sixty times per minute, in groups of four.

You can tell it's rock'n'roll when every explosion destroys as much as it creates. It has to do that to rock. You might swing or two-step without hurting anything, but you'll never rock until you are willing to whip the moment into submission even as you make time. Keith Richards calls it the "discipline" of a rhythm section. You have to chain something up, and whip it until it feels bad enough to be good. That is the rhythm of rock'n'roll. It stings the hindside of the gods, because even they don't get to live forever without at least dying a little death at the end of every bar.

Mad Men

Whenever the music gets too acceptable, too commercial, too packaged, whenever it starts to look too sanitary, you can bet that some kind of upheaval is in the offing. Rock re-invents itself by pulling down whatever it has built. It's easy to see the pattern now, that for every Hall and Oates chart-topper, there is a sneering Johnny Rotten take-down, or if you can't quite handle any more Culture Club, there is Kurt Cobain to take a bullet for you and for many.

And so it goes. That balance between pop swill and rock music has always been uncomfortable, but it's clearer now what rock does to cleanse itself of the disgusting sweet excrescence that just is the music business. It makes your fingers sticky, no matter who you are. But back in the day, you know, 1965 or so, it was difficult to know what to do about Herman's Hermits, and the ridiculous Freddie and the Dreamers, and the list goes on.

But rock'n'roll is able to survive its occasional confinement in that thin air, high above Madison Avenue and Fleet Street. It's like electricity trapped in the clouds; somehow rock music finds its way to ground. The Mad Men devise their insulators, little three-minute morsels of mind-numbing neutrons, weighing down the real protons, with only a few sugary electrons in orbit, and they sell it to the kids. But the kids are already jumping with their own charges and pretty soon, well, let's just say they'll get their ya-yas out. When they do what all of nature commands and commends, Herman's Hermits won't turn the tricks anymore. They need some real rhythm, and that means something has to be under the whip. Enter their Satanic Majesties. I promise to reveal, in the end, what gets sacrificed on that altar.

"It"

For now let's concentrate on the energy, that electricity that always finds its way to ground. It's difficult to offer a schematic of the circuit path. Whatever it is that makes a man or a woman into a conduit of all that energy isn't captured in any theory, or even any folk wisdom I know of. But it's obvious when it's working. Celebrity, star power, may intensify that energy, make it shine, but the basic stuff, whatever "It" may be, is something apart from that. It isn't the glitz that draws the lightning down. I'm sure of that because I know that this "It" can live in obscurity and often does. By chance some night, maybe you drop into some joint by the wayside, and some guys you never heard of are there just rocking the place, wailing and rattling the walls, and everybody is gripped by "It." These cats aren't headed anywhere, but they have the present moment tied to the post, already black and blue and begging for more of the same. I know you've been there.

This is a chapter about "It." I don't mean the "it" in "it's raining" or "it's too hot," and this is not just one of the words the Knights of Ni cannot hear. I'm talking about the what-ness and the that-ness of the It in "he has It" or, in the case of The Stones, "they have It." What It is, in no uncertain terms, is a path to ground for whatever floats in the atmosphere as potential energy, and then suddenly finds a circuit completed, when the right components are hooked up and tied down in the right order. This is musical metaphysics, and we can't rest until we find the very bottom of the being of the beat.

There was this dude named Alfred North Whitehead (1861–1947), and he spent a lot of time and energy thinking about, well, time and energy. He was part of an earlier British invasion, when Harvard stole him from his London gig in 1925, and he came over the pond and started writing awesome books about how the whole cosmos is really sort of rocking and rolling. It was called "process philosophy." It hovers on the edge of being well understood, because it's very difficult and pretty radical, but every time you thinks it's done for, it keeps coming back for another US tour. Consider this the advance billing. Google the dude. Or just keep reading.

Musical Metaphysics

One idea Whitehead hit upon pretty early was that experience is made of little bursts of energy. Energy vibrates, and when it comes into more or less regular repeating patterns, we have "rhythm." Things that appear to be solid are really patterns of vibrations. Back then (1925 or so), most people thought things were made of "atoms," little indivisible bits of matter, arranged in "molecules," but Whitehead thought they were wrong. There really aren't any "things," like atoms and molecules, there are dances that just look like stones and guitars and people. Everything that exists in time is a repeating rhythm of some sort, so molecules just are shakings and rattlings in patterns, like little rock bands of Being. So molecules aren't "things" made of "stuff," they're more like performances; little Stones concerts in tiny stadiums having a huge party. Whitehead even talked about The Stones themselves (before they were born), and said there was more "Rolling" than "Stones" in the rock-'n'roll of existing. Check out what the dude says when he was using the example of a stone:

> The [mistaken] molecular theory has robbed the [rolling] stone of its continuity, of its unity, and of its passiveness. The [rolling] stone is now [in that very uncool theory] conceived as a society of separate molecules in violent agitation. But the metaphysical concepts, which had their origin in a mistake about the [rolling] stone[s], were now applied to the individual molecules. Each atom was still [wrongly supposed to be some] stuff which retained its self-identity and its essential attributes in any portion of time –however short and however long, provided that it did not perish. (*Process and Reality*, p. 78—I've helped the dude say what he meant to say with the stuff in the brackets.)

But you'll never rock'n'roll that way, Whitehead says. Each member of the band just being his own individual self, bringing to the stage whatever he already has, all by his lonesome. When you see a band that doesn't have "It," you're probably looking at a collection of individuals failing to connect and not channeling anything from sky to ground. They're surrounded with a layer of individuality that insulates them from the sky and from each other. And you just can't rock in rubber shoes; you all have to dig your toes into Mother Earth and raise a hand to Father Sky. Nothing rocks and nothing rolls when it's not like that. But Whitehead goes on:

> The [uncool] notion of undifferentiated endurance of substances with essential attributes and with accidental adventures was still applied. This is the root doctrine of materialism [boo, hisssss] . . . but this materialistic concept has proved to be as mistaken for the atom as it was for the stone[s]. The atom is only explicable as a society with the activities involving rhythms with their definite periods . . . The mysterious quanta of energy [Keith, Charlie, and Bill] have made their appearance, derived, as it would seem, from the recesses of protons [called "grooves"], or electrons [called "riffs"] . . . Further, the quanta of energy are associated by a simple law with the periodic rhythms

which we detect in the molecules [called "concerts"]. Thus the quanta are, themselves, in their own nature, somehow vibratory; but they emanate from the protons and electrons. Thus there is every reason to believe that rhythmic periods cannot be dissociated from the protonic and electronic entities [or the grooves and riffs]. (*Process and Reality*, pp. 78–79)

What Whitehead is saying (with some help from me) is that it's not what we are that makes us do what we do, it's what we are doing that makes us what we are, for a short while, and then the show is over, fading ever so gradually into the past. I will now use this theory to describe why The Stones totally rock. There are three quanta (Keith, Charlie, and Bill), and their "rhythmic periods" are going to get the names Whitehead gave them:

1. Keith = the "dative dater" of the divine data.

2. Charlie = the co-ordinator and organizer of the data Keith dates, called the "synthesis."

3. Bill = the distributor and contributor of the all goods Keith and Charlie achieve, called by Whitehead (and I swear to God I'm not making this up) the "satisfaction."

Their "rhythmic periods" are called by Whitehead "the phases of concrescence," and the "groove" and "riff" are the varying patterns of "intensity," the protonic and electronic vibes from which these wondrous quanta cannot be separated. I speak henceforth of the rock'n'roll rhythm section, and by anyone's account, The Stones have the best one that ever existed.

The Sum of the Parts

One of the great mysteries associated with The Stones is that of the group-ness of It—how well It works when they are all in one place and time, and how not much happens when they separate and make music with others, or even when they try to go it alone. Of course Keith's Winos and Bill's Rhythm Kings can rock, but we all know It isn't the same. Why is that? I think it's a genuine question, and an important one—and not just for rock history or music criticism. The question is about "It," and touches on the value of one kind of existing over another, and what that costs those who would pursue "It" over some more neutral equilibrium.

Somehow The Stones together are greater than the parts, and not by just a little bit. But it never was the easy choice to keep rock'n'rolling, so the value they achieve by hanging in there for one more record, one more tour, comes with risks and costs. The lure of some sort of experience has drawn them back into the dance with death again and again.

The Stones "experiment" is now about fifty years old and we've had an opportunity to test what "It" was that completes the circuit. The comparatively early exit of Brian Jones showed that It wasn't the triumvirate of Jagger-Richards-Jones, as some people initially thought. "It" had little to do with Jones. The nearly seamless entry and exit of Mick Taylor, followed by the permanent installment of Ronnie Wood, showed that at least the "other guitar" was a modular component. In his auto-biography, Keith says he had worked out well before Jones finally vacated that what he needed was just one other gui-tarist for "weaving," and that he could adapt to a whole range of styles and levels of ability in that other player.

So, for thirty-odd years (and they certainly were odd years), the other four Stones were a constant, although their recording process often did not reflect the live line-up, even from the beginning. Some of the more memorable recordings may lack one or another member of the magic circuit. Keith is generally on all the good records, but Charlie and Bill aren't always, although the results seem indistinguishable from the core group. That's probably because the other drummers or bass players are generally playing "the sort of thing" Charlie or Bill would play, and not introducing a foreign element into the Stones' sound, but reveling in being a contributor to that dis-tinctive sound.

Yet, the permanent departure of Bill Wyman in 1992 seems to have weakened the circuit, if my perceptions are at all trust-worthy. I'm not finding their stuff since then quite as satisfy-ing, to say it as Whitehead might. The power still flows through, but I don't think the Stones could have done what they did without the full rhythm section, and I would claim that the special something-or-other they possess as a trio, is the It that Is, when all three quanta become components connected in series—and the series is Keith-Charlie-Bill, in that order; data-synthesis-satisfaction. More on that in a minute.

And here I'm going to go out on a limb. I think that even without Mick Jagger, this would have been a famous rock band, if not at all the same band. The reason has to do with what happens when Keith, Charlie, and Bill strike a groove. Mick is more like the light bulb or the box fan (or any other dirty, pretty thing you might plug in) that actually draws the current and "works" when it is flowing. Mick isn't pulling the power down from the air, he's just using it on its way to the ground. He's a symbol of what's happening in the rhythm section, and he is, as a Stone, the presentation of the rhythm section's causal effect on the world. Mick's musicality, his delivery, his showmanship, even his athleticism, is pretty much fluff when he tries to plug himself into any other circuit. He can't adorn just any musicians hooked up in series, at least not with the same depth and meaning. And unlike David Bowie, whom Mick has apparently always envied a bit (if Keith is to be believed), Mick is not a musical force unto himself. He has to have the Stones to strut his stuff and make us all believe it.

Some people can do the whole thing alone, like Elvis or Robert Johnson, or some can do it with almost anyone, like Chuck Berry. There's no denying Mick Jagger is a natural front man, a visible presentation of what jumps across the abyss from being nothing to becoming "It," from one moment to the next. Alone, Mick just isn't very "important," to use Whitehead's word for it. But put him in front of Keith-Charlie-Bill, and at least one other guitar player who "gets It," he becomes one of the most important interpreters of the existence and meaning of "It" who has ever lived. I don't know whether he chafes at being dependent on that circuit or not, but I can certainly see that he isn't the cause of the cool, even if he is just the right dirty, pretty thing to spring into view as soon as Keith hits the first chord. Don't get me wrong. They aren't The Stones without Mick, by any stretch, and I wouldn't change a hair on their graying heads, but Keith-Charlie-Bill surely would have been a famous band without him.

And, as Whitehead says, the whole is always greater than the sum of the parts, even when all the parts are functional alone, as in the Beatles, and even though clearly each component has its own energy supply. But then sometimes you have the thing that only works when it's hooked up in series, just so, like the Stones. So, structurally and functionally, The Stones are a bit like lithium, with three inseparable protons in the nucleus, an electron (Mick) down and dirty, and another electron (that second guitar) spinning opposite Keith in a more distant orbit, and a whole cloud of saxes and pianos and black girls singing in the ionized spaces. Like lithium, they're loosely bound in the middle, unstable, and highly flammable. So next time you want to know what mother's little helper really is, well, she's doing lithium, but it's about taking out the right record and dropping the needle into the groove. An interesting way to stabilize your mood, huh?

The thing about the rhythm section for The Stones is that all three of those protons are very quirky. None of these guys plays quite "right." Let me explain, but I have to begin with a crucial point, and if you don't get this, if you can't find a way to hear this, most of what I say later won't resonate: Charlie interprets Keith, and then Bill interprets Charlie and closes back on Keith, and it happens in that order, pretty much all the time. That's what is between the buttons. Now let's divide up what can't really be divided and move among the vibrations that make It happen.

A Date with Keith

Keith just is Prometheus with a five-stringed lightning rod. He's the one who pulls the grooves and riffs in from the atmosphere and shares them with the band. Until Keith arrives, it's all just the bare past and lame possibility, just data for a world that may never exist, nothing happening. And if Keith is off, the Stones will be off, but that doesn't happen too much. Almost no matter what Keith is on, he's almost never off. He can call down the lightning even in a stupor. (And Keith having an off night is like other people having the best night of their lives.)

But Keith doesn't play "right" and he doesn't play "nice." He's usually just a little bit (in other words, perfectly) out of tune, and he doesn't bother much with details, and he doesn't fret about the frets. It's a little sloppy, if you only notice what it sounds like and forget to notice what it does. He doesn't play flashy at all, and once the song kicks in, it's difficult to descry exactly what Keith is playing and what the other guitarist is adding. Keith isn't even describable as either a lead or a rhythm player, he's a little bundle of pure activity confronting a wide universe of possibilities and memories and taking just what he wants for a little date, by force if necessary.

To the guitar purist, and to the critics who are expecting something to gratify their critical reflections, Keith is something of an enigma. I have heard so many people, the types whose rock understanding is just the conventional cool, and whose actual rock experience is limited to garage bands at most, say that they don't understand why Keith's name is mentioned in the same company as the greatest guitar players of the age—Clapton, Hendrix, Page, Beck. How does Keith Richards command the respect, even the awe, of such virtuosos, and their successors like Eddie Van Halen? Is it just because he's one of the Stones and so he's automatically in the club? That isn't it. The people who will tell you Keith isn't really a great guitar player (I have even heard some say he sucks) have no clue what a guitar really does in the context of creating the rhythmic feel of a band. They think of great guitar playing as the fast and flashy more than the furious and gutsy, and they probably have no notion of the promethean groovemaker and riffmaster. And they imagine that it's more challenging to be creative with lead lines than with great grooves and amazing, ear catching simple riffs.

They're wrong. And if they don't at least admit that they can hear the greatness, if not account for it, then they are also fools. Even just finding (let alone discovering) the grooves that make your body jump, involuntarily, and creating the riffs people can't get out of their heads is far, far more difficult, musically speaking, than playing fast or freaky lead lines. The riff and groove are the batter and bake of the rock'n'roll cake, and it's more important, and tougher to master, than making a batch of tasty icing from the butter and sugar of those hot licks (that you probably copped from somebody else) to put on top of the finished product.

Anyone who has played in a serious band, a band that has enjoyed at least some real power to draw in the people, knows that you might have a trillion hot licks, but no one wants to listen to that for more than about two minutes. What every lead player and lead singer has to have is a promethean lightning rod in the band, a point of origin in the rhythm section. For The

Stones, that is and always was Keith. He's the one who kidnaps the silence itself, with his leathery sneak attack and then herds it around at his whim. You think you can handle a date with that? If not, stay well out of his range. The whip is long and the lightning rod is very stiff, and he'll keep you up for six days straight.

Maestro Tempo and Mr. Groove

But even Keith has to bend a knee at the right altar to receive the energy. He exists way beyond you, but he isn't a god. It's one thing to discover the grooves, and another thing to be able to call them up again, on demand. The power to recall a groove isn't that rare—every good bar band has one or two members who can do as much. Sometimes it's the drummer or the bass player, but commonly it's the rhythm guitar player (and quite often he is also a singer). Watch next time you go to a bar. The "grooves guy" will be the one who starts most of the songs, whether with a count, or an intro lick, or even just a nod of the head. This is "finding" a groove again, not technically discovering it. From rehearsal, and huge repetition, the groove is already down inside his body. He doesn't have to call it down from the air; he pulls it back up from the ground and re-connects it to its source.

Before the song starts, you will see one guy get still, for just a second; maybe he'll look up, or look down, or close his eyes; then he will start moving his foot, or bob his head, or he might wave his pick above the strings in a rhythmic pattern. When the groove has made its way from the edges of his body to the center, has planted itself in the center as a pulse, and has worked its way back out to his extremities, he will move, as one unified being, into that groove. He will become the groove. All this only takes a second. That is how it happens, and this part isn't too much different in a rock band than for the conductor of a symphony orchestra or the leader of a jazz band, or even a church choir director.

There is a difference, though. Whereas the conductor or choir director is finding the tempo from a full range of interpretive possibilities, and that initial tempo will then flow into and out of regular bends and eddies, the rock guitarist is just looking for the groove, which is an uneducated, hard-drinking, poor relation of tempo, who lives in a trailer across the tracks and wants to boink your underage daughter. Grooves are built on raw repetition in a way that tempos are not. The altogether "proper" determination of a tempo ought to consider how the music will sound. So Maestro Tempo treats Miss Sound like a lady, asks her for a proper date, spends some serious bucks on her, chats her up and listens to her titter and gossip, offers her the best wine, hopes for a peck on the cheek at the end of the night. Nobody gets hurt. Herman's Hermits are looking for a tempo, and they'll walk you to the door when they're done with the song and tell Mrs. Brown's daughter what a lovely time they had.

But Mr. Groove operates independently of how things sound. Sounds are a dime a dozen, and they'll need to go to their knees if they want a ride on the wild horses. Mr. Groove has had plenty of sounds in his paws, and he isn't easily impressed and never tamed, even when he decides to be gentle. In rock music, Mademoiselle Sound must conform to what Mr. Groove wants, and what he needs, to make it all feel good, and said Sound need not be, ought not be, clean or pristine. It's better if she's been around the block a time or two and has an attitude about it. Groove knows what he likes, and it isn't a sorority girl saying "ewwww"—unless she's got another side she isn't showing. And Groove will have his way with Sound before it's all said and done. In short, for rock and roll, Sound is Groove's "Bitch," and when her name is called, she salivates like Pavlov's best friend.

Who Could Hang a Name on You?

So that is how you find a groove again, but discovering a groove is a different deal. That is the promethean moment in rock-'n'roll. Truly novel grooves are out there, but you can't really make a groove out of nothing. It has to be possible for you, and you have to take it in from what you are and what you can be, but in discovering a groove, you can make it your own. Whitehead calls it the "self-creative act," in which nothing that came before and nothing that comes later wholly explains the act. So you can't really name it.

For rock'n'roll, there aren't so very many possibilities. They're constrained by the choice to rock rather than flow. Yet, the tiniest variation in terms of how the four beats are rushed or relaxed in mutual relations will make the difference between a groove that is erotic or invigorating, and one that is limpid or relaxing. Keith describes this in the current issue of *Rolling Stone* magazine (as I write this), in a tribute to Bob Dylan:

> Before he went electric and submitted himself to that relentless discipline of a rhythm section, there was a beautiful flow in Bob's songs that you can only get with just a voice and guitar. He can float across the bar here and there. You let certain notes hang longer, and it doesn't matter because it all goes with the song. . . . I love the man— and I love that he rock and rolls too. (26th May 2011, p. 66)

Some people may think it's sloppy, but the rhythm section of a rock band is in truth a highly structured and disciplined unit. It cannot slide around and still be any good. To rock'n'roll is to let yourself be whipped, a relentless repeating kick and slap.

The typical rock groove has a kick (bass drum) on the first and third beats of each bar, and a snare slap on the second and fourth beats. The bass guitar is at the mercy of beats one and three. His dominatrix likes to kick him around. The rhythm guitar is owned by beats two and four, and she slaps him when he gets out of line. The variations are built from there, stretching, pulling, switching, dragging those four beats apart and pushing them back together. I wouldn't exactly say that there is a finite number of arrangements of those four beats that "work," but I will say that all the most obvious variations are already familiar to you—that is, they've already been found and used many times in many songs you know.

Alright Now

Yet, Keith has contributed perhaps a dozen new grooves to the common repertoire. The groove to "Start Me Up" comes immediately to mind, as well as the "kick in" on "Jumpin' Jack Flash"—which makes every beat seem like the start of a new measure, like it's going one-one-one-one, at the front edge of each iteration. You want to talk about relentless driving, especially since the intro groove, before the kick-in, is all way, way back, flowing around, at the tail-end of the beat, like a primeval soup, with paramecia flitting around, barely coalescing at all. Then boom, out jumps Mick fully evolved, with no tail at all, and ready to screw anything foolish enough to move. It's a gas (the more you read about the structure and habits of lithium, the clearer all this chemistry becomes).

The song "Honky Tonk Women" is an important contribution to grooves—it's so much slower than most people realize, although this is a song they play at different speeds live. Frankly I think it diminishes the song—the recorded speed was the right speed, and the gin-soaked barroom queens of Memphis do not hurry, you or themselves. To play that song "right" (so that it does its proper work) is almost excruciating, the way you just keep having to hold back. You have to think about golf or something between thrusts to keep your load in. How can something that slow so totally rock? And how can it not? And then even beyond that, there is "Wild Horses," which is the slowest rock groove I know of (I can't believe Keith got this to be so very cool).

Not all distinctive Stones grooves are Keith's, probably, but these are among Keith's most distinctive grooves. For example, there is also "Beast of Burden," which is devilishly hard to get right, and that is partly because it's actually much faster than it seems like it would be, it's just that the snare slap is trailing in an almost unnatural way, but I have a feeling this groove was Charlie's doing more than Keith's. And there's the stupendous groove of "Shattered," but I think that one may need to be credited to Bill. More on all that in a minute.

There are lesser known original Stones grooves, like "She Said Yeah," which was way ahead of its time. It only re-emerged in the era of the Ramones, and the list could go on. I say these are "original grooves" but what I mean is that I haven't heard anything earlier that was precisely the same, and when rock musicians communicate grooves to each other, they often call these grooves by their Stones names. ("It's goes like 'Start Me Up'" they'll say, and so on.) I haven't made an exhaustive survey, but I'm fairly confident about these grooves I've named. Of course, plenty of Stones songs have ordinary rock grooves, or blues grooves, or even country (like "Far Away Eyes") or disco (like "Miss You"). It's not like our boys discovered them all.

There may be no definite limit to how many rock grooves there are, but I doubt any other single person has contributed more previously undiscovered grooves to rock music than Keith Richards. Maybe Chuck Berry did, and he is a great study in grooves because if you don't hit exactly the right groove in playing one of his songs, they all sound too similar to one another. Apart from being a daring and brilliant lyricist and tremendous innovator on the guitar, the third prong of Chuck Berry's great genius lies in the tiny variations in the rock grooves he discovered. But with the Stones concert, it is Keith who first draws the grooves down from the atmosphere to the ground, and then back from the ground and out into the ionosphere, and we all just have to hop around like worms on a hot rock— especially Mick, who shows us just how It should be done. I defy you to stay still when "Brown Sugar" kicks in.

Riffing

In spite of the dominance and heedlessness of Mr. Groove, Mademoiselle Sound does get her say, because only she knows what she likes. Maybe it's the Stockholm Syndrome. Having been captured and tied down by Bad Boy Groove, she says, not so coyly, "not like that, do it like this . . . if you wanna hear me squeal . . ." and suddenly she has all his attention. After all, he does want to hear her squeal. (And so do I, at this point. Is it getting warm in here, or is that just me?) Anyway, when it comes to the Mistress Sound, she'll only get happy for a fellow if you turn all her knobs the right way and caress her taut body just so. Keith knows the right moves, most nights. He had the gift, but it takes patience and practice too. At least, judging by what I hear, I'd say the good Lady Sound actually likes to go slumming with him.

So the riff has two legs, and one of them is the tone. You have to get a hold on that leg first, adjust it this way and that until you hear something you can work on. There are so many different things an electric guitar can sound like, from these smooth Chet Atkins country hollow-body tones, to Duane Eddy's reverb-laden, rebel rousing pluck tone, to Jimi's famous feedback-on-the-edge-of-forever, to Tom Petty's cool clean "Breakdown," to the Angus Young "fuck-tone" in "You Shook Me All Night Long." All electric guitar players explore tones, and it's common for them to be very picky about it. Keyboard players once shared in this arcane science, but then they got spoiled by the electronic overhaul of the keyboarding world, synthesizers and samplers. The keyboard player who is a master of amplifier and instrument tones is rare these days, and probably over fifty years old. But true rock guitarists will never give in to this kind of ones-and-zeroes mentality.

If you're looking to be in a good band, your guitarists need to be the kind of people who can patiently screw around with tone adjustments and reverb knobs until everyone else has given up and gone home. It helps if you can stay up for days and days in a row. Both the devil and the good god are trapped in there, down in the protons and electrons, in the signals exchanged by the instrument and the amplifier, and how each responds to the slightest variations in the other. If you want something to feel like "Nineteenth Nervous Breakdown" (and I can hardly imagine a riff that sounds more like what it is supposed to be than that one), you had better know how to get that exact sound from your equipment, and that can only be done by very patient experimentation. But if you go looking for that sound, just remember, Keith is the one who made it first, and he was the one who first heard that this—just this and only this—was the tone for the guitar on that particular riff in this one song. He regularly creates unique tones, and then in some cases he doesn't re-use them, because they are too identifiable. So there's a vast range of tones he creates with the choices of amplifiers and knobs and guitars, even though there really is no recognizable set of tones we would usually identify with Keith's work. He knew very well after he had used that fuzz pedal for "Satisfaction" that he couldn't go there again. And for him, getting the tones was and remains an endless quest.

To be a rock guitarist in our day you have to go to school on the tones Keith made and learn how he used them. It's Rock 101. The story in his autobiography about how he found the tone for the guitars on "Jumpin' Jack Flash" is a keen piece of rock history. It had been a mystery. Anyone could play the actual licks (they are easy), but people couldn't find a way to recreate those tones. So finally Keith revealed that there are no electric guitars on that recording. He played acoustic guitars into the condenser mic that was built-in on an early model Phillips cassette tape recorder, and to achieve a distortion in the tone, he played the guitars too close to the mic and too loud. He listened back to the cassette and said, in effect, "that's it, that's the sound." He didn't provide the further details in his book, but I assume he then hooked up the same mic to his four-track machine, and the result you have heard. Or maybe he just played the cassette sound into his four-track recorder. He has never been shy about losing generations in his recordings. Clean sound isn't always the best sound.

You Make a Dead Man . . .

So let's say the groove and the tone are jiving, but you're not riffing yet. Mademoiselle Sound is giving you that look, but she isn't there yet. The riff has another leg dangling and kicking, so you've got to get a hold on it. You still have to figure out what to play, and here is what we will call the "sig lick" (the signature lick is the full name). Get this right and she'll squeal, if she's going to squeal at all—I mean, who doesn't like a great lick? A sig lick is an identifiable musical phrase that belongs exclusively to a single song, and which usually starts the song, and it makes the most of what the groove and the tone have brought together. It may be just a violin arpeggio (like "Ruby Tuesday"), or it may be a little melodic phrase (like "Nineteenth Nervous Breakdown"), or it may be a chord change (like "Start Me Up" or "Honky Tonk Women"). A song can have more than one sig. lick and it can also come later in the song, like the six ascending notes that precede the words "brown sugar." Whatever it is, it's supposed to tell you in a split second what song you're hearing. It's the culmination of pulling the lightning down. It uses the tone and the groove and it makes you lose yourself in both anticipation and memory. You die a little death in that moment, for sure. But it's worth it.

No matter how many Stones songs you've heard, you know which one you're hearing within a couple of seconds because of the riff, and there is always a different combination of groove and tone and sig. lick that brings it home. It takes genuine talent and amazing patience to make all this—indeed, it takes a fair amount of ability just to recreate it, even after someone like Keith has done all the pioneering work. Keith, with his rhythm section, has probably created more truly great riffs than any other rock'n'roller, maybe up to six dozen utterly recognizable, one of a kind, winning riffs. And somehow he not only dated all these delicate beauties, he also knew they were

winners when he first set ears on them. You have to be prescient to know when you've got one. Some of these conquests
were simply bizarre, twisted trysts, like the "Jumpin' Jack
Flash" riff, while others were a risky rendezvous, like the
"Nineteenth Nervous Breakdown" riff, which is actually
painful to listen to, and is intended to be. "Ouch Keith. Turn it
up, would you? Oh yes, here it comes." She loves the way you
play that guitar.

The Singer, Not the Song

All of what I'm trying to get at is completely apart from and
basically unrelated to Keith's songwriting, both with and without Mick. The songwriting isn't a wholly separate activity for
the Stones, because sometimes the riff and groove produced the
occasion and inspiration for the song. Commonly Keith would
have a hook line to go with the riff and groove and say to Mick
what the hook was, and show him the riff and groove, and then
Mick would just start singing it or jotting down the words. That
is, for sure, its own kind of promethean feat. But the songwriting part, even as it touches on the issue of rhythm, is a different matter than the "It" I am chasing right now.

I'm still trying to explain why Keith's peers regard him as
among the greatest guitarists of his generation. And when you
consider that the same song can be played (successfully, consider Clapton's slow version of "Lala") with many different
grooves, and that the riff can be varied and re-interpreted as
needed, it becomes clear that this isn't so much about songs as
about the "how" the song comes to feel like rock'n'roll.
Christopher Guest, Michael McKeon and Harry Shearer (the
Folksmen) have made it clear enough that even a song as tied
to its groove as "Start Me Up" can be played in a bluegrass
groove (if "groove" is even the right word for it) . . . and the less
said about that, the better.

So this isn't about being a great songwriter, it's about
exploring the possibilities that the invention of the electric guitar made available, in amazing and unexpected ways. These
sounds had never been heard by human ears, as Keith points
out. Keith was in the first generation of musicians who really
saw how rich the possibilities were, and who set off into that
terra incognita and returned with some of the best treasure. It

requires a peculiar curiosity, a certain tenacity, a singular power of focus and concentration, and above all a complete passion for just this kind of journey, to explain what Keith Richards did. The people who have tried to explore this territory, and who really understand what it takes to succeed, rightly stand in awe of Keith Richards as a guitar player. To say Keith Richards isn't a great guitar player is sort of like saying Christopher Columbus wasn't a great sea captain. Whatever the faults, we're all permanently changed by the exploration, for better and for worse.

A Steady Synthesis of the Data

I confess: For years I believed Charlie Watts wasn't a great drummer—hell, I didn't even think he was very good. I admitted, along with everyone, that he certainly was rock steady, and there is a lot to be said for that. But steady drummers are out there. Every city has a dozen or so, and the good bands stand in line to try to capture such drummers, especially if they don't have debilitating drug habits or personality problems. But even then, if they can be counted on to show up for the gig, the rest can be dealt with as needed. Rock drummers don't have to be extra-ordinary, but if they don't speed up and can play a decent quick shuffle beat, well, that's all you have to have.

But watching Charlie, back in the day, when I was young and stupid and arrogant (now I'm not young), I observed all kinds of uneconomical movement in Charlie's hands and feet. There were hitches and jerks, like parries and feints at the drums, and then there was that totally annoying habit where he lays off the hi-hat with the right hand on the second and fourth beats and just slaps the snare drum by itself. That basically looked to me like no one ever told him how to play the drums. But he was pulling it together all along, wasn't he? The second phase of Stones concrescence, just as Whitehead said.

I was deeply and profoundly wrong, and my thinking and interpretation were clouded by conventional expectations and at least some pure boorishness. I had to admit even back then that it was just a mystery to me why The Stones so totally rocked. Keith was out of tune, Bill stood like he was made of concrete and I thought I knew two dozen guys who could play at least as well as Charlie. I was an idiot. No, that's not strong enough. A fucking idiot. My little theories and judgments wouldn't have helped one bit in dispelling the mystery of why The Stones have "It."

I stupidly thought "It" was about "knowing" something, as in consciously knowing it and being able to act on what you know. So I believed I understood what I was hearing and it didn't dawn on me that I had missed a whole universe of music fermenting beneath the radar of my conventional little conscious expectations. Whitehead says consciousness isn't very common in the universe, and it's not very important either, in terms of what's really going down. So it's worth remembering, just as a principle for life, that if something is very good and your pet theories say it shouldn't be, you need to dump your pet theories.

The River of Tight

The Stones were doing everything wrong, not by the rules (or the conventions), and there was all sorts of apparent looseness in how the rhythm section went about its business and I foolishly believed that everyone wants to be tight, not loose. What I didn't understand back then is that there is a kind of looseness that's on the other side of tight. It doesn't come from being a virtuoso player, it comes from being a truly great listener and responder. And here is where we could have the Grateful Dead argument, if anyone is so inclined. The Dead were (and wanted to be) even looser than The Stones, and so loose that they defied people to believe they were even capable of playing tight. But they were more than capable of that. The recorded evidence exists. They chose an outward trajectory for their rhythmic mode of being, on the farthest wilds across the River of Tight, to see what was there. By comparison, The Stones found some nice spots for partying just on the other side of the River of Tight, and they went straight to those places when they played. And they certainly could play utterly tight when they wanted to. I speak in the past tense because I feel that this changed when Bill left the band, as I will get to in a minute.

What I needed to learn is that tight doesn't rock. It's impressive, for sure, but it's for your ears and your head, not for your ass and your feet. Tight is for Rush and Styx and Kansas and Yes. It's cerebral to play tight. It's discursive and advisory, a little detached; playing tight won't solve your problems and it won't guide your life. It's good to rehearse your part in life, by all means; but when it comes time to act, to decide, to do something you can't take back, you need to be in the moment. You can plan your life until you think you have every detail under control, but the minute you step out on the stage of life, it's not going to go like you planned. If you try to make it all conform to your plan, your life will surely suck, and if you'll be honest with yourself, you'll have to admit you really wanted it to rock. So get out of your fucking head, would you? Learn how to play tight, that's good. But then forget about it and go live a little.

Charlie Chuckles

Charlie plays the drums that way. He knows that Keith has been awake for four manic days and needs a little something to pull him back from the next moment into the present one. So Charlie usually lays on the back of the beat, holding back (especially the snare slap, which is the rhythm guitar player's mistress, as I said); he holds that slap to the last possible micromoment when the skin can still be pounded. And here's his secret, the one he discovered entirely by himself, and that everyone identifies as "playing like Charlie Watts": What everyone else would regard as the last micromoment in the range of the beat isn't really the very last micromoment. The one you and I would call "last" is actually only the last *serious* moment. There is another micromoment behind that one, and it is comical, it is a rhythmic snort or a jocular grunt, and it takes all of Keith's gravity and intensity and insane focus and releases it into the room as levity and fun. Charlie hits it and Keith (serious, dangerous, violent, drug-addicted, passionate, hopeless Keith) smiles. That's when the whip comes down. And when the whip comes down, it hurts sort of *good*, doesn't it? I admit that I like it when Keith likes treating me that way. And I'm straight, too.

Charlie Watts is an excellent drummer, and I now know he can play any style he wants to play. He isn't all that limited. (I mean, everyone has limitations.) Charlie's job is to take the grooves and riffs that Keith feeds him and make them congeal into something Bill can distribut around the room, in ways that everyone can use (I'm afraid that only Keith can use his own grooves without Charlie's help). So, even though Charlie's reach is from the first micromoent before one to the last micromoment after four, he always lags behind Keith, and that is very much by design. This keeps Keith on the front edge of the whole sound and still holds him in, makes him available to the rest of us in little bursts. And after all, we need a second to follow Keith's mania. The lag also creates a musical space in which other things can happen. And they do.

I can't think of a better example of how Charlie interprets Keith than "Beast of Burden," which is a song that rarely gets covered successfully, even by bar bands that make their living covering Stones songs. The groove is extremely difficult to capture, and without the groove, the song basically sucks. One of the secrets of the song is the oodles of empty sonic space. That space is created by the distance between the clean riffing guitar and the trailing drums, and how Charlie comically hops to the front of the beat where Keith is and then falls way back, repeated every measure. How very far Charlie has allowed himself to trail becomes obvious when he hits the almost random double snare slap on the "and" of three and the "and" of four, instead of just the four. That "and" of four is actually into the next measure and Keith has already attacked.

The song also very much requires that the bass stay out of the way, being so understated as nearly to disappear. It's like watching Bill Wyman onstage, which you must admit is like watching paint dry. So I will take back one thing I said earlier. I know of one person capable of standing absolutely, stock still when Keith hits the opening chords of "Brown Sugar." The one person in the world who is best able to stay out of the way of anything Keith may do is his bass player. More about that in a moment, but to finish the previous thought before getting on to the next one, Keith mentions in his autobiography that this lagging behind the beat is Charlie's sense of humor, and that on given nights they even try to test one another's rhythmic limits, to see if one can screw up the other one. I'm sorry, but that's just way cool.

Paying the Bill: An Ode to Satisfaction

Now we come to the unhappy part of the story. As far as I can tell, Bill Wyman just wasn't destined for happiness and certainly not for satisfaction. (Holy cow. Just don't even think about it, okay? I know you know what I'm talking about.) Still, the crap that happened to Bill wasn't any worse than what the rest of The Stones got, but unlike them, it took the heart out of him, and really, it's not too clear his heart was ever really in it. But he was, ironically, the musical distributor of the joy in that rhythm section. Charlie was playful, but Bill, because the Keith-Charlie connection was so total, actually got to just play around.

He may have felt a little bit excluded or undervalued. Maybe all those women were so many proofs of his manhood. And I think Bill might have just belonged to slightly different time. His being significantly older than the rest of the band would have made it tough in the early days, I suspect. There is a very great difference between being twenty and being twenty-eight when you achieve stardom. It's sort of like why they draft kids between eighteen and twenty-one first off, for the wars. At that age, you can form the kids around the ideas they *have* to believe. But you'll never get someone who is twenty-eight to believe that death in battle is glorious, if he hasn't already bought in when he was younger. And maybe that was Bill's life as a Rolling Stone. I certainly don't know.

If Bill felt like a fifth wheel, I have to say, that's not the way I hear the music, so I must respectfully disagree. I think I do grasp what I hear (remembering I've been very wrong before . . .). But I'm a bass player too, so I'm pushing forward on this one. Bill had to do a very un-bass-playerly thing to succeed with The Stones. He had to resist the urge to play with Charlie. No drummer would be easier to play with than Charlie Watts, but somehow Bill understood what almost no other bass player would get, which is "hey, being tight and close with Charlie's kick drum will kill this energy." Bass players just instinctively want to hear that kick drum, and if not to match it, then at least to play off of it. But Charlie wasn't a kick-heavy player. Light right foot. He was and remains a snare and hi-hat guy. The kick is a time-keeper only. Perhaps it's because Charlie always wanted to be a jazz player, but there just isn't very much to work with in Charlie's kicks.

If you hear a Stones cover from a bar band and it lacks energy, it may be because of a heavy kick and a bass player who thinks he should match it. That's not how this music is played.

Bill had the amazing gift also of staying out of the way, rhythmically. He walked and wandered and he generally visited the root of the chord somewhere in every four to six beats, but Keith was pounding that, so it wasn't necessary. Bill has certainly produced two dozen bass fills that everyone hears and remembers, but his greatest contribution is the decision to use that thick, muddy, bass sound (common to many bassists of his generation) to bring the sound back around to what Keith had started but would never have time to finish (he's always already on to something else). It is what Whitehead calls the "satisfaction" of concrescence, the moment when what is being made culminates and becomes a contributor to what will come next.

So Bill often lags even behind Charlie, who is already lagging, and does so in a way that stretches out the sound even more, and Bill gets away with it because he brings the bar back around to where Keith had started it, making a thick, deep, four string memory out of a thin and twitchy five string jump. Bill uses the power of repetition to blur the point of entry from the point of exit of a musical idea. It all sounds very sloppy, and it is, but it works. So Bill never really played the bass rhythmically, as most bass players do (and are conventionally told they should do). His decisions on which notes to play are often more chordal or even melodic than rhythmic, interpreting themes, whether dark or erotic or playful that are suggested by Keith's riffs, and helping everyone see what was being suggested. This distributing of the goods is made possible by Charlie's mediation and synthesis, which is so complete as to offer a matrix for meaning and valuing the whole.

There are times, such as "Paint It Black" when the bass actually drives the backbeat, but that is the exception rather than the rule. More often, Bill is picking up on some little opening in the bar and messing around in there. The song "Miss You" is probably his masterpiece of simply fucking around in the interstices. So he waits to see how Charlie will synchronize Keith's energy and then spreads that around the room, as sound and as feel, and he does that without reinforcing the drums, creating a vague but highly tangible sonic atmosphere, sometimes playful, sometimes spare, sometimes bleak, sometimes brooding, sometimes outright dark. But it is the echo of the dying of your very own heartbeat.

What a Mess!

There was a development of this sound too, as Bill became more independent while also becoming a perfect master of his role in the rhythm section. The relation between the bass and the rhythm guitar in Stones history is like the way couples at first, when they are dating, finish each other's sentences with amazement and delight, but then after twenty-five years they can have a complete conversation without finishing any sentences at all. Bill's bass falls into an unconscious finishing of Keith's musical thoughts sort of like that. And as the years went by, the conversation between bass and guitar became so abbreviated that one could barely tell a conversation was happening. But it was still very musical.

That's how I would interpret what happens in the song "Shattered," which is a sort of menacing tangle of bottom end dissonance. It isn't made for the ear, it is made for the gonads and the solar plexus. It chases you down the street like a rabid dog. And the groove closes on itself in those lower (almost subsonic) ranges. Bill's job is to shut the door behind the band, to clear away the musical mess in a haze of bottom-shelf, down-on-the-floor-throwing-up-sick-drunk-head-spinning-I-can't-believe-I-did-that-again ooze. It works. But not since 1992. Ah well. Nobody gets to live forever.

And that brings us to the promise I made early on. What gets destroyed as we partake in the dreadful energy of rock? Well, ourselves, of course, in the form of our youth. Youth itself is sacrificed on the altar of rock'n'roll. You already know that, but it is time to look at it again. This is something like what Freud calls *thanatos*, the death wish that is being experienced beneath the organization of the energies. When you look for a tempo, you want the flow of death, but when you want to rock and roll, you want to stop your own heart every four beats and find a resurrection on the far side of the bar. And your chances of survival are pretty good, with some help from the right rhythm section, the masters of making the life force itself die a little at a time.

We can't live forever, but let's bring the whip down on the asses of the gods and see what happens.

11
The Stones in Pepperland

BILL MARTIN

The great philosopher Georg Friedrich Hegel believed all of reality is created by the dialectical tensions within Reason. Marx thought it was all about the conflict between the classes. Other philosophers have their own formulations, all of which overlook the most important and revealing tension in the universe: The Beatles versus The Stones.

Lots of ink (and tears and blood) have been spilled over this debate and rightly so. These two bands, "the greatest rock'n'roll band in the world" and the creators of the the greatest album in all of rock, *Sgt. Pepper's Lonely Hearts Club Band*, have no peers.

And there's been a lot of confusion. Take the image of The Stones as "bad boys" or even as a "working class" band—as if The Beatles were not? For that matter, the four members of The Who could have taken all five Stones in a street brawl. (The Who could have taken the Beatles, too, even if George Martin was thrown into the mix! But this is silly—Ginger Baker, back in the day, could have taken the whole lot by *himself*.) No matter how much Mick Jagger styled himself as a "street fighting man" or how prescient Pete Townsend was that "there'll be fighting in the streets," The Beatles—musically speaking—kicked all of their butts with *Sgt. Pepper*.

Please Pass the Pepper

I call their achievement "Pepperism." Rock music was always wild and experimental, and politically provocative, but there came a moment in the middle Sixties, spurred on by larger cultural factors and the influence of developments in other genres of music (from Miles Davis, John Coltrane, Ornette Coleman, and Cecil Taylor in jazz, to John Cage, Karlheinz Stockhausen, and others in Western classical music, to increasing awareness of music from India, Sub-Saharan Africa), when rock expanded and *broke* with its founding framework of the blues. With *Sgt. Pepper,* The Beatles did as much as anyone to establish the idea that, if, when writing music there is a question of either doing something more conventional and relying on established blues forms, or doing something more experimental and drawing from beyond rock music, then the time for experimentation had come. For a brief period, not coincidentally having as its epicenter the great year 1968, experimentation was the main trend in rock. After that, everything had changed. *Sgt. Pepper* captured and concentrated the aesthetic and spirit of its musical and historical moment in a way that affected the whole field of everything in rock music that came after it—and even everything that came before it.

If you're reading this book, you know that there was a reaction to this. It marched under the banner of "that ain't rock-'n'roll." I call this movement "blues orthodoxy" and wrote about it at length in *Music of Yes* (pages 110 and 188 for instance). Around this point, The Beatles and The Stones really can and should be seen as rivals. Each was making a case—a very different case—for what rock music is and should be.

Yet this way of looking at the eternal cosmic tension overlooks a very important fact: at one point, in 1967, The Stones and The Beatles were on the *same* page about what rock music should be. The result was *Their Satanic Majesties Request*, an album on which the bad boys were trying very much to follow the Fab Four.

It's Only *Their Satanic Majesties Request*, But . . .

One reason *Majesties* is overlooked is that few people see it as a great album or even a good one. Stones fans, surprisingly often, are not even aware of it, despite its amazingly cool 3-D cover. For that matter, The Stones themselves seem sometimes eager to forget they ever made it. In the nearly 550 pages of

Life, Keith Richards has very little to say about it, and nothing that's complementary:

> Much of that year [1967] we struggled haphazardly to make *Their Satanic Majesties Request*. None of us wanted to make it, but it was time for another Stones album, and *Sgt. Pepper's* was coming out, so we thought basically we were doing a put-on. (p.229)

A little further on, he says the album "was all a bit of flim-flam to me."

Yet this flimflam helps focus the debate about The Beatles versus The Stones. The album reveals that there is something to the "bad boys" question, after all. But it doesn't have to do with street fighting. For while one of the Beatles was willing to talk loosely about his band being more popular than Jesus, The Beatles weren't so brazen as to invoke Satan himself in their album titles. Even if the "sins" of The Stones were more on the order of simple debauchery and hedonism run amok, there was something of a dark side with The Stones that was never part of The Beatles' ethos.

Second, the album seals the case that The Stones were always less innovative and perfectionist than The Beatles. Lennon and McCartney were writing their own music before Jagger and Richards got started, and though they evolved, The Stones simply never caught up. The very fact that The Stones were attempting to make a Beatles album, and not just any Beatles album but specifically *Sgt. Pepper's Lonely Hearts Club Band*, is enough to establish that the album, "put-on" or not, was going to be a kind of failure.

But I Like It. Even though my own tastes go toward experimentalism and away from "blues orthodoxy," given the choice of listening to either *Sgt. Pepper* or *Satanic Majesties*, I would happily choose the latter. And that is because, even though *Sgt. Pepper* is undoubtedly really good, great even, as a musical work, and not only in itself but because of all the doors that it opened up, as an actual listening experience *Satanic Majesties* is *really cool* (whether that's a valid category in philosophical aesthetics, it should be).

I don't necessarily disagree with Stones fans who overlook the album. It has plenty of flaws. It's derivative—a knock-off within the field of what can be called "Pepperisms." And it's a departure from what most Stones fans expect from a Stones album. Philosophers like Alain Badiou argue that every philosopher and every artist has, at most, one great idea to contribute. Certainly this could be said of The Stones, their idea being a combination of blues and rock—something that *Satanic Majesties* is *not*.

The album is also kind of sloppy. Perhaps "lackadaisical" is the word, and the criticism hinges on being able to distinguish between just letting things go musically and seeing what happens—running a musical *experiment*, in other words—and not pulling things together as well as they should be. Of course The Beatles (and George Martin) excelled at pulling things together in this way. If the The Beatles are T.S. Eliot, The Stones are more Allen Ginsberg and his 'first thought, best thought' school of writing poetry. With Ginsberg and The Stones, you don't get the good stuff without all of the surrounding mess; and some of the best stuff is right on the edge of being a mess. While *Sgt. Pepper* has "edge" in places, it is not "edgy," as is *Satanic Majesties*. Perhaps you have to have the "mess" in order to also have the feeling that there is something wild and untamable that is about to burst through your speakers or headphones, and that at some points does burst through. (Perhaps these are the moments when "really cool" as an aesthetic category starts to mean really good or even great.) Even so, there are many moments with *Satanic Majesties* where it seems as if the band could have pulled things together a bit more.

In the Court of the Satanic Majesty

The Stones were no strangers to other manifestations of Pepperism in popular culture. While the debate raged over just how much experimentalism rock music could bear, Jagger himself was a part of cinematic experiments undertaken by Nicholas Roeg and Kenneth Anger.[1] And at the historic Hyde Park concert in 1969 to commemorate the life and sudden death of Brian Jones, one of the opening bands was King Crimson who delivered what was by all accounts a mind-blow-

---

[1] Dan Denillo talks about Kenneth Anger's work with The Stones in Chapter 21 of this volume.

ing performance. While Crimson's *In the Court of the Crimson King* would become a classic of experimental and progressive rock, The Stones' ragged performance at this concert pointed to the turn they would soon take—away from Pepperism and back to the blues that was, and remains, the band's first and guiding love.

Yet, for all that, *Satanic Majesties* can and should be seen as a great Stones album. In fact, it should be understood as The Stones' *only* album in so far as it really strives, following *Sgt. Pepper*, to stand as more than a collection of independent songs unified only by the period in which they were written, the sound the producers and engineers were going for, the kinds of guitars (or drugs) Keith was using, or the women in The Stones' lives. Let it be said: *Satanic Majesties* is not only a concept album, it's a *concepts* album that prog rock fans, as well as Stones fans, should pay attention to.

Beelzebub's Bugged-Out Bequest

Thematically, there are two threads that run through *Satanic Majesties*. One, a hippie-utopian theme, has much in common with *Sgt. Pepper* and other Pepperist efforts of the time. The other is *science fiction*. Perhaps because science fiction in late-1960s creative rock music is so emblematic of progressive rock, it has remained obscure in the case of The Stones. But thoughts about science fiction are rampant in progressive rock (see my *Listening to the Future*). There is a utopian strain of "sci-fi medievalism" (as I call it) in bands like Yes, and a dystopian strain running through Emerson, Lake, and Palmer (especially *Tarkus* and *Brain Salad Surgery*) and King Crimson. At that moment when The Stones shared the stage with King Crimson in July 1969, the future of prog rock was poised to go in two directions, to utopia or dystopia; just as rock itself was poised for both the peace and love at Woodstock, the next month, and the death and dysfunction of Altamont later in December.

The "medieval" aspect of *Satanic Majesties* is plain in the album's cover, a cover that is perhaps more "out of character" for the band than anything else about *Satanic Majesties*. The Stones have replaced The Beatles' military uniforms with the robes of sorcerers and wrapped the whole idea in the mystery of the original 3-D cover. As you manipulate it, you find all kinds of surprises in its nooks and crannies (including The Beatles, if you hold it right, just as The Stones appear on the cover of *Sgt. Pepper*). But unlike The Beatles' cover, there is stuff going on in the sky—a Saturn-like planet and a moon in the upper corner.

These traditional icons of science fiction point to four songs in particular: "Citadel," "In Another Land," "2000 Man," and "2000 Light Years from Home." "Citadel" is a great rocker, and it's not surprising that it has been covered by many bands, often with a punk feel. The roaring introductory chords on a very raw-sounding electric guitar completely shatter the tone that had been set by the album opener, "Sing This All Together"—though in fact, unlike with "Sgt. Pepper's Lonely Hearts Club Band" (the opening song of the album), "Sing" begins and ends with dissonance. The Stones are of course a guitar band, while "Sing" is dominated by piano and horns and a rough "chorus" of vocals. "Sing" immediately tips us off that *Satanic Majesties* is not going to be a typical Stones album, because of its seemingly silly attempt at a flower-power vibe. But look what happens when "Citadel" comes erupting up out of the (significantly) dissonant sounds at the end. We're transported from England's green fields to a Bastille-like prison. This takes us both to "the rusted chains of prison moons" evoked by "In the Court of the Crimson King" (the final song from the album of the same name) and the Marquis de Sade.

"In Another Land," is built around a dream sequence in which the central fact is holding someone else's hand. This to me is a utopian image, and also a reminder that, even insomuch as this album deals with "women" (as a category of interest for rock stars), it is different from all other Stones albums. There is no sexism or misogyny here, at least in Mick's dream. But when he realizes he's in a dream, and opens his eyes—perhaps to another dream—Jagger delivers one of the best lines of his career: "Is this some kind of joke?" hitting exactly the right note, especially on the last word.

In the final part of "In Another Land," the dream-within-a-dream turns from utopian to apocalyptic imagery: "We heard the trumpets blow and the sky turned red." Who then is playing the joke? The feel here anticipates cyberpunk, even *The Matrix*, or the paranoid feel of Philip K. Dick in which the controlling consciousness is an evil machine (*VALIS*—the "Vast,

Active, Living Intelligent System"). *Satanic Majesties* thus sings all together with ELP's *Brain Salad Surgery* and Crimson's "21st Century Schizoid Man"—though you would never gather that from reading any standard book about The Stones.

In "2000 Man," written and sung by Bill Wyman, we encounter an actual computer. Here the two threads tangle and fight each other, as the utopianism of "Sing This All Together" confronts the future. Wyman sings: "I am having an affair with some random computer." In its science-fiction element and in the way that element is intertwined with the album's "hippie" and "carnival" themes, The Stones were struggling with this question. That they later chose a certain form of "safety" in blues orthodoxy doesn't cancel the boldness of their experiment.

As science-fiction oriented songs in rock music go, there isn't really anything better than "2000 Light Years from Home." In terms of the album's Pepperism, this is a moment when The Stones strain against it and, for a moment, go beyond it (I would say this is true of "Citadel" as well). On the one side, the song could have been played better. I can't help but feel that drum and timpani roll into the vocal part could have been far more powerful—not just the playing but also the recording. To me those two beats on the timpani in "2000 Light Years" stand in for everything that's haphazard and lackadaisical about *Satanic Majesties*. And yet, there is a trade-off between polish and edginess. While the dynamics of this trade-off may not always apply, it applies here. If The Stones had polished this song very much, they certainly would have lost the edge.

You're So Very Lonely

All of the "science-fiction" songs on *Satanic Majesties* are concerned with loneliness and alienation. That is perhaps the reason why two songs are titled after the number 2000, the one referring to time and the other to distance. Both songs are really not literally about distance, but also isolation, loneliness, alienation, and the uncertainty of the then upcoming millenium.

As we move from "2000 Light Years from Home" to the last track, the deliberately throw-away and cynical "On With the Show," the album draws a circle around all this alienation and uncertainty. By this time, the *fiction* in the album's science fiction seems to take center stage to cast a cynical eye on the utopian optimism of "Sing This All Together" that started us on our journey. "Good evening one and all we're all so glad to see you here" obviously nods to *Sgt. Pepper*'s opening and closing numbers ("You're such a lovely audience we'd like to take you home with us"). But The Stones have it backwards, with their show's emcee addressing the audience only at the end of the album. And with lyrics like "But we've got all the answers, and we've got lovely dancers too; There's nothing else you have to do," the album suggests that all the fanfare and hope of utopian revolution is confused, too easy, and perhaps just a kind of scam (a note that Lennon himself would hit on "Revolution," and Townsend would as well in 1971's "Won't Get Fooled Again").

So, while in the spectrum of Pepperisms, I've been making connections between The Stones and King Crimson, it may be more apt to say that *Satanic Majesties* is tilling the ground for Frank Zappa and the Mothers of Invention's *We're Only in It for the Money*. That sendup of Pepperism would appear a year later to deliberately parody *Sgt. Pepper* (including the album's famous cover collage and gatefold portraits) and replace Lennon's profound "A Day in the Life" with the Zappa's self-parodying song, "The Chrome Plated Megaphone of Destiny." "On with the Show" came first.

2000 Light Years from the Blues

Still, despite the album's underappreciated values and ideas, Stones fans are not wrong to see *Satanic Majesties* as a kind of albatross or, as Keith put it, a bit of "flimflam" in their catalog. Just look at the band's relationship to the album in recent decades. In 1989 they performed "2000 Light Years from Home" on the Steel Wheels tour, but the version is, frankly, ridiculous. Mick's vocals and stage moves (viewable on YouTube) especially his opening interpretive dance (I don't know what else to call it) take all of the alienation out of the song. Its rhythm has become blues, not psychedelia. "She's a Rainbow" from about a decade later on the *Bridges to Babylon* tour is a little better, but Mick sings it in that exaggerated "Southern" voice he often uses, and the band rushes through the song so that it doesn't breathe and exude its charm. In the Seventies and after, it seems, *Satanic Majesties,* to the Stones, had almost become an album by some other band.

The Stones don't belong in Pepperland and they never did. One reason is suggested again by the album's cover. The Stones sit in their satanic-medieval garb surrounded by wisps of smoke, flowers, mountains, and not-so-distant planets. It's not just that the cover looks altogether too sugar-coated and silly; it's that the influences and inspirations for Pepperism—the artists, writers, comedians, poets, psychiatrists and philosophers—whom The Beatles looked to in crafting their album and expanding the boundaries of rock music, and who appear in the cover's famous collage, are missing. The Stones are just alone, by themselves, and looking somewhat ridiculous without the cultural and intellectual carnival surrounding The Beatles (and even the Mothers of Invention) that created some kind of context for their neon-colored military uniforms.

You might say this is just part of The Stones' critique of Pepperism and the new experimentalism (it's just the tissue of a "show," you see). But it also reveals that The Stones' heart was never in Pepperland. Who *should* have surrounded them on the cover of *Satanic Majesties*? Their blues idols, obviously, the ones they looked to before and after 1967 in making their classic music. But an album featuring songs by The Stones, inspired by their blues idols, however good it may have turned out, would not have been the answer to *Sgt. Pepper* that The Stones were trying to create. An album cover featuring five interplanetary sorcerers of rock surrounded by cutouts of Muddy Waters, Screamin Jay Hawkins, and other blues artists would have been as silly as blues-inspired songs about girls on other planets, or "Hey You, Get Off of My Nebula!"

The Stones simply didn't have the burning interest in the avant-garde arts and in the kind of musical and conceptual experimentation that made albums like *Sgt. Pepper or We're Only in It for the Money* or *In the Court of the Crimson King* so compelling and original. *Satanic Majesties* is not inspired by the avant-garde, but rather by another album (namely *Sgt. Pepper*) that was. The Stones explored Pepperland, but always at one remove. They took the Magical Mystery Tour, but then never got off the bus to take a walk around, to imbibe the new ideas and methods of art, to let Lennon turn them on, so that they could come up with an "I am the Walrus" or "Lucy in the

Sky with Diamonds" that was their own, and not an imitation of another band's. "She's a rainbow" is good, but it would never have existed without *Sgt. Pepper*'s inspiration (despite the fact that Lennon and McCartney sing backup on the recording).

Given how good *Satanic Majesties* is, and how well it holds up, none of this is to disparage The Stones. Their moment in experimental music-making still paid off for those of us who love the album and for those who remain inspired by it (such as The Brian Jonestown Massacre who release *Their Satanic Majesties' Second Request* in 1996). It just didn't have much of a payoff for The Stones themselves.

12
Beatles versus Stones: The Last Word

CRISPIN SARTWELL

When I was but a wee lad, The Beatles versus Stones thing was the greatest aesthetic debate of the generation. No doubt it rages still through the halls of nursing homes. In any case, the debate itself was a rather unfortunate turn of events. At any given moment, there are many interesting acts in popular music doing all sorts of things, and the idea that it all came down to only two was sort of silly. And no pop musician can possibly pay off on the adulation accorded, in particular, to The Beatles; in the face of their reception as transcendent, God-touched geniuses, as emblems of an entire era, as strange essences of our collective consciousness, and so on, the actual music is absurdly inadequate.

Well, that itself will tell you where I will come down on The Beatles and The Stones. But before I do, let me note that the idea of the essence of a generation or a zeitgeist pressed into the grooves of an LP is borrowed from modernist conceptions in the fine arts and elsewhere. One might think of Beethoven, or Van Gogh, or Nietzsche, Picasso, or James Joyce: more-than-human forces of nature, transcendent geniuses who foresee the future and take us there by courtesy of the incredible roiling forces contained in their giant heads.

The way we conceive such figures serves a number of functions other than our desire for something—anything, really—to worship. They make telling the story of art or of philosophy or of science much easier: you narrate it as a history of breakthroughs and compelling characters. In the bewildering chaotic welter that is the world of art or of ideas, they provide nodes;

they are a way of simplifying experience and history into a shorthand consisting of a few names or biographical sketches. And they are absorbing as character studies, or studies in symbolic pathology, always poised in our imaginations between hyper-effectiveness and mental illness. The promotion of any given actual person to this status is—I think—well-nigh arbitrary. But it makes things easier and satisfies our basic impulse to have something or someone to admire unqualifiedly.

This is not to say that everything is just as good as everything else, or that some artists aren't better than others. But I do want to say that no one is as better than everyone else as figures such as Picasso or The Beatles are imagined as being.

Avant the Avant-Garde

In part, this deification of The Beatles was made possible by the rise of avant-garde art. The avant-garde arts arose in the West in the nineteenth century, roughly with Manet. They proceed by a series of radical innovations, or looking at it the other way round, through a series of radical rejections of the past: a series of negations. Overcoming or destroying the past is a mark of the genius, and avant-garde arts consist of an ever-accelerating series of movements, each defined in part by its destruction or negation of the previous movement:

impressionism/fauvism/cubism/dadaism, for example

or

expressionism/minimalism/pop/conceptualism

In the avant-garde, the authenticity of the artist and the work is established by his or its overcoming of the dead weight of tradition; the avant-garde artist frees himself and us from the oppressiveness of what has come before and the rules or restrictions associated with it.

In the traditional arts, very differently—and here I include crafts such as pottery or fabric arts—the authenticity of the work and of the artist is established through continuity with the past or mastery of the techniques associated with the tradition. They tend to have a guild structure, in which the artist serves an apprenticeship with a master and absorbs precisely the sort of strictures and skills that the avant-garde artist is dedicated to destroying.

Now let's apply these distinctions to popular music. Country music is a pointedly traditional form, and new artists constantly pay their respects to the generations that have gone before. Indeed it is very likely that a country song will be about country music itself, and it might mention Hank Williams or Patsy Cline. And it will often try to establish its connection to traditional themes, settings, and objects: beer, for example, or trucks (which put in many an appearance in Taylor Swift's country-inflected pop songs), or small towns.

Even in very mainstream or poppy or crossover country music you will hear the traditional sounds of pedal steel guitar, or fiddle, or mandolin. And of course the basic song structures or even specific melodic themes, fall into a fairly narrow range. Likewise, the blues is a traditional form. The twelve-bar structure of the blues, with its pattern of recurring lines and the typical turnaround, are identifying features, and though artists have some freedom to alter or depart from these forms, a too-radical departure disqualifies the item as a blues song.

Blues and country music have changed radically over time. They have been electrified, and virtuosos have introduced many innovations; think of the guitar styles of Robert Johnson, B.B. King, Eric Clapton, and even Jimi Hendrix in this light; or the harmonica work of Sonny Boy Williamson, Little Walter, Magic Dick, and, recently, Jason Ricci. But these innovations preserve an underlying continuity. If they do not, then the musician no longer counts as a blues or country artist. That is obviously in question with regard to Hendrix, whose excellence one might take as being in part his poise between traditional and avant-garde forms; he inverts a blues lick, tears it to shreds, de and re-constructs it until it is barely recognizable, and then sets it on fire.

Through the twentieth century, American popular musics cross-pollinated. Country music itself emerged in a mixture of black and white Appalachian and southern styles. Syncretic forms like rockabilly, or gospel, or the melding of country and swing in Bob Wills and the Texas Playboys also appeared. And finally, there is rock'n'roll. The rock of Chuck Berry or Elvis Presley is both an eclectic and a traditional style—innovative by combining elements of the blues and country in a fresh way, traditional by paying strict attention to the structures that emerge from these traditions. Early rock combined the syncretic-traditional styles of black and white southern popular musics—jump blues, gospel, rockabilly—into something that both captured and pushed forward the traditions of American popular song.

Salt of the Earth

Both The Beatles and The Stones emerged as aficionados of this music and of the streams that led into it. Keith and Mick first bonded as young record collectors: always obsessively focused on the obscure blues record they didn't have yet. Like a lot of kids in a lot of eras since the dawn of recorded sound, they were archivists, buffs. And they often deployed a rhetoric of traditional purity (though this was a rejection of the culture around them): they wanted the record by the purest, the simplest, the most bluesy blues artist.

They peeled back from the eclectic surface of popular rock music to the sources of its form in blues, country, and gospel. And they admired the American black artists whom they regarded as the most authentic purveyors of the eclectic style of rhythm and blues, or what would come to be called soul music. Both the early Beatles and the early Stones were essentially cover bands, always on the alert for the latest American black music that they could perform for their British or European audiences.

The Beatles were particularly excellent at this. They took American black pop music—"Twist and Shout," let's say—and stripped it down, cleaned it up, and emphasized the big beat at its heart. The early Beatles records are about the best non-black or non-American appropriations of American black pop music ever made: incredibly clear and propulsive, and sung with a delightful tunefulness. Nor do I think they should be condemned at all for this: they always paid explicit tribute to their sources, and both the music they took and the music they made were worthy of celebration.

If we got into the business of condemning out of hand white appropriations of black styles, we'd have to condemn many of the greatest popular musicians of the twentieth century: Bix

Beiderbecke, Benny Goodman, Jimmie Rodgers, Hank Williams, Elvis Presley, Janis Joplin, Duane Allman, and so on. No race owns art, even the art it originates, and if white artists sometimes exploited this art and its artists, or made fortunes on styles they didn't invent, they just as often revived the careers of artists they venerated, paid them substantial royalties, and introduced them to new audiences. Many of The Rolling Stones' heroes and sources have toured with them over the decades.

As innovative and excellent as The Beatles and Stones were as purveyors of the traditional forms of American music, they understood from early on that it was precisely from these traditions that they drew their power and popularity. The traditional forms of American popular music, and especially African-American music, have essentially been the sources of the world's popular music through a whole century, into the eras of disco and hip hop. Their combination of simplicity and sophistication, the emotional power of the melodies and the lyric themes, the directness of the expression, the excellence of the sound structures as arenas for improvisation (and indeed the very idea of musical improvisation, the sense of simultaneous craft and immediacy), the way the music makes bodies move: all these now underlie popular music all over the world. Some of these elements trace to Africa. The way an audience behaves at a rock concert—with very active participation—is closer to African festive and ceremonial contexts than to European art music of the nineteenth century.

The Riff Not Taken

Nevertheless, though The Stones and Beatles started out in such a similar vein, they diverged quickly. Now many things might make someone prefer one to the other. For example, they positioned themselves differently on what might be termed the moral spectrum. The Beatles' image—whatever the reality— was of wholesome young men: nonthreatening and charming. This was one reason they could appear everywhere in many media. It was the persona projected in *A Hard Day's Night* and *Help!* In the early days, they were pre-teen and teenage-girl crush objects that even many parents could endorse or dismiss as harmless.

This essential wholesomeness continued as The Beatles got more hippie-like, grew out their hair, joined the peace movement, and explored Eastern religions. Still, in songs like "All You Need is Love"—the inspiring yet empty soundtrack for a hundred treatments of hippiedom and the Sixties—they captured the positive side of 1960s youth culture. The Beatles always projected a certain childlikeness, and many of their songs could without strain be covered by Raffi: "Yellow Submarine" (and its bright, happy animation) or "Magical Mystery Tour" were essentially children's songs, though mounted like mini-operas amidst a swirl of distortions.

The Stones projected a darker and more dangerous image, constantly flirting with images of Satan, for example in *Their Satanic Majesties Request* or "Sympathy for the Devil," in both of which they actually identified themselves, albeit with some irony, as the devil incarnate. Whereas The Beatles were associated with the summer of love, *Sgt. Pepper* having been released in June of 1967, The Stones were associated with Altamont, where a Hell's Angel's security guard stabbed a concert-goer. The two represented the kind of twinned fantasies of young female lust: the good boy and the bad boy, the wholesome young man you take home to Mom and the delinquent drug abuser you meet in the alley: the male equivalent of the Madonna-whore complex.

This idea of The Stones as The Beatles' evil twins was probably deliberate. The bands knew each other (members appearing together, for example in The Rolling Stones Rock'n'Roll Circus), and probably in part defined their personae as complements. But though they both started as rhythm and blues or soul tribute bands, they quickly diverged and this, I think, is where the real question of The Stones versus The Beatles arises. The Beatles developed a new musical vocabulary that drove rock'n'roll for a decade or more. The Stones developed as well—they got much sharper and more focused and also more original as they went along. But they referred constantly back to the basic rock and soul and blues vocabularies that they started with. The Beatles developed into what we might think of—at least in the context of popular music with a massive audience—as avant-garde artists. The way The Stones' developed is much more like what we see in the traditional arts.

You're 2000 Light Years from Home

The turn in The Beatles' style dates to *Rubber Soul* in late 1965, or *Revolver* in 1966. Certainly it is fully realized by *Sgt. Pepper's Lonely Hearts Club Band* in the middle of 1967. Here are some of the characteristics of the shift: a change away from a blues tonality to one that is European-oriented or perhaps British (McCartney associated the sound with British music halls of the 1940s); a shift away from basic rock instrumentation (guitar, bass, drums) to much more elaborate set-ups involving in some cases a full orchestra and experimental instrumentation such as the use of the sitar; a shift of lyric themes from dance-and-flirt to melancholy love and eventually to surrealist ('psychedelic') poetry:

> I told you about the walrus and me-man
> You know that we're as close as can be-man.
> Well here's another clue for you all,
> The walrus was Paul.
> Standing on the cast iron shore-yeah,
> Lady Madonna trying to make ends meet-yeah.
> Looking through a glass onion.

One could think of this as a radical expansion of the vocabulary of rock music, or (as I prefer) a departure from it. In a *Rolling Stone* critics' poll, "Yesterday" was listed as the greatest rock song of all times, a claim which might be refuted on the grounds that "Yesterday" can't possibly be the best anything and that it involves a category mistake: if "Yesterday" is a rock song, I am the Walrus.

At any rate, The Beatles' turn produced some charming moments and some lovely melodies, such as "Norwegian Wood" or "Across the Universe." But it also featured rafts of meaningless hooha: much of their production from *Revolver* to *Let it Be* is absurdly overblown yet utterly trivial. Picasso's *Guernica* or Joyce's *Ulysses*, is one thing; *Being For the Benefit of Mr. Kite* is something else again. And I propose that the shift was a disaster not only for the artistry of The Beatles, but for the whole genre of rock music. In one way or another, we must hold The Beatles partly responsible for the soulless anti-rock of, say, Elton John or Billy Joel, and for the pretentious yet empty art-rock of bands such as Yes or Emerson, Lake, and Palmer.

Here is something that is certainly a bad idea: Take a bunch of fairly average lads and their good pop band and abase yourself before them as though they are messiahs (Lennon: "We're bigger than Jesus." They were, but that wasn't their fault, or Jesus's; it was their audience's.) Several things will occur to such lads: first that whatever they are, they cannot just be a slightly-better version of Gerry and the Pacemakers or the Dave Clark Five; they must be, in spite of all appearances or anything that could be revealed to honest self-reflection, world-changing artistes. So they had better get busy making *art*: something that in some way sustains the reception or makes it comprehensible. And such a reception invites an immense self-indulgence: the idea that virtually anything we think of, our merest whim, our littlest jingle or nursery-rhyme, must be world-shatteringly excellent. The shattered world has seemed to support this absurd assessment from 1965 right up to the present.

Now let me admit that there are elements of taste that are irremediably subjective, and I am not going to make you hate *Sgt. Pepper* merely by asserting that it sucks, though it does. And let me also admit that it's bad to insist that an artist of any variety or quality must merely repeat himself or herself, that they must always do what you first liked them for doing. And of course, no one should be forced to do what some critic thinks they ought to do; The Beatles had a perfect right to make whatever music they wanted, and people have a perfect right to like it. But let me also point out that once you have heard a song a thousand times, it sounds like an inevitable classic. You may associate it with important moments in your life, for example. Once every documentary of the 1960s features Beatles songs, even people who hadn't yet been born will associate the music with the era. We are stuck with The Beatles in a way that makes a real assessment of their achievement next to impossible. Nevertheless, the assessments that have actually been made of their late work have been absurd.

Let the Blues Be

Some of the observations made above apply as well to The Stones. It's a familiar refrain that they stopped developing at a certain point (perhaps as early as *Exile on Main Street*), that they stayed too faithful to their roots in rock and soul, that they have repeated themselves too often for too long. Well, The Beatles played for less than a decade, but The Stones will soon reach fifty years. And though it's obvious that they're not as good or as important now as they were in 1970, there's also something admirable about the way they have kept faith with their roots and their talents.

The Rolling Stones are a cosmic essence, a Platonic Form, of rock music. The Beatles started as classicists, and soon went through mannerist, baroque, and rococo stages of aesthetic decadence. I think that one reason for their break-up—whatever women or ego-inflations were involved—was that they had reached an aesthetic dead end; there was nowhere else their actual talents or direction could take them. Soon they would have been writing symphonies and fantasias and operas, and then their artistic limitations would have been even more excruciating in relation to their ambitions than they were already. The Stones actually had their moments of trying to ape the developments instituted by the late Beatles, replying to the psychedelic *Sgt. Pepper* with their own quasi-psychedelic *Their Satanic Majesties Request*, for example. Brian Jones tried to learn the sitar before getting kicked to the curb.

But the fundamental impulse was always to strip to the essence of the rock song. Where The Beatles added layer after layer of instrumental and lyrical ornament, Keith Richards tried to find the absolute essence of the rock guitar lick, on "Satisfaction," "Brown Sugar," "She's So Cold." Finally on a late song like "Gunface" he stripped the thing down to a single incredibly alive chord. The Stones return again and again to the sources of their own music in the blues, in country, in soul. They have both celebrated these basic structures and pushed them forward.

One might be less than blown away by Mick Jagger the lyricist: there's a lot of celebration of the supposed hyper-sexuality of black girls, for instance. But there are also many interesting twists and fresh departures, displayed above all on The Stones' surprising moments of beauty and reflection: "Wild Horses," for example, or "Beast of Burden": songs that display an admirable artistry and sensitivity even in the midst of a reversion to roots. (There are even reflections on being an aging rock star: "I was a hooker losing her looks / I was a writer can't write another book / I was all dried up dying to get wet / I was a tycoon drowning in debt": from "You Got Me Rockin'"). And one thing we can say for Jagger: he did not write "Glass Onion." The art of The Rolling Stones has developed in the ways that traditional arts develop: by simultaneously nurturing the roots and pushing into the sky.

As Plato conceived his Forms, they were not things invented by himself or other philosophers; they were things that were both remembered and discovered, or that were discovered by being remembered: they were essences that were our origin and our destiny. The Stones both remembered and discovered the essence of rock music. They reverted continually to the origin, but they also stripped away the accretions. Their songs pushed forward by seeking the basis; they moved toward a center that we might associate with Chuck Berry, Bo Diddley, or Little Richard, and then they exposed that center. They showed the center of that center.

Once The Beatles had stopped touring, once The Beatles had stopped making rock music, and after The Beatles broke up, The Stones stopped trying to imitate them or compete directly with them. Once the did, they made a series of roughly perfect albums: *Beggar's Banquet*, *Let It Bleed*, *Sticky Fingers*, and *Exile on Main Street*. I propose that this sequence of albums just *is* rock music: its very essence, the definition of the form. Discovering the essence of what you're doing is of course only one way of making art. Departing from that essence in various directions—experimentation, originality, innovation—these procedures have certainly yielded important works of art. And yet the achievement of one's own essence is also a legitimate aesthetic project. It has never been achieved in popular music with more dedication, more focus, or more power in than in the work of The Rolling Stones.

IV

Politics: Sexual and the Other Kind

13
You Can't Always Get What You Want

LUKE DICK

> There are the thousand taboos which proscribe love outside of marriage—and there is the litter of used contraceptives in the back yards of coeducational colleges.
>
> —Jean-Paul Sartre ("Americans and Their Myths," 1947)

Romantic relationships are the most curious and precious of things. I'd bet five bucks that at least seventy-five percent of all popular songs written are about love or a variation on that fine theme. As westerners, we're born into the notion that monogamy is the benchmark for romantic relationships. All of our political and economic institutions have been tailored to support and reward a lasting, contractual relationship between one woman and one man. By some stroke of cultural history, and many strokes of the church's moral sword, we've inherited this tradition. Thanks to Henry VIII, we've also inherited divorce.

The Stones are a touchstone in this tradition of contractual love, because their songs and actions create an image of womanizing and tension that calls into question the very legitimacy of monogamy as "normal" or "natural." A song like "Some Girls" certainly isn't propaganda for monogamy. Given the perverse logic in this tune, you can't help but question whether or not we humans are even cut out for the task of monogamy. What, then (if anything), are we cut out for? Let's watch the tales of these lovers unfold and see what we may learn:

- OCTOBER 1927—Over smoke and clinking glasses, two young French philosophers, Jean-Paul Sartre and Simone de Beauvoir, make an infamous pact of open love, an open relationship: We are soul mates. And we want freedom. Pure freedom. Personal freedom. Intellectual freedom. Sexual freedom.

- JULY 26TH, 1943—Sir Mick is born. Fashions himself into Don Juan incarnate. Notches on his bedpost from famous women alone are too numerous to count, let alone the unknowns who made their mark there. Asked in a 1965 press conference if he's "satisfied," Jagger responds, "Sexually, yes. Financially, no. Philosophically, trying."

- OCTOBER 14TH, 1964—The dandy drummer, Charlie Watts, marries Shirley Ann Shepherd. Maintains his marriage to this day. Watts has been known to look "bored" while providing beats for The Stones.

- 1967—Uncle Keef finally steals Anita from Brian Jones: "Anita, sexy fucking bitch. One of the prime women in the world" (*Life*, p. 197). After a predictably tumultuous end to this stolen affair, Richards and Patti Hansen marry and persevere.

Saw Her Today at the Reception

With rock songs, it's difficult to know whether the lyrics are actually based on a particular event. Was there really a reception or a glass of wine? It doesn't matter. What does matter is that Mick is as good as any other songwriter at getting to the heart of his own tension, particularly in this song. "You Can't Always Get What You Want" portrays the peculiar feeling of wanting to keep something and letting it go at the same time. It is a perfect expression of the limitations and frustrations of the quest for sustainable romantic happiness. In my mind, you could lose every verse except the one about the woman, and the song loses none of its potency. The scene of the reception is what really matters here. Forget Mr. Jimmy and the demonstration. It's the reception where Mick really confronts his revelation that love won't ever fulfill his expectations—for one reason or another.

Perhaps a rock star isn't the best place to look for revelation in matters of love. After all, Mick has problems that normal folk don't—he has many, many more options for mates by virtue of his fame. But Mick is still human. He may be archetypal, but human experiences aren't that different. Even under the more normal circumstances of regular folk, monogamous relationships are difficult to maintain. Get up, get the kids up, read the paper, make the coffee, go to work, pick up the kids, dinner, shower, bed. Mix in some bills, some grill-outs, and sex with the same partner over and over again, and you've got domestic life, in a nutshell. This routine can create a blissful stability in a meaningful, productive life. But it can also deteriorate and leave the heart looking bored behind the drum set.

Communicative, financial, and sexual frustrations are not easy to deal with. Under the abnormal circumstance of rock stardom, maintaining a monogamous romantic relationship becomes exponentially more difficult. The seductive power of good music seems to make even the strangest looking musician extraordinarily desirable to hordes of women. Throw in biological urges, musicians' peculiarly hyperactive need for attention, and long periods of touring away from the family unit, and maintaining a relationship becomes very difficult, indeed. Mick's case brings with it a seemingly unbridled sexuality that threatens to annihilate the legitimacy of the long-lasting, traditional relationship. Which brings up an important question: what is a tradition and should tradition dictate anything?

A Footloose Man

In his 1946 lecture "Existentialism Is a Humanism," Jean-Paul Sartre talks about his approach to ethical judgments and gives a precise explanation of what "existentialism" means. For Sartre, there are two ways to understand humanity. He calls them "essentialist" and "existentialist." The essentialist describes human beings as if there is a blueprint for how humans are supposed to act—that there is such a thing as a pre-existing "essence." What is an essence, you might ask? An essence is a quality that makes something uniquely what it is. Cut my hair off, and I'm still essentially me, so my hair isn't one of my "essential qualities." Take out my brain and my sense of humor, and perhaps I'm not essentially me anymore.

Usually, essentialism presupposes that there is some divinity that has designed humans, created a static human nature, and defined each individual's essence before bringing them into existence. That is, an essentialist supposes that the life and essence of Jagger was in the mind of God long before the material Jagger ever came to be. For the essentialist, Jagger's essence preceded his existence. Imagine essentialism in the context of a car factory: the design and nature (the essence) of Keith's black Bentley is determined long before the metal is shaped and the car finished. All cars are essentially and conceptually dreamed up before they are created.

Sartre supposes the opposite, that we exist first, then we create our essence based on our actions: existence precedes essence. For Sartre, human beings show up, develop on the scene; we are born into the species and into the world first. Only after we exist do we begin acting in the world, conceptualizing in language what are known as our "essences." There is no such thing as a pre-existing human essence, according to Sartre. "Essences" are simply conceptualizations created by human beings after the fact. Marriage and family structure was (at some point in our pre-history) simply conceived or "made up." If we follow the trail of bones of our species back to the trees, one has to come to terms with the idea that conceptualization, symbolization, and language was a development of the human species—not something implanted as an essential quality. But then again, what do monkey-men have to do with marriage or The Stones?

It hasn't always been the case that monogamy was the norm. There are a great number primates who have various forms of group mating practices. The bonobos seem to be doing quite alright with their arrangement.[1] Even amongst our own species, there have been any number of cultures whose practical mainstream did not include monogamy. Like it or not, however, the intellectual, economic and moral ideas regarding romantic relationships have been dictated by the West over the course of the past two thousand years, which has meant that monogamy is now the popular tradition.

---

[1] Go ahead and Wiki search bonobos and you'll find creatures who seem to be as happy and sophisticated as any rock'n'roller in regards to their sexuality.

What Sartre wants us to see is that the existence of monogamy has been a human choice mandated through authority—it is not some absolute ethic handed down from the heavens. That is, at some point, the authorities made the choice to believe the institution of monogamy was best for everyone. As the western powers flexed their muscles over the past two millennia, they've also imposed their own moral choices on anyone they subjugate. Therefore, any tribe conquered by, say, Cortez, would most likely be subject to the moral choices of the Western authority, forced to follow western tradition, which included the authority's notions of relationships. Nowadays, we cannot legally marry more than one person, but there is no law against living with a dozen partners, if that's what you choose. In a sense, through the course of history, we've chosen a freer society than we had five hundred years ago.

The upshot of Sartre's existentialism is that we've always been free to choose whatever type of morality we like. Throughout human history, humans have made individual choices in regard to their own morality. It has always been the Jews' choice to believe or not to believe that circumcision is a covenant with God.[2] Anyone can choose to believe this. Similarly, one can choose to believe (as some Mormons do) that supernatural undergarments are part of divine covenant.

There may or may not be a God. Magic underwear and penile foreskin may or may not matter to that God. For humans, we must choose to believe or not believe in a ritual. Even beyond religious rituals, humans must choose what they believe about anything in their world. It was my choice to care enough about the Rolling Stones and philosophy to write this chapter about the test case of monogamy. In a way, my writing is affirmation of my belief that the subject is important.

Human action and morality has been a process of thought, choice, and change for humans. One needn't look any further than Deuteronomy to see that the moral rules and choices are certainly made in a historical, cultural context. After all, we don't stone women to death for having pre-marital sex as Deuteronomy 22:20 prescribes, because we choose not to ascribe any relevancy to this rule anymore.

---

[2] Though, it's not a universal belief amongst Jews. For more on the up-to-date debate on the Jewish foreskin, visit <www.jewishcircumcision.org>.

If Sartre is right, and all morality is simply a matter of human choices, moral traditions are simply sets of rules or moral frameworks we have chosen to believe or have faith in, and we continue to choose and change our minds about morality as time passes. Unless some all-powerful divinity directly controls the hands and minds of men (which we can never know), how can we help but give Sartre some credence on this issue? Keith, Mick, and Simone (and obviously Sartre) all took up existentialism on some level and chose to discard their inherited traditions of monogamy in favor of something else. Charlie Watts chose to stick more closely to the more staid, Western tradition.

Practiced at the Art of Deception

Mick (or at least Mick's persona, if there is a difference) seems to have embraced the world of seduction in all of its mysterious luster. Tales of bolted doors, secret coded love notes, and various rendezvous are all a part of Mick's mythology. Since secrecy is a part of seduction for the monogamist, the historical data to prove Mick's perfidy is most often obscured. We're left to either believe or ignore his alleged lovers' testimonies. I'm inclined to believe many of them. The lips, the tongue, the whip coming down. No smoke without fire, right? Mick's image is surely derived from some place of truth. But Mick isn't the world's first Lothario.

What makes Mick's case interesting is the fact that he wants to walk the line of both traditionalism and radical sexual freedom. To be all things—to be the knight and the sorcerer. But you can't be the establishment and the counter-culture at the same time, which is partly why Mick's persona and music is wrought with tension. So, he sires seven (known) children by four different women over his life and sings, "You can't always get what you want." Well, if what you want is a lasting love and to be a seducer, you have a problem. If you want to be accepted by the tradition of the aristocracy, while simultaneously living out the lyric of "Some Girls," it seems pretty obvious that to some degree, Mick will always be unfulfilled.

He is guided by incongruous moral bearings. So, as the pendulum swings one way, and he sleeps with Keith's girlfriend

(Anita), Mick gets what he wants sexually. His need for passion and excitement is fulfilled, but his impulse and desire for tradition leaves a vacuous hole. As it swings the other, Mick comes back home to Marianne, happy to be back in the fold of tradition (or some semblance thereof). But at the same time, he's wishing he was feeling up the silky sleeves of some other mistress. Tension. Meanwhile, Keef is jumping out the back window, sockless, having just had a go at Ms. Faithfull.

Glass of Wine in Her Hand

Keith is a different beast altogether—certainly not a beast of burden. He has rolled more by the instinct of camaraderie (often delightfully sordid) rather than by any defined moral impulse. If anything, both in friendship and romance, Keith's guidance seems to be some kind of will for collective hedonistic comforts. The lines of his sexual and platonic relationships are often blurred. I get the sense that Keef is always on the east side of the tracks, windows steamed, guitar in hand, intoxicated and nestled in the lap of a black woman, channeling ecstasy of one sort or another. Bacchus incarnate, he often keeps the cauldron full of wine and the songs bubbling. Most anyone who is around him takes in the vapors.

This may not seem like tension at all, and it often isn't to those who are drinking from his cup. It's only tense when those few interact with the rest of the uninhibited world. You don't notice the yellow lines on the road (let alone drive between them) once the vapors hit you. But, much of the world heeds and needs the yellow lines and recognize them as necessary for avoiding head-on collisions. Keith seems not to have worried much about that.

Though there's less tension in Keith's own mind, there's tension in his relationships to those who aren't stirring the cauldron. Keith's passed out with some gal after a night of the vapors, meanwhile, Marlon (Keith's son) is running amok without guidance, or his old lady is sleeping with someone else. (See *Life* for the story of Marlon on the '76 European tour.) There aren't many rules at all, which makes everything blurry. This chaos is fine in a vacuum, but anytime one has to interact with the rest of the world, the tension can be deadly. I'm almost positive Keith would be dead if he hadn't been a Rolling Stone.

If You Try Sometimes . . .

Charlie just turned seventy (June 2nd, 2011). He married Shirley Ann Shepherd in 1964, bringing them close to their fifty-year wedding anniversary. It seems very clear by Charlie's actions that monogamous marriage is an institution he believes in—or at least sticks to. In a profession known for womanizing, Watts is known for having kept it in his pants. In fact, while staying at Hugh Hefner's Playboy mansion during The Stones' 1972 "Journey through America Tour," Watts is said to have taken advantage only of Hef's billiard room, rather than the other sweet-smelling accoutrements on display at the mansion. Watts is a man of few words, so there's some guesswork needed here. Perhaps Watts' steadfastness is the result of someone who simply doesn't have much impulse for sexual diversity. Maybe the passion implicit in a relationship's initial stages is unimportant to him. Or perhaps Watts is a resilient man compelled by promises and tradition. My instinct and experience of marriage is that it hasn't been easy for him. That being said, Watts doesn't drop the beat when his arms get tired. He plows right on through the burn. That requires a lot of a person and can certainly be tense in its own right. Marriages often are burning, tense things. Fatigue is common. Dropping the beat is even more common.

In Her Glass was a Bleeding Man

Like the Watts-Shepherd marriage, the love life of Jean-Paul Sartre and Simone de Beauvoir lasted right around half a century. They died never having broken their promise. Sartre, the consummate seducer, and the precocious de Beauvoir formed a legendary "pact" in their early twenties. Like a marriage, the pact was meant to be lifelong. But much unlike the Watts and Shepherd arrangement, their promise was one of an open relationship. They were allowed "contingent" love affairs, the only provision being that they were required to tell each other everything about their other affairs. No secrets—emotional, physical, or otherwise, when it came to their other lovers.

The two led lives similar to rock stars, traveling the world, speaking to droves of people, and seducing at will. Their pact facilitated a free-loving lifestyle without breaking the promise they made to each other. In keeping with existentialism, the two defined the parameters of their own relationship. Rather than relying upon some traditional or religious criteria, they chose their own rules. De Beauvoir explains the nature of her relationship with Sartre in *The Prime of Life*, saying, "The comradeship that welded our lives together made a superfluous mockery of any other bond we might have forged ourselves."

The honesty of this pact eludes the kind of tension found in Jagger's and Watts's situation. There is no want of other lovers, since they are free to pursue whomever they please, nor guilt from breaking the promise of monogamy. Their only promise was to be free and communicative with each other. They would have certain days and nights where they would meet together, eat together, work together, but their relationship was mostly intellectual once the initial passion wore off.

By many accounts, there are few instances of problems that seem any more emotionally trying than a monogamous relationship. But, there were other kinds of casualties—both emotional and physical. De Beauvoir's father told her she would never amount to "more than a worm's whore." Ouch. Even within Sartre and de Beauvoir's relationship, allowing one's lover to share the bed of another can take its toll, though they seemed to manage better than most with this aspect. Despite their pact of truth with each other, neither philosopher fully extended that pact to their other lovers, and there were lies and abortions abound. They would steal each others lovers, and seduce the mates of each other's lovers. Tension, indeed.

Get What You Need

I've seen more marriages fail than succeed. For one reason or another, some person leaves, not getting what they want or need. Individuals have become more independent in our age, and there is less practical need for a couple to remain intact, as in an agrarian society. The emphasis on romantic connection seems to trump the sheer domestic benefits of lifelong monogamy. Even in the relationships that work, there are a million small heartbreaks. Perhaps by sexual incompatibility, perhaps by financial problems, or perhaps by a lack of an intellectual connection, monogamy has a way of breaking hearts and happiness every bit as much as breakups. I've heard of embittered fifty-year relationships maintained even in the face of blatant and repeated adultery. In these cases, one is left holding onto the promise they made, choosing to believe that keeping promises and keeping the kids and the family under one roof is best. For Charlie Watts, to "get what you need" is to keep the beat at all costs.

For Mick, it often takes seducing some new beautiful starlet to "get what you need." Without his flamboyant karate kicks and finger pointing, it would never have been the Rolling Stones. Their brand of rock'n'roll requires seduction, and he seems to love being the voice of it. But being the voice of seduction is certainly different from being the whole thing. Mick is not the drummer, nor a guitar player, nor the sole creative force. His solo efforts haven't been nearly as impressive as The Stones' records (though I have a soft spot for "Wandering Spirit").

Perhaps there's revelation in the fact that Charlie Watts knocked Mick out after Mick phoned him, asking, "Where's my drummer?" Try as he might, Mick just can't be all things to the band or in his romantic life. He can't keep time like Charlie, and so is neither a drummer, nor a successful monogamist. Neither can Mick revel in the cauldron of chaos, like Keef. Mick needs more control than that. He wants to choose everything at once, but he's left getting only what he needs—serial seduction. Mick is older now, and (according to the news) settled a bit with L'Wren Scott. I suspect his urges have wained, but old urges die hard. Though he may long for more than seduction, that will be all the satisfaction he can get.

For Richards, he and Anita Pallenberg fueled the fire together, and it was tumultuous. He eventually chose a companion who is the buffer between his chaotic cauldron and the world. Patti harnessed Mercury. Most everyone made it out alive, though I'm sure not without Patti bearing the brunt of the tension at times. Richards has cooled the fires and relaxed the vapors a bit, which keeps him out of jail and the grave. His part in The Stones is to re-conjure the fire when necessary. His days in the Shaman-trance are over, and he's chosen to live out his life with a quasi-normal family and only a few cracked bones as reminders of his days maniacally stoking the fire.

The Sartre and de Beauvoir pact ended on April 15th, 1980, when Sartre died. Rather than being surrounded by family,

Sartre was surrounded by his lovers and students. Though many of his lovers knew of each other and got along, there were still rifts. Instead of family fighting over inheritance, as is the often the case with traditional arrangements, Sartre's women quarreled over his dead affections. The emotional complexity of that many open lovers seems baffling to the trained eye. I often wonder if de Beauvoir would simply have preferred a life of monogamy. Regardless of what she might have wanted, she chose a life and lived it out. On a few occasions, in the throws of passion with another woman, Sartre considered breaking the pact and marrying another. But he never did. For Sartre and de Beauvoir, getting what they needed meant maintaining their freedom and choosing independent lives, rather than embracing emotional, domestic, and financial stability that can come with monogamy.

The philosophers are now buried next to each other in Montparnasse, Paris. It's difficult to look at their headstone without some sense of respect and bewilderment. They made it longer than most with a pact they created and ended up sharing a tombstone like my grandmother and grandfather. Hard to say which manner of relationship creates less heartache for those involved. The same goes for Charlie and Shirley, Pattie and Keith, Mick and whomever. The truth is that each of us has to choose what kind of love (or loves) will fulfill us most. Making that choice is part of being human. Heraclitus had it right when he said that life is a matter of tension. For the existentialist, the tension (Sartre even called it "nausea" in one of his plays) comes from realizing that we are responsible for every choice we make—for relationships or otherwise. In fact, civilization itself is the tense product of all human choices.

I was once in Oklahoma, having dinner with a group of friends. As the night went on and the wine kept coming, the stories and discussions got better, as they often do. I was talking about relationships with a friend. She was on her second marriage, which had lasted twenty-five years. She's a very sweet and devoted woman, but had an interesting Okie aphorism regarding relationships: "Luke, every relationship has an element of shit to it. Staying married is a matter of finding a plate of shit you can deal with. I couldn't deal with my first husband's shit. I divorced him. Now, I have new shit to deal with. But this is shit I can deal with."

Some people want domestic stability and sexual satisfaction and financial well-being and intellectual stimulation and perpetual passion and sexual freedom and personal freedom. Having everything is probably impossible. So, one has to choose a romantic path. Which path? I guess it depends on what you need.

14

Riding the Devil's Tank and Complicit in His Mayhem

James Rocha

> Before, we were just innocent kids out for a good time, they're saying, "They're evil, they're evil." Oh, I'm evil, really? So that makes you start thinking about evil . . . What is evil? Half of it, I don't know how much people think of Mick as the devil or as just a good rock performer or what? There are black magicians who think we are acting as unknown agents of Lucifer and others who think we are Lucifer. Everybody's Lucifer.
>
> —Keith Richards, 1971

Let me begin by confessing to my personal role in the international drug trade. You see, I spend a lot of money downloading music, and, I have to admit, I do it all legally. For example, I have almost all The Stones' records on iTunes. Now, just imagine my surprise when I read Keith Richards's autobiography, *Life*, and learned that The Stones did drugs back when they made all of this wonderful music! I was shocked, I tell you!

Okay. I have a new confession: I suspected all along that they did drugs. Whenever I forked over my $9.99 to purchase a record online, I knew that there was a good chance that my money would support rock stars' drug habits. Drug habits almost always support murderous drug cartels. The collection of Stones songs on my computer may right now be financing some assassin's per diem as he hunts down a poor, unsuspecting prosecutor who's trying to indict a Colombian cartel drug lord.

Obviously, I can't be held responsible for rock stars' drug habits. I'm also not responsible for drug cartels assassinating prosecutors. But saying that "I'm not responsible" doesn't mean that there are no other ethical questions to ask. The concept in moral theory called 'complicity' falls in that mysterious gap between guilt and innocence. I cannot be guilty for what other people do, but maybe I can be complicit if, in some way, I support, aid, or fail to stop the guilty actions of people I'm connected to. Complicity is a strange concept, but fortunately there's a song that tells us all about it. And, of course, that song is from The Rolling Stones.

Philosophy by Satanic Example

Perhaps no song in The Stones' catalog elicits as much controversy as "Sympathy for the Devil," released on *Beggars Banquet* in December of 1968. Though Mick Jagger, the song's writer, has denied any connection to devil worship,[1] both the title and lyrics easily suggest that interpretation. The Stones did not mean for this song to literally provide sympathy for the Devil. The song, instead, implies an argument for a particular ethical point of view that surrounds the concept of complicity. Whether Jagger or the other Stones knew the theoretical background of this concept or the moral theory involved, they are complicit in it.

I have to admit, complicity is both a controversial and mysterious concept. We all know what responsibility is, of course. When something bad happens, the initial response is to search around and seek the person responsible—hoping, all the while, that it isn't you. And, if it isn't you, it seems you're off the hook. But there could be more to accountability than responsibility. Maybe we can hold people accountable when they aren't responsible if they're related to the wrongdoing tangentially.

However, we don't usually look that far: if you find the responsible party, then you should hold him or her accountable. But accountability is not (as the philosophers would say) a zero-sum game: we can find one person fully responsible, and still have room to think others are involved enough to also be accountable to some degree. We can go over one hundred per-

---

[1] Douglas Cruickshank, "'Sympathy for the Devil': Mick Jagger's Mad, Erudite Incantation Strutted '60s Rock toward the Dark Side of History," Salon.com (January 14th, 2002).

cent when it comes to demanding people pay for a wrongful deed.

Let's make up an imaginary example. Anita cheats on her lover, Keith, with his best friend, Michael. Anita is fully responsible for the adultery; Michael (who likes to be called 'Mick' in this fictitious case) is fully responsible for the betrayal; perhaps Keith can also be partially accountable if he somehow led to the adultery by not being the most attentive lover. One unethical act, and we get 220 percent accountability! Not bad, unless you're mixed up in the affair.

In "Sympathy for the Devil," Lucifer (I'm only guessing that's the narrator's name, but it is an educated guess since he asks to be called that) goes through different acts of evil for which he is one hundred percent responsible (he is the Prince of Darkness, after all). Yet he also wants to hold the rest of us to account for his wrongs. I believe that Lucifer is saying we can be complicit in wrongful acts that we do not directly engage in. But, first, we need to examine this concept.

Please Allow Me to Introduce Complicity

A person is complicit with wrongdoing if she cannot be held directly responsible for a wrongful action, but is partially or indirectly related to it. I will lay out three ways she could be complicit. First, the person may not commit the immoral action but may be a necessary component for it happening or being covered up. The legal crime of aiding and abetting applies to situations where a person is complicit in this direct way. We find such a person guilty because we think she played a pivotal role without actually committing the crime. Consider the time a groupie allegedly took a driving test for Keith Richards so that Keith could have a driver's license without learning how to drive. This groupie is so complicit in Keith's crime of driving around illegally that the groupie could be arrested for it.

The second way a person can be complicit is by being a part of a larger group whose collective action is immoral. Suppose the majority of a state's residents votes for a ballot proposition that bans listening to The Stones. Obviously, that's an evil choice, but it's made by the masses, not by any single individual acting alone. Since it's difficult to judge one person—whose single vote has limited political significance—as responsible, we say every person who voted with the majority is complicit in the collective bad deed.

The most interesting sense of complicity combines these two. Suppose a handful of individuals are directly responsible for some evil action, but the action requires the additional activity, support, or even inactivity of the collective masses. We can consider the tragic killing of Meredith Hunter at the Altamont concert (whatever you think of Hunter, it has to be a tragedy for an eighteen-year-old, who's too drugged out to think straight, to be killed). Surely the Hell's Angels, who were acting as security and ended up killing Hunter have a good deal of responsibility. Even more responsibility should be on Hunter, since he had a gun and had already rushed The Stones on stage. And of course, this tragedy would never have happened if not for the wild and unruly atmosphere at Altamont. Euphoria, fueled by alcohol and drugs, fanned into delirium by fantastic rock'n'roll, aided by a sense of paranoia since Mick had already been attacked, mixed with the toughness of gangster security—all this made for a feral mix. But, once blame is dispersed through the three hundred thousand members of the crowd, we can't claim individuals are "responsible." Maybe though a person can be held *complicit* for playing a small part in creating this toxic atmosphere that led to a young man's death.

This way of being complicit brings us back to our collective complicity in the drug trade. Regardless of what you think about the morality of taking drugs, the larger drug wars include some horrendous activities, such as drug dealing children and the assassinations of prosecutors and judges. In our society, we fall into three groups: those who actively participate in the drug trade at the criminal level (the kingpins, dealers, and assassins), those who merely support the drug trade through their purchases (the users), and those who support it indirectly by spending money in ways that help others buy drugs (everyone else). This last kind of support, obviously, is spread out over a lot of people, but without everyone playing his or her part, there could be no drug trade. Without the drug trade, there would be no drug wars. There are evil agents, including the drug kingpins for sure, who are fully responsible for all these horrible things. But the rest of us are in our own small ways complicit, even if we are in no way responsible.

Killing the Kennedys—What's Your Alibi?

Someone could reject any one, or even all, of these positions on complicity. I will concentrate on the combined notion since it includes the other two and makes the most sense of saying that we are all more or less complicit in large acts of collective evil. But, we could only say that if complicity makes sense to begin with. "Sympathy for the Devil" provides an argument that it does. Consider the lines concerning the Kennedy assassinations:

> I shouted out:
> "Who killed the Kennedys?"
> When after all
> It was you and me.

Since he's willing to proudly confess to so much, it's not surprising when our narrator, Lucifer, accepts direct moral responsibility for the murders of both John and Robert Kennedy. Since responsibility is not a zero-sum game, Lucifer can still look around for compatriots in the Kennedy homicides. Lucifer, being the devil that he is, blames us all.

How could this be possible? I myself have an airtight alibi simply by not having been alive in either 1963 or 1968. The surface reading makes no sense. What if, on the other hand, we thought of the Kennedy's as the symbolic representation of all that is positive about the 1960s? What if we saw them, as some people did, as the individuals who were bringing about the utopian Camelot in the US? If we see them as a symbolic ideal, then our inability to continue their legacy, our failure to protect what they stood for, our falling into the entanglement of the Vietnam war then, and similar wars now, all represent our collective complicity in their metaphorical deaths.

Washing the Evil off Your Hands

There is, though, another point of view on complicity. One man's infamously washing of his hands perhaps best represents the point of view of the complicity-skeptic. Allow The Stones' satanic narrator to explain:

And I was 'round when Jesus Christ
Had his moment of doubt and pain,
Made damn sure that Pilate
Washed his hands and sealed his fate.

Pontius Pilate's hand washing suggests skepticism about the very idea of complicity, as if by washing our hands we could also wash away negligible traces of accountability. Pilate, who—at least in the Bible—is reluctant to execute Jesus, does so anyway at the pleading of the Jewish authorities. Since those authorities demand Jesus's execution, Pilate feels he can wash his hands of the affair. Pilate figured that once responsibility has fixed onto someone, everyone else's hands would be clean.

Complicity is a controversial idea. Why should I have any residual stain on me for something that I'm only tangentially related to? Consider my "involvement" (if it can even be called that) in the drug wars. I may have purchased some songs online, but I had no choice in how the rock stars used that money. And those rock stars had no choice in what the drug dealers did with their money. We shouldn't be at all accountable, declares the skeptic. It is the other people—the kingpins, dealers, and assassins—that need to account for the wrongs done! Why invent a new ethical concept to lay any accountability on me when I didn't directly do anything? Pilate's got a good objection: if others are truly responsible, why can't we just wash our hands and move on?

The Stones, given this stanza, don't seem to agree with Pilate's take. The final "his" in the stanza is ambiguous: "Washed his hands and sealed his fate." Whose fate? Jesus makes sense, but isn't grammatically accurate. We learned in elementary school that a pronoun whose referent is unclear attaches to whomever was named most recently—in this case, Pilate. Pilate's hand washing shows his complicity since he's trying to downplay his part in the murder: he allowed it to happen. We're often complicit for wrongdoing precisely because we do nothing to stop it. Pilate, who's complicit for allowing the murder to happen, cannot wash that off his hands. Pilate's hand washing is not key to figuring out responsibility for Jesus's death, but it is for assigning complicity.

The Stench of War

Perhaps we can best understand the incentive to wash our hands from collective wrongs by thinking about war. Within the last few years, the US and the UK have been enmeshed together in two massive wars in the Middle East that many believe are unjust. I have played no role in either war—or so I'd like to think to assuage my pacifist commitments. I never "rode the tank" or "held a general's rank," as the narrator of "Sympathy" did.

I personally didn't even vote for the guy who began the current ongoing wars—in fact, I protested against him, trying to be as much of a street fighting man as I could be. But even then I might remain complicit. While we as citizens do not directly get to choose whether the country goes to war, we may still be complicit in an unjust war if we support it either through words (or bumper stickers), deeds (such as voting), or money (via taxes). Complicity may even result from inactivity—from not sufficiently protesting or speaking out against the injustice.

Again we see exactly how controversial, and somewhat mysterious, complicity can be. We are not only assessing people for wrongs they barely control, but also for wrongs they merely allow to happen. As we can see with war, often this "allowance" is incredibly weak. Even if I did start protesting right now, it surely would not stop either war. I am not allowing the wars to happen—not by myself anyway. Stopping these wars requires just as much collective action as supporting them does. To give me any moral culpability (complicity must imply some culpability, even if much less than responsibility) seems rather harsh in this instance.

The Puzzling Nature of the Complicity Game

If assessing people negatively for complicity seems to be a stretch—especially as we get farther away from the actual wrongdoing—then why would any philosopher want to keep the concept? Though some would scrap it, there are two main reasons why we should keep it. First, it accurately describes something real within our moral discussions. Second, the concept may be necessary for urging people to stop their tiny roles in grave wrongdoings.

"Complicity" describes something real that lies between innocence and responsibility. There are situations where a person is involved in wrongdoing, but is neither directing it nor making it happen. We need a category for that type of moral activity. This need is obvious in aiding and abetting cases: when someone enables a crime, we must give them our moral disapproval.

A complicity skeptic could say that anyone who enables a crime is morally responsible for the enabling, which should not be confused with being complicit with the crime. That is a tricky philosophical question: were any of Keef's drug runners responsible simply for picking up the stuff? Or were they complicit with Keef's habit? Or both? Maybe the difference is so negligible that it is impossible to decide. Perhaps we'll have better luck with collective complicity.

There does seem to be something real about complicity in these collective wrong cases as well. Returning to war, we all know who's directly responsible because Lucifer tells us:

I watched with glee
While your kings and queens
Fought for ten decades
For the Gods they made.

National leaders are responsible for war, not the people. If we want moral accountability, blame the kings, queens, presidents, or prime ministers. While it would be wrong to blame the people, who can hardly be responsible for what their leaders do, at the same time, no war effort could succeed without popular support.

The people surely need convincing, and the stanza points out that religion is often employed in a war-rousing deception (the song suggests that our leaders wage war in the names of "Gods they made"). The fact that they need to trick the citizens shows the necessity of gaining the citizens' support. While the war effort does not depend on any one citizen, it needs the majority's support. In the same way, the drug trade cannot survive on a single person's iTunes collection—my collection hardly supports a single rock star party, much less the assassination of a prosecutor (the price of which I'm only guessing at). These acts only have moral weight when added together. However, the fact that we get something when we add them all up suggests that there's something there to begin with. Zero multiplied a million times neither supplies a war nor a drug trade.

"Complicity" then appears to be a real part of our moral discussions—it fits right between innocence and responsibility (probably closer to innocence). So, we have a theoretical reason to believe in complicity. We will also have a practical reason if acknowledging our complicity is necessary to correct some wrongs in our lives.

Restraining Lucifer with Some Courtesy, Sympathy, and Taste

Complicity also helps us to see the need for changing our wrong ways. Even small bad acts can add up to very serious wrongdoings. Citizens of countries engaged in unjust wars almost routinely support those wars. Those wars can lead to millions of civilians perishing, along with the needless suffering of soldiers who are merely following orders.

We need a concept for assessing these actions because we need to stop them. Because no matter how good we are at avoiding the big evils (how many of us have gone all week without committing murder, torture, or grand larceny?), we all—every single one of us—have problems of complicity. We could not make that point without a concept of complicity. We would not be able to say that:

> Just as every cop is a criminal
> And all the sinners saints
> As heads is tails
> Just call me Lucifer
> 'Cause I'm in need of some restraint.

The concept of complicity enables us to break down these seeming contradictions at the beginning of this stanza—even Lucifer's call for his own restraint appears to be morally confusing. Most of us may be genuinely good people in terms of the big evils, and there may be little to hold us responsible for, but we all have wrongdoings that we are complicit in.

All this makes "Sympathy for the Devil" a most politically and morally significant song for The Stones. It flies in the face of claims that Mick Jagger and The Stones don't have any deeper political awareness. Instead, a song that relates the dangers of complicity through a tale woven by Lucifer shows a clear depth that is usually reserved for the likes of Bob Dylan, John Lennon, or Bob Marley. But it would not be sufficient to merely point out the problem: we also need a solution.

Fortunately, "Sympathy" offers one. The end of the previous stanza points to the biggest reason why we need the ethical concept: Lucifer is in need of some restraint. We don't need to query whether The Stones, or Jagger in particular, believe in Lucifer, or in any religion. Lucifer is a metaphor for the collective evils that all of us create or enable when we are complicit with wrongdoing. In that very real sense, we cannot restrain the wrongdoing that Lucifer represents unless we fight against our own complicity.

That is exactly what the song implores us to do in the very next stanza:

> So if you meet me
> Have some courtesy
> Have some sympathy, and some taste.
> Use all your well-learned politesse
> Or I'll lay your soul to waste, um yeah.

We can use courtesy, sympathy, and taste to better discern instances of complicity. Much of being moral is easy: few of us struggle to resist stealing a car, for example. The hard part is watching our everyday actions, however small, and figuring out where we might be contributing to larger wrongs. Wherever we find such complicity, we must fight against it. For, if we don't— if we allow ourselves to be complicit in grave wrongdoings— then Lucifer really will lay our souls to waste.

15
The Most Dangerous Rock'n'Roll Band in the World

SETH VANNATTA

When I was in the third grade, my neighbor's mother told me that rock'n'roll was the devil's music. My rock band of choice at the time, played on vinyl, was AC/DC. My God-fearing neighbor assured me that this stood for "Against Christ/Devil's Children," which worried me a bit although it didn't bother my parents—products of going to college in the late Sixties—at all.

There was definitely something transgressive about rocking out to "Dirty Deeds Done Dirt Cheap," but at age nine, the sinfulness of rock music mostly eluded me. What was so bad about rock? Why did the church-going types fear it so much?

Reading Keith Richard's autobiographical account of his run-in with the law in Fordyce, Arkansas, in 1975 helps crystallize the dark energy coursing through the veins of rock music. Richards reflects on just how imprudent his July 4th trek through the Bible Belt was. Traveling from Memphis to Dallas to play a show at the Cotton Bowl, The Rolling Stones, against the advice of their attorney, drove through Arkansas and stopped at the 4-Dice restaurant for a bite to eat. Not "fancying" the clientele or the food, Richards spent forty minutes in the loo getting high and "carrying on." The staff called the police. When Richards and two friends began to drive away from the 4-Dice, the police pulled them over immediately—and not to get an autograph.

I guess they broke the law.

But had they? Richards had been getting high in a public restaurant, but the cops did not charge them with anything resembling that offense. Instead, the police made them drive to a car park beneath city hall, eventually holding them in a loose "protective custody" in the police chief's office. The local authorities alerted the media of their catch, and national news reporters began to gather around the courthouse.

The car Richards drove, along with his friend Freddie Sessler, and their head of their security, Jim Callaghan, was stuffed with drugs like a Hefty bag teeming with autumn leaves. Plastic bags filled with coke, grass, peyote, and mescaline were hidden in the door panels. Freddie had a locked brief case full of pure, "fluffy, pharmaceutical cocaine," which was in the trunk alongside around sixty bottles of regionally distilled (but legally sold) corn whiskey. Freddie had Christmas-tree barbiturates on his person, and Richards was wearing a ridiculous-sounding denim cap whose pockets were filled with dope.

On the ride to the garage below city hall the car spewed drugs from its windows like a rotating sprinkler. But again, they were not charged with anything akin to this wrongdoing. They were up against the law in a bad way, and they knew why. They were initially charged with the possession of a "concealed weapon," (a hunting knife laying on the backseat), and "reckless driving" (their tires had spun up gravel on their apparently hasty twenty yard departure from the restaurant). Why hold Keith Richards in custody on trumped-up-sounding charges such as these? And why had they tipped off the wire services that they had Richards in detention?

What's the Law against Rock and Roll?

Understanding why the local Arkansas cops nabbed Keith Richards will help us recognize rock music's sin and how the fear of that sin is embodied in Richards's legal run-in with the Arkansas fuzz. Richards sets the stage for his Arkansas arrest in his autobiography, *Life*:

> Rolling Stones on the police menu across the United States. Every copper wanted to bust us by any means available, to get promoted and patriotically rid America of these little fairy Englishmen. It was 1975, a time of brutality and confrontation. Open season on the Stones had been declared since our last tour, the tour of '72, known as the STP. The State Department had noted riots (true), civil disobedience, (also true), illicit sex (whatever that is), and violence across the United

States. All the fault of us, mere minstrels. We had been exciting the youth to rebellion, we were corrupting America, and they had ruled never to let us travel in the United States again. . . . We . . . were the most dangerous rock-and-roll band in the world. (p. 3)

Those of us who go to rock concerts know the general disruption and unrest that accompanies them—public drunkenness, if not public urination, and back in the days when smoking was allowed, arenas filled with pot-smoke filtering light to and from the stage. But Richards does not seem to be describing these relatively minor disruptions of the public peace. These were not their sins. Their sin was rock itself. The state of Arkansas had even tried to draft legislation outlawing rock'n'roll. In his description of these events, Richards describes the Stones as if they needed an extirpation befitting Socrates, another famous corruptor of the youth.

What was rock's original sin? Well, the term rock'n'roll was originally slang for sex, a sexual metaphor extended from the back and forth rocking of a ship at sea. This gets us closer to the heart of the matter. Rock music emphasizes rhythm, as opposed to harmony, and that rhythm signals other, more libidinal, rhythms. We may need to recall that just a few years prior to Richards's arrest, networks broadcasting Elvis Presley's performances on television were not allowed to show him below the waist. Moms knew the tingle they felt when they saw those Tennessee hips rock, and they did not want their daughters sharing in that dark energy. Consider the utter frenzy and deafening scream of the women when they heard those other four, nerdy Brits with long hair sing and strum just ten years prior to Richards's Arkansas detaining. The Beatles' lyrics were less sexualized than The Stones', but the women were still passing out at the sight of John Lennon, for crying out loud.

Listening to rock music in the years running up to the 1975 incident was like eating from the tree of knowledge. It was a sexual awakening of epic proportions. Rock was the soundtrack of the sexual revolution. When the state of Arkansas tried to make rock illegal, it was trying to outlaw horniness. When Fats Domino "found his thrill on blueberry hill," we know what just what thrill he found. In fact, even Richie Cunningham was corrupted by the sexuality of rock'n'roll, as he sang "I found my thrill," whenever he snagged a date. Those were "Happy Days," but only insofar as rock music had not found its way into too many girls' pants—at least not too many white girls' pants.

Muddy Water and Brown Sugar

Highlighting the internal relation between rock music and sexuality just skims the surface of the rock's transgression. Rock music originated, not far from that Arkansas courthouse in Fordyce, in the Deep South, and it came from black folk. The most immediate origins of rock lay in "race music," a name for jazz, swing, boogie-woogie, jump blues, and rhythm'n'blues. But more than that, rock was the product of a collision of cultures, of white southerners' country and Appalachian folk and black southerners' gospel and blues. Rock'n'roll was the artistic embodiment of the greatest fear of the white powers of the South—racial integration.

Rock music helped initiate and propel a revolutionary social transformation. Often live music concerts in the South would separate the audience into white and black sides of the room using only a rope. But when the music and dancing began, the ranks would begin mixing. Rock music helped integrate the south, and this was dangerous. Rock was in fact breaking the law. It was breaking Jim Crow. Footage in the BBC/PBS documentary "Rock and Roll" shows a Citizens' Council chairmen, standing in front of a sign that read "WE SERVE WHITE CUSTOMERS ONLY," who tells us: "We set up a twenty-man committee to do away with the vulgar, animalistic nigger rock and roll bop." And a member of the Alabama White Citizens Council said: "The obscenity and vulgarity of the rock and roll music is obviously a means by which the white man and his children can be driven to the level with the nigger. It is obviously nigger music."

Still image from the BBC/PBS documentary "Rock and Roll" originally broadcast in 1995

But only when we combine the two transgressions do we begin to understand the psychology behind the fear of rock music and the consequent desire by southern police to lock up Keith Richards. Racial integration was certainly a fear, but the current giving this fear its most primal energy was the fear of miscegenation. As Lloyd Price, a member of the Rock'n'Roll Hall of Fame, said, "Again now here's what you're doing. Remember, when I say white people, white girls liked that music. They was comin' round seein' those black boys shakin' and stuff like that. That was a no-no in this country."

Sam Phillips of Sun Records said of the experiment that was rock'n'roll: "Believe me the resistance on this was absolutely incredible." If rock's logic was allowed to spread, eventually white women would begin spreading their legs for black men. A racist white father watching his daughter dance and shout to Jerry Lee Lewis, let alone Little Richard, was psychologically akin to watching her be seduced by a dark, musclebound, and sweating-like-Patrick Ewing field hand.

The Rolling Stones and Keith Richards were the physical embodiment of racial integration. They were white, but foreign. They played blues-based music. Their hero was Muddy Waters, a black blues man. All of their musical heroes and inspirations were black, and they were playing and selling this black music, this "Brown Sugar" to southern white girls. The redneck cops had it out for 'em, but their legal pursuit of Richards was the culmination of a long history of race-relations, including the racist assumptions of black libertine sexuality, the racist psychology treating black as a marker of dirt and mud, and the mythology of pure southern womanhood needing protecting from dirty black sexuality.

Consider Richards's own reflections on his touring through the American South:

> You try going to a truck stop in 1964 or '65 or '66 down south or in Texas. It felt much more dangerous than anything in the city. You'd walk in and there's the good ol' boys and slowly you realize that you're not going to have a very comfortable meal in there with these truckers. (*Life*, p. 8)

The markers which signaled Richards's harassment by white southerners were his long hair, his extremely non-local and exotic clothing, and his British accent, but we could imagine this exact description being given by a freedom rider or any black person in the south.

Unlike Richards's experience at white truck stops, The Stones would stroll into black juke joints, and after some hesitation, would revel in their "education" there. Richards writes:

> There'd be a band, a trio playing, big black fuckers and some bitches dancing around with dollar bills in their thongs. . . . They get very intrigued and we get really into being there. . . . Lovely black ladies squeezing you between their huge tits. You walk out and there's sweat all over you and perfume, and we all get in the car, smelling good, and the music drifts off in the background. I think some of us had died and gone to heaven. (*Life*, p. 9)

The Stones were in heaven in the black juke joints, tasting and smelling all that brown sugar, and getting to meet and play with Muddy Waters himself, but they were harassed at white truck stops. When they played Muddy Waters songs to white kids, they were symbolically integrating the white audience into the sweat and sex and smell of the black juke joints. Such was their crime.

That and all those drugs, but we'll come back to that.

When The Stones toured with The Ronnettes, "the hottest girl group in the world in early 1963," Richards fell in love with their lead, Ronnie Bennett. Now I admit this might not signify Richards's at-home-ness with black folk (as Ronnie was a black woman), because anyone, white or black, male or female, who has seen 1960s footage of Ronnie Bennett singing "Be My Baby," has probably fallen in love with her. I know I have. However, Richards and Ronnie got hot and heavy on that tour—to the chagrin of Ronnie's pathologically eccentric producer and uber-jealous future husband, Phil Spector. Richards shared with her a sense of being forlorn and out of control amid their sudden success, and he sympathized with Ronnie's plight of not being in control of her career. The animus of Richards's rock music might have found some harmony with Ronnie's gendered and racialized experiences, whether or not these included future overly controlling producer-husbands.

However, if falling in love with Ronnie Bennett is just the inevitable by-product of having a soul watching her sing, then, as a window into their conscious affiliation with the Black cultural experience, consider The Stones' motive for writing "Sweet Black Angel," whose lyrics include:

> She countin' up de minutes, She countin' up de days,
> She's a sweet black angel, woh, Not a sweet black slave.
> . . .
> Now de judge he gonna judge her For all dat he's worth.

Written for *Exile on Main Street* a few years before Fordyce, "Sweet Black Angel" was an overtly political song about the imprisonment and prosecution of Angela Davis, a black feminist philosopher and civil rights activist.

Inspired by Muddy Waters, the Stones were the musical embodiment of a white-black synthesis. Entranced by and at home in Black juke joints and outcasts at white truck stops, the Stones were an aesthetic and cultural manifestation of racial integration. Richards in love with Ronnie Bennett, was a romantic and sexual enactment of racial mixing. Eventually writing a song in solidarity with Angela Davis and civil rights, the Stones became a political voice of racial injustice. The fear of The Stones' embodiment of these racial, sexual, and political dimensions was reflected in the Arkansas laws and in the psychology at work in their arrest.

Keith Richards the Prophet

Richards's Arkansas arrest serves as a leading clue to a philosophical question—what is law? The question concerning the definition of law stops being merely factual and starts being philosophical when we realize how the general rules in print, such as Arkansas statues, fail to map-on to the specific conduct sanctioned by the letter of the law in a one-to-one correspondence.

Statutes and regulations are inevitably more general than any particular action that might or might not fall under their purview. So the law involves the art of judgment; that is, legal authorities must determine which instances fall under the general rule, or which general legal principle to apply to a specific case at hand. That there are legislated statues that prohibit misconduct is straightforward enough: reckless driving is illegal. Deciding which specific ways of driving (such as spinning up gravel outside an Arkansas restaurant) is to be counted as reckless is where the rock meets the roll, where the art of judgment come into play. This particular judicial decision of what specific acts fall under the more generally written statute is what matters to those of us, British rockers or not, who want to avoid the long arm of the law.

Some theorists, such as John Austin in his *The Province of Jurisprudence Determined*, define law as a function of political power. For Austin, a law is a command from a political superior to a political inferior imposing a duty to obey and backed by a sanction for disobeying. Austin's definition places the primacy of law in the legislative branch of government. So the Arkansas state legislators serve on committees and try to draft laws making rock'n'roll illegal. According to Austin, these laws impose duties on us inferiors, and we are penalized for disobeying them. Austin and other legal positivists (the superiors posit the laws), thought that law and morality were separate matters. Legislators write statutes in an effort to transform social practices in accord with some ideal, but, according to this legal philosophy, they do not conceive their laws as embodying or participating in some higher, say divine, morality.

However, the definition of law that most helps us understand Richards' predicament in Fordyce comes from Oliver Wendell Holmes, Jr. Holmes agreed with the positivists that in order to understand the law, we need to set aside questions of morality. Moral duties, according to Holmes, were the limitations upon our actions by conscience or some ideal. But legal duties cannot be understood independently of the consequences of breaking them. If you want to know what law is, says Holmes, you have to look at it from the perspective of the bad man. No pangs of conscience limited our bad man, Keith Richards, in his public drug use. But he did have every desire to avoid the consequences of "breaking the law." Holmes said that the study of the law is just the study of prediction. He wrote that the only thing he meant by law was the "hypostatis of a prophecy" (by the bad man or his lawyer) of what the courts will in fact do ("The Path of the Law," in *Collected Works*, Volume 3, p. 391). This means that the bad man turns the prediction of the behavior of the judge or jury into a thing, and that thing is the law. Keith Richards was a prophet in that he predicted the consequences of his actions. This is all we mean by law, according to Holmes.

The positivist conception of law overemphasizes the primary role of the legislative body, by conceiving of law as decreed in a top-down way. What mattered to Richards was what the judge would in fact *do*, not what some statute said. The judge uses the statute as one among many motives for his decision. What matters to the bad man is how the judge decides the case, and this is what Richards had to predict. Richards, as we have seen, had every reason to predict a bad outcome. When The Stones played in San Antonio, they were told they'd be arrested if they erected a huge blow-up phallus on stage. They predicted that this was in fact the case, and did not raise the "giant inflatable cock" on stage (*Life*, p. 12). I told you sex was their sin.

Holmes did think law and morality were related. He thought that the law was the external deposit of our moral life. In this way, we see why the officers of the law had it out for The Stones. The history of race-relations, segregation, and sexual mores were externally deposited in Arkansas law, and this history was embodied in the desire to lock up Richards. The original sin of rock'n'roll became crystallized in the effort to prosecute and convict "the most dangerous rock band in the world."

Holmes showed how the law in its mature form was expressed by external standards. The police needed to detect some external evidence serving as a sign to detain Richards. Lacking x-ray vision into the car panels and trunk, and predicting that the judge would not admit into court evidence found by tearing up the car, they were left with only a hunting knife and spinning tires. However, they eventually found that briefcase, and the judge's behavior hinged on whether it was obtained with probable cause. The police needed some external sign to infer that more nefarious activities were hidden in the truck.

Legal pragmatists, such as Holmes, admit that there is a large amount of indeterminacy in the law, while other theorists are uncomfortable with indeterminacy and think legal decisions fit neatly into right and wrong, correct and incorrect. These "formalists" insist that the law is an internally consistent chain of logical decisions and that a judge's decision simply finds the relevant general principle and applies it to the specific case. But the context of Richards's arrest illustrates just how much indeterminacy is at work in the law. It would be naive to think that it did not matter that they were a famous British rock band with a history of arrests in Europe for drug possession, that they were in fact in the rural south, and that fame and promotion might accompany those responsible for their conviction in the states.

Pragmatists hold, correctly I think, that the origin of the law is in custom and social practice, and so the origin of the laws emerged organically alongside social customs. In Fordyce it was not customary to spend forty minutes in the john, and this transgression of custom was enough for the staff to call the cops. Another pragmatist, John Dewey, emphasized this cus-tomary origin of the law. Social activities, such as playing music in public venues, should be conceived as interactions and ongoing processes. Laws, such as prohibitions against inflating giant cocks on stage, both intervene in these practices and are themselves in ongoing transition, as I imagine this would not be prohibited today—even if Eminem attempted it. Law must be viewed within the conditions of the social practice at hand and cannot be viewed apart from them as if standing above and outside of them. Dewey articulated a consequentialist and pragmatic standard for determining what law is. What we think of as the judge applying the rule is not an act that hap-pens after the rule is passed as a legislated statute, but instead, his judgment is a necessary part of the law. A judicial determination contains a living consideration of the advan-tages and disadvantages of policy, the costs and public attitude concerning the enforcement of the decision, and has the possi-bility of serving as a precedent for future legal cases.

The judgment is so necessary a part that we can often fig-ure out what the law is by describing judicial behavior ("My Philosophy of Law," in *Later Works*, Volume 14, pp. 117–18). It is an empty prospect to discuss what the law is apart from what the judge does. So what was the law in Arkansas? That is, what can we learn about law by looking at the judge's behavior in Richards's case?

Judge Richards Presides

The cops in Arkansas needed probable cause to search the trunk, and they manufactured this by saying that they saw marijuana smoke bellowing from the windows of the car.

Richards's attorney, Bill Carter, himself an Arkansas native, insisted that it was impossible for Richards and his friends to light up and fill the car with smoke in the twenty yards they drove before being pulled over.

With a large crowd of media and fans gathering outside the courthouse, the ensuing "trial" turned into a comedy. The judge they eventually recruited to hear the case had been playing golf all day and was drunk. (Did I mention indeterminacy in the law and in judicial behavior?) He even left the court in recess to walk across the street to buy a pint of bourbon which he hid poorly in his sock and sipped from while he listened to the angry arresting officer demand Richards's conviction and threaten to arrest the judge for being drunk on the bench.

The young, idealistic prosecuting attorney insisted they release Richards and his friends because the court lacked justification for holding them. Eventually the judge interrupted the proceeding in order to take an interview with the BBC, in which he praised the golf courses in England, and announced a press conference "with the boys" to "explain some of the proceedings here, how the Rolling Stones came to be in our town here an' all." Eventually the judge's brother took him aside and said, "Tom, we need to confer. There is no legal cause to hold them. We will have all hell to pay if we don't follow the law here" (*Life*, p. 17). Holmes was right. The law is prediction through and through. At every level, from the bad man to the judge, the law is just the prediction of the consequences of its transgression.

Richards conducted the press conference promised by the judge from the bench and was filmed pounding the gavel and announcing to the press, "Case closed."

The bad man, Richards, reflected on the indeterminacy at work in the case:

> It was a classic outcome for the Stones. The choice always was a tricky one for the authorities who arrested us. Do you want to lock them up, or have your photograph taken with them and give them a motorcade to see them on their way? There's votes either way. In Fordyce, by the skin or our teeth, we got the motorcade. The state police had to escort us through the crowds to the airport at around two in the morning, where our airplane, well stocked with Jack Daniel's was revved up and waiting. (*Life*, p. 18)

TIME TO ADJOURN—Keith Richard, right, appears to be "rapping" the gavel to call for adjournment of their eight-hour stay in Fordyce last Saturday. Richard, the lead guitarist for The Rölling Stones rock group and another guitarist Ron Wood, left, went to the Fordyce Municipal courtroom for a picture-taking session following their release by City police. Richard was charged with wreckless driving and possession of an illegal weapon after being stopped on the Fordyce By-Pass. (See related article on Page 1).

Reflecting on Keith Richards's arrest serves as an index to a philosophical reflection on the "sin" of rock'n'roll and on the way law embodies a history of attitudes and social practices surrounding that sin. The original sin of rock'n'roll also helps me see why my neighbor's mom thought rock was the devil's music. She didn't want us eating from the tree of knowledge and being initiated into rock's primal and libidinal energies, drives, and desires.

My parents, as I mentioned, had no such fear. They lived the sexual revolution, detested the psychology of racism, and they weren't afraid to bring racist tendencies to consciousness when they were operating subliminally, but divisively. Prejudices against rock and roll, legal or otherwise, in Arkansas contained the external deposit of a moral history rife with a deep psychology concerning sexuality, a psychology of racism, and fear of integration and miscegenation. The Rolling Stones have sympathy for the devil, but the devil was just a projection of white southern fear and repressed libidinal urges. These projections, according to my parents and so many others of the 1960s protest generation, are the truer sin—even if we predict that transgressing them will have grave consequences—even if those projections have become law. But, seeing how much indeterminacy is in the law, we cannot always predict how "de judge he gonna judge," or even if the defendant, as in Richards's case, will end up being the one pounding the gavel.

16

How Come You're
So Wrong,
My Sweet Neo Con?

Joseph J. Foy

One of the best tracks on 2005's *A Bigger Bang* is the overtly political "Sweet Neo Con." Critical of the policies and political climate during the presidential administration of George W. Bush, as well as US foreign and domestic politics and the rampant corruption and cronyism of corporatist politics, "Sweet Neo Con" breaks from the more poetic and personal lyrics on the rest of the album. Jagger's lyrics are not subtle. They are an unconcealed indictment along the lines of "You call yourself a Christian / I think that you're a hypocrite / You say you are a patriot / I think that you're a crock of shit." As Jagger told *Newsweek*'s Lorraine Ali, "It is direct." Then, impersonating Keith Richards, he claimed, "It's really not metaphorical."[1]

The Rolling Stones have always had an anti-establishment aura. That's why Richards and fans of the band chided Jagger for accepting the knighthood honor for "services to music" from Prince Charles. But The Stones only rarely engage in direct political expression. "Sweet Neo Con," however, is a rock anthem that inserted The Stones directly into politics. Although some praised the politics of the song, others thought the band should have remained apolitical.

On the left, filmmaker Michael Moore and journalist and commentator Bill Moyers felt the song was a welcome change for the band and for the political dialogue in the United States. On the right, people like conservative blogger Matt Drudge

---

[1] "Satisfaction Guaranteed," *Newsweek*
<www.newsweek.com/2005/08/14/satisfaction-guaranteed.html>.

argued that the "Bush-bashing" song was nothing more than a way for the band to deflect geriatric jokes and pander to young audiences.

Both sides, though, get it wrong. Ultimately, "Sweet Neo Con" actually crystallizes the band's politics across the years and the role The Stones have played in defining the public sphere.

No Place for a Street Fighting Man?

For many casual listeners, the only thing The Rolling Stones seem to have in common with politics is the familiar strain, "You can't always get what you want." There were hints of revolutionary strains in songs like "Street Fighting Man," inspired by an anti-war rally at the US Embassy in London in 1968. But for the most part The Stones seemed to preach a message of solitary disaffection. "Hey you, get off of my cloud."

Despite being formed in 1962, and coming of age during a time of tremendous political change and social upheaval in London and America (The Stones being heavily influenced by American blues musicians like Muddy Waters—a track from whom they got the inspiration for the name of the band—and early rock'n'roll artists like Chuck Berry), they never seemed to embrace the all too common role of becoming celebrity spokesmen for political activism. While John Lennon was trying to rally Americans to end the war in Vietnam ("War is over, if you want it"), and President Richard Nixon was trying to have him deported, Mick and Keith were more likely to make headlines for having amazing parties or new girlfriends. The assumption was they were narcissistic, apathetic rockers who were more concerned with booze, drugs, and beauty than anything truly political.

Though it's incorrect, there's a logic to this view of The Stones as being disaffected, checked out, and apolitical. If you're not tuned into mainstream political discourse and engagement, then you aren't a 'true citizen'. Such a disparaging view arises from a limited conception of political activity. People come together, communicate ideas, and make decisions about their mutual interests. They then pursue these interests through traditional political activities like voting, contacting elected officials, or standing in picket lines and engaging in demonstrations. This is what is known as the "public sphere." The public sphere forms the connection between the state and the private lives of individuals, and is seen as essential for democratic society.

But what if you aren't engaged in political discussions or political action? What if you willfully remove yourself from mainstream politics? The conventional view is that you're no longer being political. This is why people think The Stones are apolitical. They don't engage in the direct political activism of groups like The Beatles, nor the on-stage finger-wagging (in spite of iconic photographs of Jagger doing exactly that) of bands like U2.

Because they rarely came out engaging directly in social activism, they weren't singing politically charged music like Bob Dylan. Richards and Patti Hansen never spent a week doing a celebrity "bed-in" to protest war, the way Lennon and Yoko Ono did. So it's tempting to assume that The Stones aren't engaged in politics.

But how can you be so wrong? By projecting an anti-establishment image of rebellion that ran counter to prevailing social norms, The Stones helped to legitimize a counter-cultural identity. They challenged traditional institutions and structures without having to be overtly political. And, because they took counter-culture rebellion and transformed it into mainstream, they were able to push boundaries and challenge conformist thinking at a mass level.

Like a Rollin' Stone

Audiences at Stones' concerts may not have been told who to vote for or where to stage a rally, but as a band The Rolling Stones legitimized a lifestyle; one of rebellion and decadence (it is rock'n'roll, after all), but also of individualism and anti-establishment identity. More so than groups like The Beatles—whose softer, gentler image made them the original "boy band" and much more acceptable to mainstream American audiences—The Stones were the original "bad-boy band" that appealed to the fringes of the counter-culture that rejected social norms and conventions. With songs like "Satisfaction" indicting popular media and mainstream society, and "Brown Sugar" flirting with a variety of lusty and scandalous topics,

The Stones presented a hard edge to rock that shook the cultural foundations.

Take "Let's Spend the Night Together." In order to even play the song on the popular *Ed Sullivan Show*, the band was required to change the lyrics to "Let's spend some time together." When they returned to the studio after the performance wearing SS uniforms with swastikas to protest the censorship of their music, they were subsequently removed and banned from ever appearing on the popular show again. These are hardly the actions of an apolitical group.

As a part of the so-called British Invasion, The Stones joined bands like The Beatles, The Who, The Kinks, and The Zombies in cracking into pop-charts outside of the UK, most notably in the United States. An early sign of globalization, these bands helped to internationalize rock'n'roll. In the process, they began to influence cultural movements and trends around the world. Within the US, The Stones became a symbol of rebellion and social antagonism, the trademarked lips and tongue appearing on sleeveless t-shirts and dorm room posters across the country. They legitimized the marginalized, and in doing so became enduring icons of rebellion.

The kinds of influence The Stones had points to an important distinction between "strong" and "weak" publics within the public sphere. Strong publics are ones concerned with decision making, whereas weak publics deal with the formation of identity. When someone attends a political rally or a protest, they are engaged in the process of trying to advance a particular goal and play a direct role in furthering public deliberation. The appeal is designed to be much more intellectual and engaged in public debate and deliberation. When someone attends a Stones concert, there is still an impact but one that is not as direct. Just as your parents may have feared, when you associate yourself with an anti-establishment rock'n'roll band, you may become more distrusting of centralized power and institutional means for social control.

Obviously, it's not often that someone will have their life changed by listening to a song, buying an album, or attending a concert. It's just as unlikely, however, that that same person would end up making long-term political decisions from attending one single political rally or watching one news broadcast. That is simply not how human beings operate.

Numerous studies on what is known as "political socialization," or the induction of an individual into their political attitudes, opinions, and a political culture, point out that there are several important factors that are working to influence individuals throughout their lifetimes.[2] However, prolonged exposure to a particular attitude toward life, especially one that a person feels a deep emotional attachment to, as fans of The Rolling Stones will attest, begins to have an impact on the ways a person thinks about and values things.

The music, performance, and lifestyle of The Rolling Stones make their rebellious worldview seem attractive and legitimate. So when a die-hard Stones fan hears politicians professing a need to use the tools of the state to enforce a cultural or political agenda, they may be less likely to accept that at face value. What may start troubling a Stones fan is the nature of the game played by so many politicians of wealth and, maybe, taste.

My Sweet Neo Con

If The Rolling Stones represented the liberal and free-spirited side of the social unrest of the 1960s and 1970s, Neo-cons were united on the opposite side of that coin. The neo-conservative philosophy began in the 1960s as a political movement in reaction to what were perceived as the failures of liberalism and the radicalism of the left. Responding to the expansion of the social welfare state, the Civil Rights movement, demonstrations against US involvement in Vietnam, and other challenges to traditionalism and American identity—the British Invasion among them—neo-conservatism rose as a means to consolidate state power in order to restore a sense of order and promote so-called "traditional values."

Early neo cons, the likes of Daniel Bell (1919–2011) and Irving Kristol (1920–2009), argued that liberalism, focused as it was on individual rights and principles of freedom, had transformed over the decades. What was once a politics of limited government and personal responsibility, they complained, had been replaced by a philosophy of big government programs that forced social and economic changes through massive top-

---

[2] Richard G. Niemi and Barbara I. Sobieszek, "Political Socialization," *Annual Review of Sociology* 3 (1977), pp. 209–33.

down policy programs like the New Deal and Civil Rights and the decadence of an unchecked consumer culture.

What makes neo-conservatism different from traditional conservatism? To be sure, both embrace traditionalism and only the most gradual pace of change to society. The difference is that neo-cons are willing to use the state as a means of advancing their political agenda. Traditional conservatism is skeptical of centralized power and authority, no matter who is in charge or what their worldview happens to be. The original neo-cons, many of whom were radical socialists before becoming disillusioned with what was happening in the Soviet Union under the leadership of Joseph Stalin, actually viewed the power of the state as being essential for cultivating a particular social order, one rooted in traditionalism and a romanticizing of the past.

Bands like The Rolling Stones represented what neo-cons were rejecting. Their music and garish stadium rock concerts were seen as manifestations of a liberal culture that had abandoned social norms and cultural mores. They were edgy and dangerous and made neo-cons fear that groups like The Stones might help spark an unsafe and unwelcome transformation in society. Adherents to the neo-con point-of-view would not only take issue with The Stones' lyrics and image, but would point to outbreaks of violence surrounding the band. The most obvious was the Altamont Speedway Free Festival where eighteen-year old Meredith Hunter, who was at the time under the influence of methamphetamines, was stabbed to death by a member of the Hell's Angels Motorcycle Club working security for The Stones while they played.

Neo-conservatism often attacks the perceived convergence of libertarianism (a political philosophy of personal liberty from external constraint) and modern liberalism, which is based on the definition and pursuit of maximizing individual rights, in the arena of popular culture. Robert H. Bork, a conservative political thinker who was nominated to the US Supreme Court by President Ronald Reagan but rejected by the Senate, used his book *Slouching Towards Gomorrah* to argue that popular culture debased western society and was helping to unravel civilization as we know it.

Similarly, American philosopher Allan Bloom not only called Mick Jagger "weird," he described him as the symbol of the hypocrisy of popular music. Although their rebellious antics might appeal to the youth, Bloom argued that the petty antics of The Stones are not authentically political because audiences don't embrace political rebellion so much as they merely envy only their money and fame.

> A shrewd, middle-class boy, [Jagger] played the possessed lower-class demon and teen-aged satyr up until he was forty, with one eye on the mobs of children of both sexes whom he stimulated to a sensual frenzy and the other eye winking at the unerotic, commercially motivated adults who handled the money. In his act . . . he legitimated drugs, which were the real thrill that parents and policemen conspired to deny his youthful audience. He was beyond the law, moral and political, and thumbed his nose at it. Along with all this, there were nasty little appeals to the suppressed inclinations toward sexism, racism and violence, indulgence in which is not now publicly respectable.[3]

By legitimizing decadence and dissident insubordination, The Stones embodied the fears and criticisms of those like Bloom who worried that modern culture would derail neo-conservative agendas. If Jagger could be happily and triumphantly "beyond the law," so could all of his fans.

Oh No, Not You Again

The clash between The Rolling Stones and neo-conservatism is nothing new. It is actually at the heart of the band's identity. What pushed it to a more overt confrontation was the recording of "Sweet Neo Con" at the beginning of George W. Bush's second term as President of the United States. The song is a no holds barred criticism of contemporary right-wing politics, both domestic and international. It condemns the hypocrisy of Christian political actors and self-proclaimed patriots, and it takes swipes at unilateralism in American foreign policy aimed at forcing regime change through military action. By mentioning the public funds being directed to the Pentagon at the expense of other programs, it also revives an icon of 1960s

---

[3] Allan David Bloom, *The Closing of the American Mind: How Higher Education Has Failed Democracy and Impoverished the Souls of Today's Students* (Simon and Schuster, 1987), p. 78.

counterculture, namely the quasi-conspiratorial connections between government, industry, and the military that former President Dwight D. Eisenhower infamously referred to in 1961 as the "military-industrial complex."

The song also alludes to the US government selling influence to, and driving profit margins of, private companies like Halliburton and KBR (Kellogg, Brown, and Root). The song was so scathing in its indictment that Richards, who lives primarily in the United States, was concerned about the potential response from American audiences.[4]

In terms of its contribution to the cultural conversation, "Sweet Neo Con" continued to advance the same kind of anti-establishment undermining of authority that has always been associated with The Stones. What made this particular song different, therefore, is not that it made a break from what The Stones have always been, but that it took the covert message and made it overt. It is a direct form of political messaging. The Rolling Stones—wrinkles and all—have not changed their identity or reinvented themselves. "Sweet Neo Con" simply makes explicit the battle-lines that have always existed between rock that challenges authority and neo-conservative principles that seek to use political power to impose social order and preserve traditional institutions and a way of life.

If You Turn Out Right, I'll Eat My Hat Tonight

A major lesson of "Sweet Neo Con," and the history of The Rolling Stones leading up to it, is that the traditional distinction between what counts as a political message and what doesn't is in fact very blurry. In an age of mass media, the internet and the news cycle, politics has saturated all facets of social and economic activity. Trying to sort out public sphere activities of political discourse and activism from private sphere activities of identity development and preference formation is no longer relevant. There simply is not a well-defined space outside of politics—nearly all activities are now political.

---

[4] "Satisfaction Guaranteed."

The Rolling Stones have long recognized that fact, and have embraced it with both indirect and direct challenges to the status quo. They have always sought to push back against the rigid organization of society into a single mold or framework of the kind that neo-cons work to establish. They were covertly part of that wave in the 1960s, but in contemporary politics where the personal is fully political, and neo-cons held sway for so long, this more overt confrontation between The Rolling Stones and the structures of modern power should not have surprised us. It may not even be the last time.[5]

---

[5] I want to thank my friend and colleague Timothy M. Dale who established the groundwork for how popular culture is transforming how we might conceive of the public sphere in *Homer Simpson Marches on Washington: Dissent through American Popular Culture* (2010). His insights were invaluable to this chapter. Thanks also to Craig Hurst and Phil Zweifel for helping me to better understand The Stones.

17
Keef for President

LUKE DICK

I was walking through the East Village when a cloud of pot smoke hit me—common occurrence around NYU. I turned to see a fellow walking with a joint in his mouth. His shirt had a picture of an indignant, twenty-something Keith Richards. Just above the picture, it read: "Keef for President." Too bad Richards wasn't born in the US, or else voting for him would actually be an option. Perhaps someone like Keef would be just what the country needs—someone rough enough, tough enough, and rich enough to keep himself from being beholden to the Big Mac and be the country's beast of burden. This would also mean Keef's soul would set the agenda for the nation. That's a decadent hypothetical worth exploring.

My Name Is Called Disturbance

Actors stateside have led many successful political campaigns. The Terminator. Ronald Reagan. Al Franken. Jerry Springer. Jesse "the Body" Ventura (I classify "professional" wrestling as a form of acting). Maybe, just maybe, the political platforms of these actors were so brilliant that the public couldn't help but vote them into office. I'm inclined to believe it has at least *something* to do with their thespian talents. After all, the more somebody practices the art of provoking emotions, the more adept at it they become. It's difficult to differentiate just how much of an actor's campaign effectiveness has to do with acting school, craft, and need for attention, and how much has to do with actual political competence and care for their constituents.

Actors aren't really poets or musicians, though. There's a difference. Ever notice how actors make horrible musical "artists"? I believe there are more Russell Crowe and Dudley Moore albums in used CD stores than in people's stereos. Sure, there are many musicians who've turned into successful actors (Johnny Depp, Dwight Yoakam, Tom Waits, for instance). But most actors' rock'n'roll attempts have been aesthetic failures.[1] There's a significant qualitative difference between the soul of the musician and the soul of the actor.

By the nature of their respective arts, the musician and actor require different talents. Good acting, by some standards, requires some kind of empathy. A good actor is expected to "act" like whomever she is portraying, to create and harness the emotional history of a character. This helps tap into another world and allows the actor to give a convincing performance within the constraints of a plot. Great actors find ways to create a unique emotional experience with and through a character. Mannerisms, vocalizations, delivery, interaction, and costuming all contribute to an overall experience for the audience.

Keith's talent, on the other hand, begins with his own relationship to music, sounds, and words—not always in that order.[2] He uses his own sensibilities and instinct to carve out the sound. It's generally more of a visceral inspiration that occurs differently each time. Sometimes, a melody or phrase hits him and sets the musical steel wheels into motion. Sometimes, he reaches for the guitar and creates a sound that he finds agreeable, something that moves him. Though he has a few tried-and-true ways of making songs, each situation is unique.

Unlike an actor, whose job is to tap into others (both the character they are playing, as well as their audience they're performing for), Keith's job is primarily to tap into what moves him. After some technical woodshedding, someone like Keith develops a "style" by virtue of a musical conversation with himself and the muses. Oftentimes with a song, Keith simply riffs and mimes words until something inspires him. When he's sufficiently moved, he hones in on formalizing the song. No matter how much Keith becomes a persona or a caricature, if you

---

[1] Jenny Lewis is perhaps the only exception to this rule.

[2] There are several chapters worth exploring in Keith's *Life* where he explains his creative experience.

trace back his experience with music, you'll be led to some kind of pure interaction with music that moved him. The main distinction here is that Keith taps into his own soul, rather than tapping into the souls of others, as is the case with actors. This is one reason why Keith's music is more believable than Jack Palance's. Keith has spent years having a personal aesthetic conversation with himself and music, letting his own aesthetic soul develop his sense of what is good. In a sense, Keith is relying on his own refined instinct of what is "good."

"Values" and more importantly "good values" are important aspects of political and moral philosophy. If we want to know if Keith should be president, we eventually need to tap into Keith's soul to see what moves him now and what would move him as a leader.

A Palace Revolution

Since we're indulging hypotheticals, I believe Keef wins the primaries in a landslide against Arnold for presidency. But if we bring back Plato, an ancient dead flower, the election gets much more heated.

Plato spent much of his life talking about what good souls do. In his *Republic*, this takes the form of a discussion of justice. That might seem an easy task. Good souls do good, right? But if you devote any kind of intellect to any issue of moral or political importance, you begin to see the complexity. New York just passed a law allowing same-sex marriages. I've heard plenty of philosophical argumentation for both sides. Wherever you stand on the issue, rest assured, there's someone out there in your own city who stands passionately against you with some valid reason in their corner. The question Plato is concerned with is whether or not there is such a thing as "good" at all. If there is, how do we find and develop it?

Plato begins to illustrate the question of justice with the story of the Ring of Gyges. This fabled ring has the ability to allow you, if you're its owner, to disappear by simply turning the ring around on your finger. Being invisible exempts you from consequences. If there are no consequences, do you have any reason to be good? Turning the ring and stealing some old Stones paraphernalia without any threat of consequence seems tempting. Plato wants to know if we do just acts only out of fear of consequence. Keith had his own Ring of Gyges in the form of defense attorney, Bill Carter. Carter would get Keith out of many legal jams (most of which were drug related). Keith gets popped with drugs, then rings Carter. Carter rings higher ups in Washington and at the state level. Carter rings his register, and that's how that ring goes. Keith never had much respect for drug laws and clearly didn't find them just, given his propensity for his various decadences.

So, Plato figures, *good* and *justice* have less to do with the legal consequences of actions and more to do with one's *soul* performing appropriately. A just soul is one that acts harmoniously. Plato understands the soul to be an immaterial center from which we act. That is, soul is what thinks, judges, and moves. Plato also believes that the soul is something different than matter—it's separable from our material body. This might sound far-fetched. It might actually be far-fetched. Whatever the case, *soul* for Plato is a human's eternal, experiential nexus, so to speak. It has three parts.

1. **Appetitive.** This portion of the soul is concerned with appetites and desires—food, drink, and sex. These are all necessary appetites to keep one alive. But they can run rampant, and unnecessarily voracious appetites can cause disharmony in a soul. As Mick well knows, appetites can be a "Bitch."

2. **Spirit.** This part of the soul is competitive and fierce. It concerns itself with victory and honor and can work for the appetites or for rationality. Consider the Glimmer Twins' competition with each other as an example. Both Jagger and Richards are highly spirited fellows.

3. **Rationality.** This part of the soul is concerned with truth. Plato believes the rational portion of our soul has a thirst for knowing the nature of the world. This is the part of us which seeks to know and do good. Keith clearly has wits and a thirst for knowledge—so much so that he busted his head open in his Connecticut library, fetching a book from the top shelf. This anecdote alone seems to me a revealing insight into Keef's relationship with the rational portion of his soul.

Plato believes the answer to the good life is aligning and harmonizing all three parts of the soul. Justice is a matter of putting each part in it's right place in a hierarchy of action. Rationality needs to control the spirit and appetites.

To show how the three parts of the soul should work, the *Republic* creates an ideal city in which the three classes of people represent the three parts of the soul, a macrocosmic literary device. The working class, which represent the appetite, make up the majority of a society. The auxiliaries—similar to soldiers—represent the spirit. Lastly, the philosopher king, ruler of the city, represents rationality.

Now unlike Keef, Plato is about complete control. He wants to harness the appetite and use it only as a means to do rationality's bidding. Appetites should only serve to aid rationality in the pursuit of eternal truth. The auxiliaries/spirit take their orders from the rational philosopher kings and keep the workers/appetites in line. All those workers out there in the city who've put in a hard week's work get no luxuries in the *Republic.* They get their basic needs met. But remaining "just" is a matter of rationality steering the working class (appetites) away from unnecessary desires.

The philosopher kings in Plato's utopia are no velvet-robed Nancy-boys, either. There is no opulent treatment for these kings. They are put through grueling moral and physical training their entire lives to make sure they act only from the love of justice. These philosopher kings live in barracks with no excessive pleasures. The function of the philosopher king is to make sure the city remains harmonious and all its people remain in their right place. There is no tolerance for excess and debauchery here. It's a safe place, with a big sign at the edge of the city that reads "NO POETS, NO ROCK'N'ROLLERS." Plato doesn't want to let Richards in. He knows rapscallions like Richards will corrupt the appetites of the masses. Keef's soul has no place in Plato's city.

Shout and Scream and Kill the King

During the campaign, Richards blows away the auxiliaries on the edge of town with a rendition of "Play with Fire" and staggers his way into Plato's *Republic.* Along the way, he works the working-class appetites into a frenzy. They love him. They want his records. They want to sleep with him. Plato was right. Poets and artists do have their way with the appetites. If you don't believe it, put on a copy of *Exile on Main Street*, drink a few rounds, and see what happens. Probably something more bawdy and raucous than if you wouldn't have. Let's see what kind of society emerges, reflective of Keef's soul.

What do we know about Richards's soul? Well, this bloke has appetites—for drugs, for sex, for booze, for music, for bangers and mash. He is also quite spirited. I don't think anyone could ever accuse Richards of being dead behind the eyes. I'd bet my Fender Telecaster that he'd still pull a knife on you. He also has moments of real rational clarity. His understanding of the legal system, music, world history, and religion as expressed in *Life* really paint a worldly picture of him. These, of course, are all things we love about Keith. He's a character out there in the world making great music and living his quirky life, and we love him for it in some weird way. Richards seems to have mellowed in his sixties, so, to make things more interesting, we'll use the young Keef's antics during the Stones' heyday to talk about Richard's soul as a possible philosopher king.

Keef's appetites are most radically displayed in his drug use. This man has cheated death and the law a few times with his ravenous hunger for substances. Week-long benders, car crashes, fights, all somehow drug-related. For Richards, getting the fix for his appetites is his priority (or was during his twenties and thirties). He knew it could kill him. He knew it was unhealthy for his young son to wake him up for gigs or hide the dope when he was too high to handle himself. Still, the appetite held a high seat of power for Keith. When he eventually kicked his habit, it was because it threatened to destroy his talent. Without talent, he's done for. But family, relationships, and many other things that hold conventional value took a back seat to his appetite for drugs. It was a reckless life, to say the least.

Quite different from the philosopher king of the *Republic*, Richards's spirit takes the form of a blue Bentley, darker and meaner than a bruise, his path guided primarily by two things: a voracious appetite for drugs and an unwavering appetite for unique artistic creation. The desire for creative expression is an appetite much like a drug and can be every bit as destructive. The roadmap for Keith's spirit has always led to one of these two, given the day and the hour. Anita or Marlon may have been in the car with him at any given time, and maybe even a history book or two, but Keef's spirit wasn't primarily directed by domestic bliss or knowledge. Something of Keith's young soul is revealed by the fact that "Blue Lena" (Keith's Bentley) has a special, hidden drug compartment.

So, Richards swerves and runs his car onto the lawn of the philosopher king, leaving the rigid rulers beneath tons of blue and bloody steel. This dangerous part of Richards is part of what we identify with when we tune in. He has just enough control of himself and his appetites to be dangerous.

No need for a recount. Plato and the philosopher kings have been pummeled. Richards holds the keys to the city and the reigns of the soul. How does it translate to his leadership? What does the Republic of Keef look like? Something like this: the working class and their habits—the appetites—are constantly on the brink of revolution. They always want more. To get it, they ultimately don't care if they die. They don't care that they risk their lives. They don't care that they risk the lives of their children. They don't care that they risk the life of the entire fucking republic, so long as they get their fix. The guardians of the city (the spirit) work in tandem with the

Keith Richards, Anita Pallenberg, and "Blue Lena," Keith's S3 Bentley Continental Flying Spur said to have a secret drug compartment located in the chassis.

working-class appetites for art and for indulgence. Rationality is only ever employed to help obtain the fix. The Republic of Keef is certainly a driven republic, but it's driven fast and hard and on the edge of a cliff. There's a good chance you might get cut or shot here. Everyday is the sound of marching, charging, feet, boy. Every day for the soul is a street fight in the land of Keef.

Wherever the appetites lead, tyranny soon follows, according to Plato. Keith's soul is a case in point. It seems Plato is right, to a degree, to fear the poets and the musicians. I don't believe it's simply stodgy moralism talking when I say I believe Plato's right that appetites can drive you to destruction. Whenever you habitually let unnecessary bodily desires dictate your action, your rational interests, the interest of your family, the interest of your very life can be at stake. That is, we neglect justice when we let appetites reign. I happen to love tobacco. I love the dull high. I love how the pipe smells. I love the heat of it in my hand. I love the slight burn of the smoke in my lungs. I know this is an unnecessary appetite, one that may even shorten my life. But, I still let that appetite dictate my action every time I light up. I have no answer for this, other than I love that pleasure more than longevity. That's a tyranny of the appetites on some small level.

Compromise Solution

I wonder if a person *could* be trained to be as pure in heart and motivation as Plato describes as the just man. I doubt it. I've never, ever seen anyone with a soul as harmonious as Plato believes is possible. The philosopher king sounds like a fairytale to me. I've never met a philosopher I would want as a leader. Something else I wonder about is whether or not beating the appetites down with the force that Plato requires would lead to a better life. By my lights, there are a few things that make life truly valuable. At the top of my short list are good sex, good food, and good conversation. Here I sit, writing in a resort, awaiting a fine dinner. My soul tells me that doing without any of this would mean a life bereft of serious value. Of course, I grew up under a form of democracy, which Plato believes has caused my soul to be soft on the appetites:

He lives from day to day indulging the appetite of the hour; and some-times he is lapped in drink and strains of the flute; then he becomes a water-drinker, and tries to get thin; then he takes a turn at gymnas-tics; sometimes idling and neglecting everything, then once more liv-ing the life of a philosopher; often he-is busy with politics, and starts to his feet and says and does whatever comes into his head; and, if he is emulous of any one who is a warrior, off he is in that direction, or of men of business, once more in that. His life has neither law nor order; and this distracted existence he terms joy and bliss and free-dom; and so he goes on. (Plato, *Republic*, Book VIII)[3]

If you think Plato has the democratic citizen all wrong, then you clearly haven't looked around. There's so much laxity in my own life, in the life of my own city, state, and nation, I can't help but find this passage incredibly insightful. No party escapes this, as our love for "freedom" only lends to our appetites for unnecessary desires. BUT, does that mean I need to stop lis-tening to the Stones and downscale?

What Can a Poor Boy Do, but Sing in a Rock'n'Roll Band?

Only a fool fails to give Plato his credence. Justice has some-thing to do with self-control, and the success of a person or gov-ernment rides heavily on this. I'm not willing to give up my refined pleasures. Perhaps I'm too entrenched in democracy. Perhaps my soul's too weak. Whatever the case, I'll be dying happy and conflicted, taking in the sweet smoke of my pipe, enjoying my friends, my food, and my sex.

I always wondered if the sexual appetites of, say, JFK or Bill Clinton, really affected their ability to lead a country. I don't believe their sexual indiscretions directly affect their ability to think about governmental policies. However, I do think that self-control counts for something in the soul of a leader. Weakness for any appetite in a potential candidate should give a voter pause. At the end of the day, I would rather have a pres-

---

[3] <http://classics.mit.edu/Plato/republic.9.viii.html>. Go ahead and read it. It's free and on the Internet. You probably won't, as your soul, like mine, is too democratic by now. You might just skim it.

ident with a bit more self-control than Keith. Though, I will say that the world has seen leaders plenty worse.

But I must admit, I'm drawn to Keith. Ultimately, I believe that he sees that the questions of real importance are unanswerable. He resigns himself to dwell in the darkness, letting his soul run amok, controlling himself just enough to bang out a beautifully confused melody into the void. He's a spirit worthy of tuning into as a reminder that control is ultimately an illusion. But I can't live under his rule. My hope, illusory or not, is bound to the ones I love, and I want them safe.

In the end, I prefer Keef on the edge of town, playing at a juke joint. I want to keep him there always. And when I need my occasional fix, I'll take a midnight ride to the edge of town, give a listen, and dance by the light of the darkness. Unlike Keith, I'll be back before morning comes.

V

Undercover of the Knight

18
Sympathy for The Stones

MICHAEL BARILLI AND STEPHANIE ST. MARTIN

> The brutalities of progress are called revolutions. When they are over
> we realize this: that the human race has been roughly handled, but
> that it has advanced.
>
> —VICTOR HUGO

Being a music lover draws a line between hearing and listening. The music we hear is merely background noise, a soundtrack of indifference. Yet taking the time to listen is the catalyst for a transformation—it can transform our language, transform our clothes, and even—sometimes—transform our values.

When The Rolling Stones released "Sympathy for the Devil," they not only wrote a song that rocks, they wrote a song that reveals things about the human condition. At first glance, it's a catchy, Forty Licks-worthy jam with some pretty funky instrumentals. But it's more than that. In talking about the devil and human tragedies, The Stones proclaim the nature of evil and freedom, and man's role in the tragedies of history.

Killing One "Traditional" Bird with Five Stones

We can remember our fathers telling us stories about how The Rolling Stones created "the devil's music," mostly because of their lyrics and performances. Many radio stations even outlawed their songs from the airwaves. (We are too young to have been around during the British Invasion and the outrage over

The Stones and their lyrics—don't judge us, but our memories are clearer of Britney Spears' cover of "Satisfaction" than the original—which, yes, appalls us). Many teenagers of the 1960s weren't allowed to listen to The Stones' suggestive lyrics— mothers and fathers considered it "wrong." Yet like anything else labeled taboo, teenagers always found a way to it. Many found refuge in their friends' cars and places where there were "no parents allowed."

Mick Jagger, Keith Richards, Bill Wyman, Charlie Watts, and Brian Jones became the cornerstone for the counterculture of rock'n'roll. They had their own ideas and were not afraid to broadcast their take on the "adolescent angst" many Americans were feeling. Like a contagion, the Stones' music triggered a fanatical response from their fans, sometimes, unfortunately, erupting in violence.

The Devil Went Down to Altamont

"Sympathy for the Devil," cites certain historical tragedies— Jesus Christ's trial and ultimate death, the deaths of the Royal Russian Family the Romanovs, the Holocaust, the Kennedy Assassinations, and the Hundred Years War—over what ironically seems to be a samba dance rhythm. Mick sings about these events in a taunting, provocative way, and The Stones' live performances of "Sympathy for the Devil" sometimes fueled the satanic fire.

In 1969 at the Altamont Speedway Free Festival, with California's Hell's Angels providing security for the band, violence broke out and escalated during the band's performance of "Sympathy for the Devil." By the end of the show, four people were dead, including Meredith Hunter, stabbed during the performance of "Under My Thumb." Needless to say, "Sympathy for the Devil" was not helping The Rolling Stones' already questionable image.

But is this "satanic" image valid for The Rolling Stones? Compared to contemporary "Devil's music" (like that of Slipknot and others) that explicitly contains Satanic lyrics, The Rolling Stones' lyrics aren't all that racy—in fact, if anything, The Stones were discussing something philosophical. Not that The Stones were "doing philosophy" in their music, but when you closely examine the lyrics of "Sympathy for the Devil," you begin to see a rough sketch of virtue and a call for societal compassion.

Maybe their drug-crazed past and court hearings had led The Stones to re-examine what really matters? If so, that's not to say they cleaned up their act entirely (Keith Richards, we're talking to you) but maybe they felt called to something higher—not lower into the underworld. Perhaps these are their uncensored confessions about how they feel mankind is doing? Any kind of periagoge like this, a turning around or reorientation of one's soul, usually calls for reflection and contemplation about the world around you and what you've discovered about yourself. As it did for one of the holiest men who ever lived, St. Augustine.

What Happens in Carthage Stays in Carthage

In his adolescence, Augustine was devilish. He went to Carthage, the Las Vegas of his day, to satisfy his physical desires. Sex, drugs, and rock'n'roll would have been his motto to live by if rock'n'roll was around in the fourth century. It wasn't. But sex was. And Augustine was probably more of a rolling stone at that time than Mick and Keith ever were.

Before they formed the band with Brian, Mick and Keith seem to have been more obsessed with music than sex. They both had an affinity for blues, collecting records, and eventually named the band after a Muddy Waters song. Though Jagger is no saint, he actually lived his adolescence more responsibly than Augustine by forgoing at least enough "orgyesque" vacations in order to enroll at the prestigious London School of Economics. Augustine, on the other hand, along with this intense sexual desire, didn't run with the best of crowds. In his *Confessions* he describes how he wandered further and further away from God and further into sin. Still, Augustine was able to have a conversion that re-ordered his unquenchable longings for something higher.

At first glance, it may seem as if The Rolling Stones were merely using "Sympathy for the Devil" to fuel their countercultural image, but in fact their message is an old one that Augustine would have known. The song actually highlights the imperfections of humanity rather than acknowledging, much less praising, the existence of some evil genius.

> I watched with glee
> While your kings and queens
> Fought for ten decades
> For the gods they made.

The devil, Jagger tells us, *watched* these tragedies, but did not *cause* them or make them happen. The Devil saw the Romanov murders and he was "'round when Jesus Christ had his moment of doubt and pain," but the Devil didn't exactly nail Jesus to the Cross himself. If Lucifer were truly lurking around every corner, then of course, evil would exist and cause mayhem in the world. But The Stones are saying that these tragedies are not coming at the hands of the Devil himself. If the Devil is not the guilty party, who is? Is there another reason why these evil things occurred?

(I Can't Get No) Satisfaction . . . Or the Satisfaction that I Ought To

"Sympathy for the Devil" outlines many of Lucifer's alleged transgressions and recalls moments in history where many would think, "Why? Why is this evil taking place in the world?" The nature of the devil's game *is* confusing. But Augustine offers some clarification. To really understand what The Stones are singing about, you have to understand St. Augustine's theory of evil. No other account of evil has been as influential in western culture.

Here you are at a Stones concert and you want to capture the event in a photo. The stage is bright, fire and lights go off during each amazing chord as the Stones rock the crowd. When you think you see the "perfect moment," you snap some pictures. But when you get back home, and your ears are buzzing, you might be disappointed about your pictures. Despite the bright neon lights on the stage, even the best photo is dark. You can't even recognize any of The Stones and there are burned spots in the corner from where the lights were.

In today's world, this problem is easily solved with technology. You edit your photos, add light or filters and now you can see the band and the stage much better. What may have been the worst photo of The Stones ever taken is now a great memento from a Stones concert. It's the envy of all your friends on Facebook.

The salvation of your photos illustrates Augustine's conception of good and evil. He doesn't believe evil is some entity that exists as a polar-opposite to good: There's no "good" side to the universe opposed to an "evil" one. Evil is instead merely an imperfection or lack of good, in the same way that the darkness of your photo was a lack of proper exposure. There was no real darkness on the stage when you took the photo (it was bright, you remember, because of all those lights); the camera just lacked the proper settings at that moment to capture the image you wanted.

Augustine believed that humans are like your camera. They often lack the proper lighting to see and capture the world right and to take the right actions. There's no evil entity or Devil making the evil we sometimes see around us. The darkness exists in the photo because here the camera doesn't have the "light-making" features that it ought to have. Evil comes about when something does not have the certain, perfect "good-making" features that it ought to have.

Who's to Blame?

So maybe the Devil isn't the cause when "bad things happen to good people"—but how can we explain the Holocaust? Assassinations? Wars? Again, let's look to Augustine.

As a teenager, he and his friends decided to steal pears from another man's tree. They didn't need the pears—they already had plenty in their own homes and they weren't hungry—but, as Augustine recalls, "it was the sin that sweetened" the pears. Stealing the pears with his friends was fun, and the fact that it was "forbidden" made it even sweeter. At no point does he mention the Devil, or even the presence of evil; rather, it was a choice "seeking no profit from wickedness but only to be wicked." Evil is not some kind of force that controls us. It doesn't come down from the sky and tell us to do its dirty work and steal pears. Evil comes about when there are choices in front us, good and bad, and we choose the bad. It's not that we don't know this is the "bad" choice, it's that there is pleasure and thrill in doing what's "forbidden." The pleasure of defiance can trump any other moral duty.

Like Augustine claiming that evil is just a *lack* of good's perfection, maybe Jagger is acknowledging the fact that not only do we all do evil, but humans do evil quite often. What is most alarming about Augustine and The Rolling Stones is that they both seem to be discussing the same problem even though the saint and the band exist centuries apart. We all know when we choose to do something wrong or wicked but regardless, we just don't view it as a problem. This has been called 'moral impotence', the notion that although you know what's right, you willingly choose what's wrong. The best way to illustrate this is to think about your childhood when your parents would yell at you for missing your curfew, saying "You know what you were supposed to do. . . . Why didn't you do it?" Human beings have never found a solution for this instinct to turn away from what's good.

The Rolling Stones know all about this. Their reputation as troublemakers is something they seemed to enjoy, especially when the cameras were rolling and they brought their songs and attitude into living rooms around the world. They were singing to their young fans who probably knew all about this kind of pleasure, and it made many parents nervous. They knew the implication of what Augustine and Mick Jagger were saying: We often choose to do bad things because there is a little "devil" in all of us?

This is the significance of "Sympathy for the Devil." By nature, people have desires for power, wealth, and conventional success. But these desires take over our better natures, we become more like the devil. Jagger sings that he should be called Lucifer "'cause I'm in need of some restraint." The taunt is completely justified. Even in the twenty-first century, we're still killing one another, robbing one another, and losing sight of the good innately in us. You can't really dispute that "the devil" caused people's actions when the Devil's fingerprints aren't the ones discovered at the crime scene. It's as if the trademark background vocals keep asking "Who? Who?"—Who is the real devil? Who is really to blame for these historical catastrophes and murders? Mick Jagger gives us the answer. It was "you and me." "I'll tell you one time," he sings, "you're to blame."

Sympathy for The Stones

People are often quick to praise God for catching a touchdown pass or hitting a home run, and in the same way, they are equally as quick to blame the Devil for their flat tire. The Stones would have us believe that evil, and by implication good, alike come from us. They put the blame and the credit squarely on human shoulders. It's not unlikely, therefore, that some will accuse The Stones of atheism.

This image of five young men threatening the fabric of civilization is reminiscent of the accusations against the Socrates, usually called "founder of Western Philosophy." One of the most influential and virtuous men in history, Socrates was put on trial for some of the same charges that The Rolling Stones faced in the 1960s. At his trial, documented in "The Apology," Socrates was accused of:

Being an atheist

Being a sophist (or malicious, persuasive man with his own personal, wicked agenda)

Corrupting the youth in Athens.

Socrates was found guilty and condemned to death in a decision known as "the great sin against philosophy." Socrates could have fled Athens, like The Rolling Stones were exiled from England in the south of France, but he accepted his death sentence (he did not know if death was all the bad anyways); he wanted, most of all, for the changes in Athens to occur.

The Stones also questioned and challenged religious and civil authorities, especially in the 1960s, and were arrested and widely criticized for their relationship to youth. Think about the three accusations against Socrates. Socrates refuted the atheist charge by discussing his belief in the gods—he would not only quote them, but he talked about visiting temples dedicated to various deities. The Stones could employ a similar defense by citing "Sympathy for the Devil." There's clearly some differentiation about right and wrong going on in the song, and it refers to the devil and Lucifer. These are things theologians talk about, so it's hard to see the charge of atheism sticking.

As for sophism, Socrates argued that because he received no money for his speeches (a common trait of sophists was charge for their "inspiration") it was not correct to call him one. Plato wrote that Socrates dressed in common clothes because, like most philosophers, his work led him to poverty. His speeches didn't exactly bring in the Benjamins. Granted, the Stones are now one of the most lucrative bands in the history of rock'n'roll, but they weren't in the 1960s and 1970s that we're talking about.

Socrates argued that he couldn't possibly have corrupted the youth, because he didn't go searching for them—they found him. Crowds would gather in the thousands to hear Socrates speak his wisdom. He didn't ask for the groupies to show up; he didn't exactly promote his tour schedule. The youth found him and followed him wherever he would go. They recognized and felt the palpable excitement of a fast-changing shift in philosophy, just as Stones fans who camped out to get tickets or drove hours to go to a show knew that The Rolling Stones were not your everyday rock band.

And yes, like Socrates, the Stones had to defend themselves against their critics. Adults often did not like the way The Stones went about using their new soapbox to promote their music and their records. But in fact they advanced the musical landscape and were a part of changing the social landscape. Without The Rolling Stones fighting back and refusing to back down, we might now have been discussing the "great sin against music" that once forced a great band off the stage.

19

How Mick Learned to Love the Devil

RICHARD BERGER

They could always play, but it took time for the songs to flow. The first incarnation of The Stones was a cover band. They played the music they liked to listen to and turned a white, middle-class British audience onto the Blues.

The Stones were always a band that had a sense of heritage, and even when they began to write their own songs, Mick Jagger and Keith Richards still drew heavily on a range of musical sources. What changed, however, was Mick's increasing reliance on literature for inspiration.

"Sympathy for the Devil" was one song of many (including "Sister Morphine" and "Wild Horses") that were written and recorded during Mick's relationship with Marianne Faithfull. Marianne's influence on The Stones is well documented, although perhaps not appreciated as much as it should be. "Sympathy" is one of the darkest moments of The Stones' mythology. Ever after it helped define them as rock's demonic bad boys. But the song is based on a once-obscure Russian novel called *The Master and Margarita*, written by Mikhail Bulgakov, itself a critique of the philosophical ideas of Saint Augustine of Hippo. It's also a very moral song. "Sympathy" can be read a response to, and an updating of, the philosophy of Augustine, particularly the notion of "evil."

Saint Augustine seems an unlikely influence on the world's greatest rock band, but he was, in many respects, quite a rebel himself. He wrestled most of his life with his own sin, a struggle that culminated in his influential *Confessions*, a book that exerts quite a pull on Mick's lyrics for "Sympathy."

Just as Every Cop Is a Criminal, and
All the Sinners Saints

Augustine's philosophy was about the nature of evil and the
limits and responsibilities of free will. Who hasn't mused on the
origin of evil when reading a newspaper or watching the news?
It was no different for The Stones in 1968, with Vietnam and
the deaths of the Kennedy brothers on their minds. It was the
same too for Mikhail Bulgakov in the 1920s, with the assassinations of the Russian Royal family still in living memory, as it
was for Augustine way back in 387.

Augustine lived between 354 and 430 A.D. and for thirty
years was Bishop of Hippo—now the coastal city of Annaba in
Algeria. He started off as a pagan, like his father, believing that
the world was the product of two Gods—one good, and one
evil—a belief known at the time as the "Manichean heresy."
Later, he converted to the Catholicism of his mother and was
fascinated by the miracles portrayed in the New Testament. He
then discovered the writings of Plato and decided that evil was
not a force in its own right but instead an 'absence' of what
should be—a topic Mick Jagger would touch upon in his lyrics
centuries later. But, Augustine had a problem:

> because such little piety as I had, compelled me to believe that God,
> who is good, could not have created an evil nature. (*Confessions*
> 5.10)

For Augustine, the existence of evil challenged the notion of
an all-powerful and good God: if such a God existed, why did-
n't He just rid the world of evil? If He had created everything,
and "everything" includes evil, then logically, God had created
evil. Why had He done this? Augustine put the puzzle this
way:

> How, then, do I come to possess a will that can choose to do wrong
> and refuse to do good, thereby providing a just reason why I should
> be punished? Who put this will into me? Who sowed this seed of bit-
> terness in me, when all that I am was made by my God, who is
> Sweetness itself? If it was the devil who put it there, who made the
> devil? If he was a good angel who became a devil because of his own
> wicked will, how did he come to possess the wicked will which made

him a devil, when the Creator, who is entirely good, made him a good angel and nothing else? (*Confessions* 7.3)

The Catholic Church taught that evil was an individual's choice, and this led Augustine to revisit that moment of 'original sin' in the Book of Genesis. He believed that it was a factual account of original sin, one that condemned the human race to everlasting perdition: we all live under these conditions and are part of a wider 'divine' plan. The snake (or demon) in the Garden of Eden tempted Adam and Eve to prefer themselves over God. For Augustine, this was 'original sin'—the sin of pride. God allowed the snake to tempt them, to correct their terrible mistake. Demons then, are fallen angels, whom God allows to punish us as part of their own eternal punishment.

Now if God created demons and humans (as part of His "omnipotence" or all-powerfulness), and God knows every individual outcome (as part of His "omniscience" or all-knowingness), then how is anyone free to do anything other than what God planned?

Augustine believed in a type of free will that gives us freedom that is fairly well prescribed and pre-destined. Predestination and free will may seem contradictory. But in order to explain the existence of evil that was not caused directly by God, Augustine had to suppose that humans had freedom to act in ways that brought about sin and evil. So, in something of an awkward compromise, he envisioned humans as free agents who nonetheless live under major constraints— all imposed ultimately by Adam and Eve's 'original sin'.

Augustine knew quite a bit about sin and lack of satisfaction. He admits in his *Confessions*, "I muddied the stream of friendship with the filth of lewdness and clouded its waters with hell's black river of lust" (3.1). Unlike The Stones, who seem to have reveled in the black river, Augustine struggled with his lust for other women for much of his life, keeping a mistress for several years while he was married: "In those days I lived with a woman, not my lawful wedded wife but a mistress whom I had chosen for no special reason but that my restless passions had alighted on her" (4.2). Because of this, Augustine was initially reluctant to be baptized into the faith. But once he had worked through his concept of evil, he decided that the sin he had been guilty of was pride: turning away from God.

Yet there was a bright side. As James Wetzel explains it, the more we 'confess' to God, the more we enter into a conversation with Him, and therefore become less likely to commit further sin. The act of confession itself is a good thing. But does that mean that if we didn't sin, we would never talk to God? Quite a comfort for a sinner such as Augustine! It's as if he figured that to reach God we must have enough free will to permit us to sin and, subsequently, to confess. For Augustine, therefore, evil is a necessary thing. It must exist.[1] So you might want to have some courtesy and some respect.

Please Allow Me to Introduce Myself

Bulgakov's masterpiece, *The Master and Margarita*, had to fight for its existence. Bulgakov started the novel in 1928 but never completed it, partly because Stalin pretty much banned all of Bulgakov's books and plays. Bulgakov died in 1940 while still revising the final draft.

The first English translations appeared in 1967, and Marianne Faithfull get hold of one of them. She read the book in 1968 and passed it on to Mick, correctly thinking that the work's glamorous portrayal of the Devil would appeal to his decadent sense of drama. The novel ignited Mick's imagination in the aftermath of *Their Satanic Majesties Request* and leading up to the *Beggars Banquet* sessions. As Marianne puts it in her own autobiography:

> I had given Mick a copy of Mikhail Bulgakov's *The Master and Margarita* to read—out of which came "Sympathy for the Devil." The book does deal with magic and the central character is Satan, but it has nothing to do with demonism and black magic. It's about light, if anything. (*Faithfull*, Penguin, 1995, p. 267)

The novel begins with two writers, Bezdomny and Berlioz, arguing about the existence of Jesus Christ . The two atheists are then disturbed by an eavesdropping "foreign" gentleman:

> Please, excuse me . . . for presuming to speak to you without an introduction, but the subject of your learned discussion is so interesting that . . . . (*The Master and Margarita*, Picador, 1997, p. 6)

---

[1] James Wetzel, *Augustine: A Guide for the Perplexed* (Continuum, 2010).

Satan, here disguised as Professor Woland, introduces himself and the novel gears up into a savage critique of the vanity and secularism of Russian society—something that must have chimed with Mick and Keith's (then) anti-establishment ethos. Russia's bourgeois, particularly the literary and cultural elite, come in for particular scorn. Woland attacks the two atheists by immediately invoking Augustine's ideas about predestination in arguing that if man truly rules himself, he must have a plan—yet no man is capable of that:

> . . . how can man be directing things, if he not only lacks the capacity to draw up any sort of plan even for a laughably short period of time—well, let's say, for a thousand years or so—but cannot even vouch for his own tomorrow? (p. 9)

The Moscow of the 1930s is pictured as being so Godless that it takes the Devil himself to restore belief in God; we are all, including the Devil, part of God's divine plan.

And I Was 'Round when Jesus Christ Had His Moment of Doubt and Pain

The Master and Margarita also has a 'novel within a novel', a device whereby a novelist, known only as 'The Master' writes an updating of the New Testament in which the mysterious Yeshua Ha-Nozri (Christ) battles with Pontius Pilate, while Christ's own spin-doctor, Matthew the Levite, embellishes his "miracles." The Master is eventually locked in a lunatic asylum after turning in his manuscript, in much the same way that a reluctant Pilate handed over Yeshua Ha-Nozri to be crucified. All the while Satan looks on. The reader gradually realizes that The Master's novel is no fiction, but is meant to be an accurate account of historical events, similar to Augustine's re-reading of the Book of Genesis and the events in the Garden of Eden.

　　Back in Moscow, a more sympathetic Woland turns The Master's mourning lover, Margarita, into a witch. The most climatic scene of the novel comes as Margarita leads hundreds of 'dead' people—characters stretching right back throughout human history—out of Hell into a huge masked ball that she hosts for Woland in central Moscow. The decapitated head of the character Berlioz reappears to suggest that death is not in any sense a final ending. Margarita's selflessness is rewarded and she is allowed to live in a kind of limbo with The Master, a limbo that they both assume to be death. This time, it is God himself who intervenes and orders Woland to grant The Master and Margarita peace. Even Pilate is forgiven, as he sits waiting to be reunited with Christ; he even wishes now that he had taken Christ's place at the crucifixion.

Bulgakov, like Augustine before him, suggests that there is evil in the world, but that there is good in all of us, which can be united with the Divine if we turn away from the material world. Pilate, the Master, and Margarita all end up rejecting the material world and are joined with the Divine at the end of the novel.

Like Augustine's *Confessions*, the novel begins by posing the question of God's existence and ends by answering it firmly in the affirmative. Bulgakov's Satan also operates within the divine constraints of Augustinian free will. He is more like an employee of a large organization than he is an autonomous destructive force. So we naturally have sympathy for this Devil. It was to these ideas that Mick Jagger turned his attention in 1968, indirectly questioning Augustine's notions, asking searching questions about the nature of evil and free will.

But What's Puzzling You Is the Nature of My Game

Their Satanic Majesties Request—an album many still wrongly assume includes "Sympathy for the Devil"—was released in 1967. That was the year of the infamous Redlands Bust, when a police raid on Keith Richards's Surrey mansion, Redlands, yielded a relatively modest haul of narcotics and a Marianne Faithfull infamously clad in just a fur rug. The UK press, pointing directly at the title of the new album, painted the band as if they were the center of some decadent, possibly demonic, cult—a reputation that further fueled Keith's persecution complex.

You might think that Mick, after such a close shave, would avoid the subject for a while. But events kept pointing to these questions about evil and morality. The following year, when Marianne would lend Mick her copy of *The Master and*

Margarita, students were rioting in Paris, the Vietnam War was in full fury, and Bobby Kennedy was assassinated on June 5th—his brother having been murdered five years earlier. The promise of the so-called "decade of peace and love" was starting to fracture alarmingly. Mick quickly saw the relevance of Bulgakov's notion of evil.

To simply label "Sympathy for the Devil" another example of The Stones' demonic obsession—or even worse, to dismiss it as just another plundering of the 'Bluesman selling his soul to the Devil' myth—does the song a great disservice; it remains an important part of the Stones' canon and is a sophisticated counterpoint to Augustine's notion of evil. It manages to do all of this while remaining true to Bulgakov's explosive novel.

In the song, Jagger's Devil is very much a presence at historical events; he's there in religious wars—clear reference is made to the assassinations of the Russian Royal family in 1918 and the "Blitzkrieg" of World War II. And this devil is present as the Stones were recording the song. The most chilling moment is perhaps when the original lyric, "I shouted out, 'Who killed Kennedy?'" was changed to "I shouted out, 'Who Killed the Kennedys?'" after the band heard about Bobby Kennedy's assassination the night before a recording session at Olympic Studios.

Adding an existential dimension, one which Augustine tied himself up in knots to avoid, the song makes a robust case for our own complicity in all of this: The answer to this question in the song is "Well after all / It was you and me." Mick's Devil is much more of a human figure than Augustine or even Bulgakov conceived, and therefore he is just like us. For Mick, there's not much to distinguish Satan from ordinary people. By repeatedly asking us to "Guess my name," Jagger urges us to recognize that the Satan of the final verses of the song is us.

Far from being a paean to black magic, the Stones' finest-hour forces us to confront our own actions, and not to view evil (or good) as benign, predetermined (and therefore Augustinian) forces. Shot though with the mythical utterances of Augustine, Bulgakov, and the Stones themselves, "Sympathy for the Devil" is something like a confession that our own impulses are, in fact, the originators of malice in the world, without regard to any divinely predestined plan.

I Tell You One Time, You're to Blame

After the sessions were completed for *Beggars Banquet*, it was the beginning of the end for Mick and Marianne. The relationship that brought a new dimension to the Stones' purely aesthetic and philosophical flirtation with the occult was on the rocks.

The French New Wave filmmaker Jean-Luc Godard, attracted by the anarchy the Stones seemed to embody, documented the "Sympathy" sessions, at London's Olympic Studios in June 1968. The resulting movie shows a band in transition: Brian Jones is marginalized, sitting in his own booth, his acoustic guitar inaudible. Bill Wyman is also something of a spare part, as Keith plays bass on the song. Besides Mick and Keith, only Charlie Watts seems involved, as the somber organ chords of the original version "turned after many takes from a Dylanesque, rather turgid folksong, into a rocking samba—from a turkey into a hit—by a shift in rhythm," as Keith later put it (*Life*, p. 252).

In 1969, Brian was sacked by Mick and Keith, and was found dead soon afterwards in the swimming pool of his home on July 3rd. The Altamont concert took place on December 6th, with The Rolling Stones as the headline act. The omens weren't good, with Jimi Hendrix and Janis Joplin having both died in September and October respectively. Fan Meredith Hunter was brutally murdered during The Stones' set by an element of the Hell's Angels gang who had been hired as security detail for the event. Rumors persist to this day that The Stones were playing "Sympathy" during Hunter's murder, but the later release of the *Gimme Shelter* documentary (1970) shows that it was actually "Under My Thumb." Mick and Marianne Faithfull finally separated for good that year, as the decade of peace and love ended in bloody violence.

"Sympathy for the Devil" defined The Rolling Stones for their next decade. Like the song it informs, the best philosophy endures, and the ideas of Augustine maintain their relevance to both religious and secular readers today. Augustine asks us what Jesus would be without his Judas—perhaps just another wandering teacher in the desert. Bulgakov asks us what the world would be without the Devil; and we should ask what the world would be without the Rolling Stones.

While those who buy into the mythology of The Stones as satanic would never agree, a world without The Stones would be less enlightened about the nature of evil. The problem with Augustine's philosophy, and in particular his narrow definition of free will, is that humanity is left out to a large extent. The triumph of "Sympathy for the Devil" is to put ourselves and our humanity back into the picture. It shows that we have far more control over our own actions and destinies that we often think, but that with these freedoms come much larger responsibilities. Mick seems to have contempt for Augustine's idea of a divine plan that is beyond our control and he completely rejects Augustine by co-opting Bulgakov's device of a human or human-like devil. But his doing so forces us to examine our own actions and ultimately their consequences. In this regard, "Sympathy for the Devil" points to a larger and serious moral burden that we must shoulder—it demands more of us, perhaps, than Augustine's *Confessions*.

If you're listening to The Stones, reading one of the many editions of *The Master and Margarita*, or watching one of the operas or television series inspired by the novel, you're effectively conversing with Augustine through the centuries, much as Mick and Marianne did when she gave him the book. These ideas still echo through history and our lives—call it a Satanic Majesty's Bequest.[2]

---

[2] This chapter is for Carol Russell.

20
A Devil's Trick of Opposites?

GARY CIOCCO

Why Should the Devil get all the good tunes,
The booze and the neon and Saturday night . . .?

> —A.E. STALLINGS, "Triolet on a Line Apocryphally Attributed to
>   Martin Luther"

It's Just that Demon Life Has Got Me in Its Sway

Blogs are still heavy today on The Stones' 1968 classic from their *Beggars Banquet* album, "Sympathy for the Devil." Religious conservatives claim that the song is Devil worship, while others object that merely mentioning the Prince of Darkness does not amount to worship.

Mick Jagger himself has always claimed that the song is about the dark side of humanity, not a celebration of Satanism. He addressed it directly on "Monkey Man," from their next album, *Let It Bleed*:

I hope we're not too messianic
Nor a trifle too satanic—
We love to sing the blues.

"Sympathy for the Devil" itself is a mix of serious ideas set to a samba rhythm—the lyrics are mostly Jagger's and the beat is credited to Richards, who upped the tempo and added percussion to what was initially conceived as a folk song. This new creation cemented The Stones' position as a group more renegade than The Beatles, especially when, after having been turned down by The Beatles, Jean-Luc Godard filmed the Stones recording "Sympathy for the Devil."

The fact that the lyrics were inspired by *The Master and Margarita*, a novel by Russian author Mikhail Bulgakov, has always given the song a philosophical aura. But in fact there is no thinker more relevant to the meaning of "Sympathy for the Devil" than Saint Augustine. Augustine was obsessed with the meaning of good and evil, and his ideas had lasting impact on both Christian and secular thought.

Born in Thagaste, Northern Africa (modern Souk Ahras) in 354, Augustine jump-started the genre of autobiography with his *Confessions*, written in 394. He converted to the Catholic Church at age thirty-two, and eventually became a Bishop. But Augustine was no saint, in one sense at least. His *Confessions* describe a youth and young adulthood filled with enough passion and indiscretion to rival the tabloid exploits of Britney Spears, Eminem, or The Rolling Stones. Most notoriously, he confesses an obsession with sex. When he was sixteen, Augustine wrote, "both love and lust boiled within me, and swept my youthful immaturity over the precipice of evil desires to leave me half drowned in a whirlpool of abominable sins." God didn't seem to mind all this evil, Augustine pointed out: "You left me to myself: and I was tossed about and wasted and poured out and boiling over in my fornications: and You were silent, O my late-won joy."[1]

If he was both a well-respected man about town and a fornicator who struggled with his sex drive, this man of "wealth and taste" was also prone to self-analysis that usually ended in self-loathing. Besides all of his lust, he was also in the habit of stealing things he did not need. Augustine and his gang, out carousing late at night, once stole a load of pears from a tree filled with fruit "that was not particularly tempting either to look at or to taste." Augustine has other, similar stories that suggest why he acted this way: "Our only pleasure in doing it was that it was forbidden . . . I loved my own undoing, I loved the evil in me—not the thing for which I did the evil, simply the evil . . . For what might I not have done, seeing that I loved evil

---

[1] *Confessions* (Hackett, 1993), p. 23.

solely because it was evil?" Augustine is convinced that he loves evil and has no other reason for committing these acts. But there's something else involved, he says, namely other people assisting him: without "the companionship of others sinning with me, . . . I would not have done this by myself: quite definitely I would not have done it by myself" (pp. 26–31).

This connection between evil and social or group behavior shows up in "Sympathy," as Jagger shrieks: "I shouted out— 'who killed the Kennedys?' And answers "When after all, It was you and me." We know it wasn't "you and me" who literally pulled the trigger on the Kennedys, but perhaps partial blame can be assigned to others. Whether conspiracy theories were in the back of Jagger's mind or not, there is a way to see that Augustine and Lee Harvey Oswald share a similar refrain: I could not, would not, and did not do this by myself. You all helped me.

Still, there's an important difference between Augustine's and Jagger's take on the Devil. In "Sympathy" Jagger puts a human face on evil and makes us feel guilty for the violence and tragedies presented to us. Evil is real—and it is us. But Augustine does not think it's real in the same way. For Augustine evil has no positive existence at all.

It's Only Rock'n'Roll, But I Complicate It

Augustine begins with questions about what defines a person and how a person behaves—the psychology of personality. His Christian view of the person, and his abiding concern with psychological tension in the individual, suggest that he can be seen as something like the first Christian rock artist. Like most of them, until he converted to Christianity, he was all about rebellion and obsessed with sex, excess, and bad-boy behavior. Eventually Augustine came to blame his indiscretions on his material nature, as opposed to his immaterial soul. In fact much of our modern understanding of the split between body and soul can be traced to Augustine, who like Plato, placed the body on a lower plane of existence than the soul. The body will drag you down, away from the excellences of the higher realm.

Yet God created everything, Augustine believed, including our bodies. God is the ground of all being, for "if there is something more excellent than the truth, then that is God; if not, the truth itself is God. So in either case you cannot deny that God exists." As the ground of being, God is perfectly good—Goodness itself—and all things created are also good as a result, in varying degrees. But since evil was not created by God, it either must have had a different source or it doesn't really exist. Augustine opts for the second alternative, writing that "evil has no positive nature; but the loss of good has received the name 'evil.'"[2]

This is where Augustine's interest in human personality meets his theory of evil. Evil is not a thing or a positive force, but instead "a swerving of the will which is turned toward lower things" (*Confessions*, p. 121). The free will is crucial: the best world must have moral freedom in it, because only moral freedom allows for moral goodness to come forth. God would want a world where evil exists, because moral virtues can only exist in a world where evil exists. Courage would not exist, if neither natural evils such as floods or hurricanes, nor moral evils such as the Holocaust or slavery, existed. So God is neither the creator of evil, nor its helpless victim. Rather, he co-exists with evil understood as a privation of goodness. On the other hand, Augustine believe that evil sometimes leads to good in ways that humans cannot see or understand. As Goodness itself, God can see the big-picture-benefits of having evil around, which may sometimes elude our human understanding.

For Augustine, all this moral freedom means that our lives face a constellation of simple yet powerful opposites that we must navigate: soul versus body, pride versus humility, God versus man, good versus evil, temporal versus eternal. We not only have to think about these issues, but live with them and through them in order to approach philosophical truths.

I Shouted Out, Who Killed Meredith Hunter?

"Sympathy" suggests a very different interpretation of evil. It begins with the Devil's introducing himself and boasting of his conquests and his taste. The suggestion is that evil is as charming and likeable to us as this "man of wealth and taste." When we reach the refrain:

---

[2] *On Free Choice of the Will* (Hackett, 1993), p. 58; *City of God* (Hafner, 1948), XI, Chapter 9.

Pleased to meet you
Hope you guess my name
But what's puzzling you
Is the nature of my game.

—the song's psychological punch becomes clearer. In the first two lines, Satan says, "I am happy to make your acquaintance, but if you can identify me, you might have a better chance against me and my wiles." And then comes the crux of the matter: Is it the nature of the devil's game to make us puzzled? Or are we just puzzled about the nature of his game? Or is it even more fine-tuned, so that the Devil is referring to how hard it is to tell good from evil—his eternal game? In any case, the song implies that this devil is no mere lack of goodness, but rather a force, a person, in his own right, present at each of the tragedies and wars he describes in subsequent verses.

In a 2002 interview in *Rolling Stone*, Richards said: "You might as well accept . . . evil . . . and deal with it any way you can. Sympathy is a song that says, 'Don't forget him. If you confront him, then he's out of a job." Richards's comment, coming on the heels of 9/11, updates the song by adding a modern tragedy to those in the song—Christ's crucifixion, the Russian Revolution, World War II, and later, the Kennedy assassinations. Evil is real, the Stones are pronouncing, and its destructive powers should be given credence and, of course, sympathy.

But are, or were, The Stones serious about being evil? While Richards has been more direct, Jagger has often been coy, revealing only generic tidbits about "Sympathy," such as the fact that he wrote the song in a Dylanesque manner, and embraced the role of the sophisticated "man of wealth and taste" rather than that of the beastly Anti-Christ. But there can be little doubt that Jagger was sincere in pointing to the political and cultural tragedies that his man of wealth and taste has been involved in. Nearly forty years later, in the song "Sweet Neo Con," his grinning and assertiveness are still in full force:

You call yourself a Christian
I think you're a hypocrite
You say you are a patriot
I think you're a crock of shit

. . .

It's getting very scary
Yes, I'm frightened out of my wits
There's bombers in my bedroom
Yeah and it's giving me the shits.

According to Jagger, the dangers of ideology are still in place, and he's still pointing his fingers at us for being involved and allowing evil to happen. Unlike Augustine, who sees evil as only a lack of goodness and weakness of human will, Jagger sees evil in the strength of will and the resolve and confidence of humans that perpetrate it:

Just as every cop is a criminal
And all the sinners saints
As heads is tails
Just call me Lucifer
'Cause I'm in need of some restraint.

"Every cop *is* a criminal," he sings—not that every cop is a good person who, occasionally, lets his guard down and is tempted, as Augustine might see it.

In Godard's documentary "Sympathy for the Devil," there is a segment titled "All about Eve," in which the character "Eve Democracy" wanders through an idyllic landscape followed by interviewers. They pepper her with eloquent questions, to which she unfailingly answers only with a laconic "Yes" or "No." One interviewer asks: "There is only one way to be an intellectual revolutionary, and that is to give up being an intellectual?" "Yes," said Eve. Another asks, "Do you think that the Devil is God in exile?" "Yes," she replies. Perhaps the follow-up question should have been, "Does the Devil, then, really live on Main Street?"

Under Our Thumb

Altamont, the free concert given by The Stones outside San Francisco on December 6th, 1969 is one of the great tragedies in rock history. Woodstock's pre-eminence over Altamont in history and rock mythology may be a tongue-in-cheek sign that good does triumph over evil. Everyone learns of Woodstock soon after they reach the age of reason, but many people under the age of thirty, perhaps older, have never even heard of Altamont. Augustine might be surprised to learn about it, as well.

"Sympathy" is directly linked to Altamont, at least in the popular imagination. It's often said, wrongly, that The Stones were playing "Sympathy for the Devil" when the eighteen-year-old Meredith Hunter was murdered by the Hell's Angels. Yet eyewitnesses, as well as footage from the documentary *Gimme Shelter*, clearly show that The Stones had finished with "Sympathy for the Devil" and were onto "Under My Thumb" when the murder occurred. As Norma Coates pointed out in her essay "If Anything, Blame Woodstock," the error is still being made.

Coates places the blame for Altamont everywhere, and not just on the Rolling Stones:

> If anything, the spirit of the times and the concomitant burden placed upon the counterculture by the mainstream media as well as its own scribes was responsible for Altamont.[3]

This verdict is almost unique. At the time, most blamed the tragedy directly on Mick and the band. *Rolling Stone*'s coverage claims that on that fateful day Altamont was like "a decaying urban slum. . . . It was in this atmosphere that Mick sang his song about how groovy it is to be Satan. Never has it been sung in a more appropriate setting."[4] Before Altamont, The Stones and Jagger's words were the center of attention; after Altamont, The Stones, and Jagger in particular, were considered ready for a penitentiary. *Rolling Stone* magazine included a caption under Jagger's picture: "Is Mick responsible for the killing?"

I'm sure Mick would say no. But that's not because he doesn't think evil is real. As he sings in "Sympathy for the Devil":

> I watched with glee
> While your kings and queens

---

[3] "If Anything, Blame Woodstock: The Rolling Stones, Altamont, December 6, 1969," in Ian Inglis, ed. *Performance and Popular Music* (Ashgate, 2006), pp. 66–69.)

[4] Lester Bangs, "The Rolling Stones Disaster at Altamont: Let It Bleed," *Rolling Stone* (21st January, 1970), p. 20.

Fought for ten decades
For the gods they made
(woo woo, woo woo)

Mick doesn't seem to care much for Augustine's view of evil as "privation"; in "Sympathy for the Devil" The Stones are presenting evil as an in-your-face reality that exists independent of the good. This is what Mick and the band saw, if not from the stage at Altamont, in the footage they are shown watching (with revulsion) in *Gimme Shelter*. Meredith Hunter did not die at the hands of a bunch of privations.

A Wild Murder Couldn't Drag Me Away

Despite their different views of evil, there are reasons to see Sir Mick and Saint Augustine as taking similar paths in life. Augustine's youth played a necessary role in his redemption. And The Stones' early flirtation with an evil persona—at its apex in the swirl of Altamont and "Sympathy for the Devil"— no doubt taught them that the force of opposites colliding makes the world go 'round—or brings it crashing down.

Drug use was a staple of The Stones in the Sixties, and the unbridled use of drugs is a certain kind of evil, a fact Jagger emphasized in telling *Rolling Stone* in 1995 that his avoidance of drugs in 1968 helped make *Beggars Banquet* the great success that it was.[5] And it's ironic that the sex-talk in this chapter has almost exclusively been related to Augustine, since The Stones were one of the most sexually-charged bands in rock history. Sexual obsession can also strangle creativity in many ways. But it is the visceral nature of their lifestyles that I have most emphasized in comparing and contrasting Sir Augustine with Saint Mick. They are like brothers, with deep connections, but also diverging in notions and lifestyles in the way only brothers can.

In calling Augustine a Christian rocker, I mean that he was concerned with the primordial forces underlying reality, such as sexuality and evil. He defines evil as the dark underside of good, and gives performative detail to it by describing his love

---

[5] Steve Appleford, *The Rolling Stones, It's Only Rock and Roll: Song by Song* (Schirmer, 1997), p. 69.

of evil itself. For all his love of rationality, Augustine believed that some truths can only be performed or willed. Before his conversion, he had followed the Manichees (followers of the teachings of Mani), who believed that we have two minds, one good and one evil. Augustine came to believe that we can have many wills but only one mind. So if our will is pulled in many different directions, we can say that we have many wills, and the directions they are pulled in may all be good. But if all these good things "attract us at the same moment, . . . they are all in conflict until one is chosen" (*Confessions*, p. 143). One good will is our goal, and can only be achieved by actually choosing.

Gimme Shelter also seems to have two personalities, and critics argue that the movie must choose what it wants to be— a harrowing documentary, or joyous concert footage—just as Augustine says we must choose—between goods or, more dramatically, between good and evil. The Stones, both as explorers into the dark side of humanity and as passive observers of the evil of Altamont, had to rise again; they had to find a way to make their "Sympathy for the Devil" the performative force for understanding evil that it was meant to be, rather than the scapegoat for a multiplicity of forces that were often beyond their control. In doing so, they would learn some restraint, but thankfully also remained restive. If Augustine could fully rest in God, perhaps it was because of how far he had fallen early in his life. And he expresses just how much tension he felt between the flesh and spirit in his infamous line, "God, grant me chastity—just not yet."

On December 6th, 1969, also early in their careers, the greatest rock'n'roll band in the world was in tatters. While Augustine turned from the flesh to the spirit to find rest, The Stones remained in the flesh, continuing to sing the blues and to confront the ecstasy, pain, and evil which define the body and the blues. They've continued rocking and rolling, telling us—for forty more years since that fateful day at Altamont— that rock'n'roll is for everyone, that it's likeable, and that it's in touch with both good and evil in a way that will make it impossible to destroy or ignore.

21
Lucifer Rising and Falling

Dan Dinello

> Before, we were just innocent kids out for a good time, they're saying,
> "They're evil, they're evil," Oh, I'm evil, really? So that makes you start
> thinking about evil . . . What is evil? Half of it, I don't know how much
> people think of Mick as the devil or as just a good rock performer or
> what? There are black magicians who think we are acting as
> unknown agents of Lucifer and others who think we are Lucifer.
> Everybody's Lucifer."
>
> —Keith Richards, 1971

Keith Richards raises some good philosophical questions about
the nature of evil and the meaning of the devil. Satan as the
personification of evil emerged out of the Old Testament and
became enshrined by theologian and demonologist St.
Augustine (354–430 A.D.) as part of the traditional Christian
worldview. His philosophy of evil begins with Lucifer's expul-
sion from heaven for his disobedience. (I'm going to use 'Satan',
'Lucifer", and 'the Devil' interchangeably.)

Lucifer challenged the Almighty's power and this prideful
opposition made him the literal embodiment of sin. Amid the
eternal flames of hell, Satan conspires with his sinister band of
fallen angels to wreak vengeance on God by luring humans
into their foul embrace. According to Augustine, the devil
seduces God's weak-willed children into evil actions that dis-
obey the laws of God, the Church, and the State—the moral
authorities.

Casting the Rolling Stones as "Satan's Jesters" (*Time*, May
17th, 1971), the moral authorities of the 1960s—the press, the

police, and the clergy—accused them of exhorting gullible young people to protest, riot, blaspheme, fornicate, and take drugs. In effect, they did the devil's work by luring innocent youth astray. The Stones, however, embraced a different view of Satan's work. Their music embraced a nineteenth-century Romantic vision of Lucifer as a rebellious angel fighting the forces of moral repression. The Stones' interpretation of evil blamed the mob of hypocritical authorities for the world's horrors.

Diabolical Beginnings

"I hope we're not too messianic or a trifle too satanic," sang Mick Jagger in "Monkey Man," "We love to play the blues." From its origins, blues music was denounced by the Christian community as disreputable—an angry music that opposed traditional values. It was sinful to play the blues, whose name derives from the term "blue devils,"[1] meaning depression or sadness. Accused of being the "devil's music," the blues was feared as a social force that encouraged disruption, irresponsibility, violence, or sexual freedom.[2]

Taking their name from a song by Muddy Waters, The Rolling Stones immersed themselves in the devil's blues of Elmore James, Howlin' Wolf, Willie Dixon, and others. One could say Satan also infiltrated The Stones' musical subconscious when they first heard Robert Johnson's 1930s recordings of "Me and the Devil Blues" and "Hell Hound on My Trail." These songs fostered the legend that Robert Johnson met the devil at a lonely Mississippi Delta crossroads and sold his soul to become a great guitarist, writing songs that overflow with references to Satan.

The Stones played these artists' songs, feeling part of a religious crusade to preach and live the blues. They had the disadvantage of being white, but Mick Jagger sounded black. Leering maniacally and dancing provocatively with arms over his head and hips thrust out, Jagger became a charismatic, sex-charged anti-Moses, leading the rhythm and blues horde into

---

[1] An early use of this term is found in George Coleman's one-act farce *Blue Devils* (1798).

[2] Giles Oakley, *The Devil's Music: A History of the Blues* (Da Capo, 1997), p. 9.

the promised land. The Stones evoked the blues' anger and sexual aggression—grind, shake, rock, ride all night long!

They grew their hair longer than The Beatles, cultivated a funky grubbiness, swore, and behaved like monkey men. With the encouragement of their anti-conformist manager Andrew Loog Oldham (who'd been dumped by the cleaner-cut Beatles), they flaunted their contempt, their anger, and their passionate commitment to sex and lavish autonomy. They were fined for pissing against the wall of a garage, thrown out of hotels, busted for drugs, and accused of orgies.

The press saw them as thugs: "These performers are a menace to law and order and a result of their formula of vocal laryngitis, cranial fur and sex is the police are diverted from other forms of mayhem to quell the violence that they generate," said London's *Daily Mirror* in 1964.[3] Assaulting Christian values, The Stones made outrageousness their trademark. Yet, the more adults despised them, the more teenagers loved them. Commenting on the adoration of their audience and their evil intent, the *Daily Mail* said in 1964, "I have seen nothing like this since the old days of a Nazi rally."

"(I Can't Get No) Satisfaction" caught the tenor of the times. It was an anthem of rejection to the authoritarian teachers, priests, politicians, bosses, and parents who wanted to trap kids in a society that denies sexuality and freedom. They criticized corporate propaganda in "Get Off of My Cloud," mocked anti-drug hypocrisy in "Mother's Little Helper," and delivered a punch to the face of the old values with a flagrantly provocative "Let's Spend the Night Together." Despite the uproar, they were invited to perform it before nine million viewers on Britain's most popular variety show, "Sunday Night at the London Palladium." Seeing this notorious group singing that sinful song on television right after dinner caused mass indigestion and indignation.[4]

Yes, other British bands—such as The Animals and The Yardbirds—were steeped in the blues; and, yes, The Beatles were busted for drugs and provoked hysteria at their shows.

---

[3] Unless otherwise noted, this chapter's quotes from newspapers come from Bill Wyman's *Rolling with The Stones* (DK, 2002).

[4] Tony Sanchez, *Up and Down with the Rolling Stones* (Morrow, 1979), pp. 47–48.

But it was The Stones' unique blend of devil's music, social criticism, public vulgarity, sexual promiscuity, lewd charisma, and overt mockery of authority that generated this rabid hatred and their reputation as a menace to society. "This is the end of the line. Beyond The Stones, one simply cannot go and still maintain civilization," claimed the *Chicago Daily News* in 1965.

Even twenty years later, in his critically acclaimed and best-selling book *The Closing of the American Mind*, Allan Bloom called Jagger a nihilist provocateur, a "demon" and "satyr," who stimulated mobs of children into a sensual frenzy with an act that

> was male and female, heterosexual and homosexual; unencumbered by modesty, he could enter everyone's dreams, promising to do everything with everyone; and, above all, he legitimated drugs, which were the real thrill that parents and policemen conspired to deny his youthful audience. He was beyond the law, moral and political, and thumbed his nose at it. (Simon and Schuster, 1987, pp. 78–79)

From Satyrs to Martyrs

Bloom's morally offended viewpoint—enclosed in a larger critique of how the University fails its students—encapsulates the reasons why many adults thought The Rolling Stones were in league with the devil. Antagonism to Christian values, self-indulgence, sexuality, seduction, mind possession, and the provoking of chaos were intimately linked with the rise of Satan and the vision of evil in early Christian mythology. In the Old Testament, the devil as phallic snake tempts Eve into sin.

St. Augustine developed the idea of sex as sin. According to one historian, he was "the dark genius of imperial Christianity, the ideologue of the Church-State alliance, and the fabricator of the medieval mentality. Next to Paul, he did more to shape Christianity than any other human being."[5] Writing at the end of the third century and the beginning of the fourth, Augustine believed that while all humans were destined to sin, only Christians could resist the devil's influence through God's grace. Therefore, non-Christians were doomed to evil and must

---

[5] Paul Johnson, *A History of Christianity* (Touchstone, 1976), p. 112.

be compelled to accept Christian dogma. Rejecting Christianity equaled rejecting society—something that could not be tolerated. So Augustine's totalitarian vision of a Christian society included the right to persecute non-conformists and rebels—heretics—and force their compliance.

"The devil has moved the heretics to resist the Christian doctrine," Augustine wrote,

> as if they could be kept in the city of God indifferently without correction. Those in the Church of Christ who savor anything morbid and depraved and will not amend their pestiferous and deadly dogmas are to be reckoned enemies who serve for her discipline. (*The City of God*, Book XVIII)

More than a philosopher, Augustine was a leading bishop who actively worked with the State to compel this Christian obedience. Since God was All-Good, evil resulted from human free will, giving in to self-indulgence at the devil's behest. Weak and easily persuaded to sin, people required the ironclad discipline enforced by Church-sanctioned State authority to help control sinful chaos.

The worst aspect of that chaos is unbridled lust: To Augustine, sex is evil—an irrational, animalistic outburst that must be restrained. Preying upon the weakness of the flesh, he believed, Satan uses sex as a weapon to seize the soul. Like Satan, Adam and Eve disobeyed God. They then became Satan's tools, bringing evil into the world through Original Sin, a concept Augustine invented. The genitals serve as the instruments for the transmission of Original Sin, corrupting human nature, infecting the body, and making us more susceptible to the evil of demonic contagion. This is one of Augustine's most significant contributions to the theory of evil because it justified moral authorities doing whatever they wish to control lustful behavior and the human search for "satisfaction."

To put it bluntly, Augustine comes off as an unhappy, authoritarian prude who despised life, sexuality, humanity, and even himself—pretty much everything except God. In Augustine's view, humanity must defeat the dark, corrupt physical world and embrace the light spiritual world by obeying God and His Earthly representatives—the Church, its priests, and the State. Only then can we save ourselves from the serpent's curse, the original sin inherited from Adam and Eve.

While a snake evoked sex as bestial and disgusting, it was not the only symbol of evil for Augustine. The pagan male deity Pan—the so-called goat-god—provided the required physical and symbolic model for Satan: cloven hooves, beasts' ears, glowering face, lascivious eyes, enlarged penis, and phallic horns. The Satyr Pan played hypnotic music and symbolized anarchic freedom, animalistic impulses, unrestrained lust, emotional seduction, and irrational chaos. Visually reflecting the characteristics of Augustinian evil, Pan was gradually incorporated into Christianity's image of Satan—and the Sixties' press image of The Rolling Stones.

The press tried to enforce conformity by mocking and ostracizing The Stones; the state, through the police, persecuted them through drugs busts and other harassment, even hauling almost invisible Rolling Stone Bill Wyman into court for profanity and insulting behavior, calling him a "shaggy monster." From the viewpoint of their youthful audience, The Stones became martyrs. Possibly in reaction to the denigrating attacks, Jagger and The Stones in 1966 started to consciously remake themselves into the "Lucifers of Rock," as *Newsweek* labeled them in 1971.

Their single "Paint It, Black" signaled this shift and suggested an embrace of the dark side. A throbbing hypnotic song with an Arabic melody played by Brian Jones on sitar, Jagger sings, "I look inside myself and see my heart is black, it's not easy facing up when your whole world is black." Fueling black magic rumors, Jagger appeared on the cover of a magazine published by a so-called satanic cult known as The Process Church of the Final Judgment, while his girlfriend Marianne Faithfull articulated her occult perspective in an issue dedicated to death. Flirting with this darker image, The Stones pictured themselves as wizards in the elaborate 3-D cover photo of their weak psychedelic album *Their Satanic Majesties Request*. Calling the album a "first-rate oddity," critic Jim Miller said, "The title alone was the single greatest image manipulation in The Stones' whole history."[6]

---

[6] Jim Miller, *The Rolling Stone Illustrated History of Rock and Roll* (Random House, 1976), pp. 196–97.

Invocation of My Demon Brother

The Stones' demonic dabbling converged with the counter-culture's fascination with Satanism, witchcraft, and the occult. In 1967, a peace rally drew almost one hundred thousand participants to Washington DC to "Levitate the Pentagon."[7] Popular horror films, such as Italy's *Mask of Satan*, America's *Masque of the Red Death*, and Britain's *Dracula: Prince of Darkness* featured the devil or satanic practices. *Rosemary's Baby*, filmed at the Dakota Apartments where John Lennon was later assassinated, tells the story of Rosemary—a lapsed Catholic—who is raped by Satan and conceives the devil's spawn.

Shaking off their psychedelic pandering, The Stones released, in 1968, a powerful new single "Jumpin' Jack Flash" with vicious lyrics that created a new mythology, reinventing Jagger as a monstrous abused mutant ripped out of a witch's womb: "I was born in a cross-fire hurricane, I was raised by a toothless bearded hag, I was drowned, I was washed up and left for dead." Though Keith Richards said his gardener Jack inspired the name,[8] there's little doubt that the title refers to Spring Heeled Jack, a demonic English folklore character, who could jump across buildings and breathe fire and who sported diabolical traits like claw hands, bat wings, and flaming eyes.

Even before "Jack Flash," The Stones had acquired a fervent fan and unsettling friend in occult filmmaker Kenneth Anger. Best known for his apocalyptic biker movie *Scorpio Rising*, Anger gained notoriety when California police banned the film for obscenity (though it eventually got cleared in a court case). An inspiration for *Easy Rider*, *Scorpio Rising* depicted the last gasp of the dying Age of Christianity—a church is desecrated when gang leader Scorpio pisses on its altar and Christ is compared to Hitler as the leader of a mindless, death-wish mob.

Anger was a disciple of Britain's most notorious black magician Aleister Crowley (1875–1947), the so-called "Great Beast 666." Crowley fascinated several British rock stars, including David Bowie, Ozzie Osbourne, Iron Maiden, and Jimmy Page,

---

[7] For an account of this demonstration, see Norman Mailer, *Armies of the Night* (Signet, 1968).

[8] Keith Richards, *Life* (Little, Brown, 2010), pp. 140–41.

who even bought Crowley's house. He was pictured on the cover of the Beatles *Sgt. Pepper* album and his novel *Moonchild* inspired the song "Child of the Moon" on the flip side of the "Jumpin' Jack Flash" single.

More than a black magician, Aleister Crowley was a free-love advocate, drug addict, and social critic. He revolted against the moral and religious values of his time and espoused a form of anarchism based upon his law "Do What Thou Wilt." The popular press of the day vilified him as "the wickedest man in the world." Inspired by nineteenth-century Romantic poets, he believed that Lucifer was the light-bearing god, not the dark devil of conventional Christianity.

To Anger, making a movie was casting a magickal spell. He claimed that "Magick"—using Crowley's spelling—was his life's work and the cinema was his magick weapon. He saw Jagger as a latter-day Lucifer, who played devil's advocate for the disenfranchised youth, and Keith Richards as his attendant demon Beelzebub. Anger wanted to cast Jagger in his intended masterpiece *Lucifer Rising*. Jagger, who had seriously branched into movies with *Performance* and *Ned Kelly* on the horizon, was impressed with Anger's reputation as a sorcerer and an avant-garde master of film.

The role of Lucifer apparently captivated Jagger, not the least for its intriguing sense of purpose. Maybe he started seeing himself as the incarnation of a metaphysical force that could destroy Christian repression with liberating abandon. In a 1967 interview with the *Daily Mail*, Jagger is quoted as saying:

> When I'm on that stage I sense that teenagers are trying to communicate with me, like by telepathy. Not about me or our music, but about the world and the way they live. I interpret it as a demonstration against society and its sick attitudes. Teenagers are weary of being pushed around by half-witted politicians who attempt to dominate their way of thinking and set a code for their living. This is a protest against the system. (*Up and Down with the Rolling Stones*, p. 62)

Jagger agreed to help Anger by composing music for the film's score—an ear-piercing improvisation on his newly acquired Moog synthesizer.

Flowers of Evil

The Rolling Stones embraced their diabolic power to conjure primal forces of rebellion, pandemonium, and orgiastic anarchy. At almost every date on a European tour, savage violent clashes between audiences and authorities exploded, turning shows into a military exercise involving attack dogs, tear gas, batons, and blood. Everywhere they played, The Stones were searched, raided, and intimidated. Their antiestablishment stance made them the focal point of revolutionary fervor.

The Stones projected a nineteenth-century Romantic vision of Lucifer as the rebellious angel, the sexual provocateur, the pagan satyr of Dionysiac celebrations. This romantic conception of evil developed in Europe mainly in literature. Artistic revolutionaries—responding to the massive social and political upheavals caused by the French, American, and Industrial revolutions—attacked Christianity as part of an authoritarian order. Rejecting 1,800 years of Western Christian tradition, Augustinian philosophy, and its absolutist vision of evil, romantic poets like William Blake and Charles Baudelaire saw Satan as a symbol of resistance to the tyranny of the Old Regime. If the greatest enemy of traditional Christianity was Satan, then Satan must be a heroic rebel against unjust authority. Emulating Lucifer, the Romantic Artist stands alone against the world and strives to liberate humanity from a society that blocks its freedom, passion, and creativity.

The most original artist of the period, visionary British poet and painter William Blake (1757–1827) was fascinated by this idea that the Devil was a positive social force. In his richly illustrated poem "The Marriage of Heaven and Hell" (1790), Blake's Satan symbolized creativity, emotion and energy—liberation from reason and orthodoxy, the twin engines of oppression. Rebelling against God's repressive authority, Satan acted on impulse and represented the human desire for freedom. Blake provoked his readers, writing things like "Sooner murder an infant in its cradle than nurse unacted desires,"[9]—an even more outrageous sentiment than The Stones' dark vision of lust and murder in "Midnight Rambler."

---

[9] William Blake, *The Marriage of Heaven and Hell* (Oxford University Press, 1975), Plate 10.

Criticizing St. Augustine's notion of Original Sin as a kind of physical infection, Blake believed that religion devalues the body and distorts human nature. He further believed that organized religion snuffs out emotional life by promoting the primacy of reason. To Blake, these repressive chains can only be broken by frenzied energy: Evil is a progressive force, the energy needed to break boundaries, unify ourselves, and truly transcend evil. In his "Proverbs of Hell" Blake said, "The road of excess leads to the palace of wisdom" (Blake, Plate 7).

In France, Charles Baudelaire (1821–1867)—the Mick Jagger of Romantic Poets—combined a strident anticlericism with an emerging gothic sensibility, finding in Satan a symbol of everything from human freedom to dark, frightening, and seductive beauty. He portrayed the Devil as a subversive spirit who embodies political revolution and opposes fear-mongering systems of power and oppression. Like Blake, he points out the debilitating influences of dogmatic Christianity and Augustinian thinking. Baudelaire linked Christian dogma to tyrannical political systems, analytical philosophy, and empirical science—all of which sever the body from soul, sex from love, desire from reason and prevent us from transcendently merging these aspects of our nature. For Baudelaire, the true god is authenticity.

In his quest for spontaneity and immediacy, Baudelaire gave free reign to his urges and passions, liberating himself from religious repression and social conformity. He obsessed over dreams, took drugs, and experienced hallucinations that were strange and bizarre, brutal and grotesque, demented and demonic. His fascination with Satanism is perhaps clearest in his "Litanies to Satan," part of his 1856 work *Flowers of Evil*: "Prince of Exiles, to whom God has done wrong; Healer of evils, that leave God in wonder; Glory and Praise to Thee, Satan."[10]

Like Jagger, Baudelaire was a controversial figure in his time, suspected of being a devil worshipper and a drug addict, only the latter of which was true. Like The Stones, Baudelaire's name became synonymous with decadence. A French court condemned *Flowers of Evil* and banned several individual poems, one of which—"Damned Women"—involved lesbian love. In

---

[10] Charles Baudelaire, *Flowers of Evil* (Citadel, 1947), p. 170.

response, he mocked the court and took pride in the fear-inspiring book.

Humans are devils, according to Baudelaire; Satan serves merely as an imaginary scapegoat. Like Blake, he believed that passivity, boredom, and malaise easily infected us and compelled our complicity in the horrors of the world: "In our miserable brains, swirl the Demons of the Deep; He is Ennui!—more malevolent than his Mother, You know him this delicate monster, Hypocritical Reader—my Brother!" Like "Sympathy for the Devil," *Flowers of Evil* was mistaken as satanic, but Baudelaire's true purpose was to claim that we, not Satan, have created hell on earth. By externalizing evil as a mythological creature, we fail to confront and defeat it within ourselves.

The Devil Is My Name

Referring to "Sympathy for the Devil," Jagger told *Rolling Stone* in 1995, "I think that was taken from an old idea of Baudelaire's, I just took a couple of lines and expanded on it." The lyrics, spoken in the voice of the devil, also correspond to parts of Mikhail Bulgakov's satirical surrealist novel *The Master and Margarita*, given to Jagger by Marianne Faithfull. Kenneth Anger said the song arose from conversations he had with Jagger about *Lucifer Rising*. Influences aside, "Sympathy for the Devil"—whose working title was "The Devil is My Name"—cast Jagger as the Prince of Darkness. Channeling "Hell Hound on My Trail" through Blake and Baudelaire, Jagger recounts the evils wrought by humanity under the influence of a satanic trickster who in the end is just a reflection of us.

The song's recording, documented by radical French filmmaker Jean-Luc Godard,[11] took several nights of fumbling and grasping, turning from a country dirge to become a voodoo samba. Over percussive bongos, conga drums, and death-rattle maracas, Jagger yelps, screeches, grunts, and moans as if he's emerging from hell. The song builds into a wild celebration of humanity's hatred, hypocrisy, and violence—Christ's crucifixion, European religious wars, the Russian Revolution, the

---

[11] Godard's movie *Sympathy for the Devil* was released in 1968.

Blitzkrieg, the Holocaust, and the Kennedy assassinations. Robert Kennedy was killed on June 5th, 1968, while The Stones were recording, compelling Jagger to pluralize the lyric to "Who Killed the Kennedys?" to account for this latest horror.

Like the poetry of Blake and Baudelaire, the song paints a picture of an inverted world gone mad: Cops are criminals; saints are sinners; God is the devil. Among The Stones' most brilliant songs, "Sympathy for the Devil" mocks the human race for its destructive wars and violence, putting humanity on trial by the devil rather than the other way around. Satan ridicules human beings for their intense hypocrisy, their willingness to cloak their warlike and greedy nature under the veneer of religion.

Lucifer's Dream Ends

By the end of 1968, the nightmares of Lucifer flourished throughout a year of catastrophes including the assassinations of Kennedy and Martin Luther King, riots that set city blocks ablaze, and the Soviet invasion of Prague. With half a million troops in Vietnam, the war penetrated and infected everything. Europe was in turmoil. The young took to the barricades in Paris and around the world from Warsaw to Washington and confronted repressive, reactionary governments.

The Stones attracted more controversy with the first single from *Beggars Banquet*, "Street Fighting Man." Released just days after Mayor Daley's Chicago police had attacked and beaten war protestors at the Democratic convention, the song was denounced as an incitement to violence and banned by many radio stations. It reveled in the "sound of marching, charging feet" and the images of "fighting in the street." Despite showing ambivalence when he sang about "compromise solution," Jagger once again introduced himself as a revolutionary: "Said my name is called disturbance. I'll shout and scream, I'll kill the king, I'll rail at all his servants."

At this point, the band seemed to be a mirror of these desires for militancy, rage and chaos. Still, the vision of the evil was romantic. At the Hyde Park concert following the death of Brian Jones, where some five hundred thousand people showed up (including Kenneth Anger with his cameras), Jagger came on stage alone. He looked like a nineteenth-century poet with his long hair and billowing white frock. He also wore a gold studded leather collar and black lipstick. From a large, Bible-like book, he read the elegy "Adonais" by Percy Bysshe Shelley:

Peace, peace! He is not dead, he doth not sleep—
He hath awakened from the dream of life—

The stage crew released several hundred little white butter-flies that flew off a few feet, then promptly dropped to earth, dead.

When his Lucifer film bogged down, Anger edited his footage to Jagger's whining electronic soundtrack and created a short film, *Invocation of My Demon Brother*. The flashing, pulsing montage of superimposed images included Jagger and Richards in performance, soldiers in Vietnam, Anger as Magus performing an occult ritual, the Devil,[12] flowing lava, volcanic fire, and alchemical symbols—all blurring together in a menacing portent of Lucifer's resurrection.   As   the   movie played the underground film circuit, the emerging news showed that the revolutionary decade was not going well: there was the American massacre of women and children at My Lai Vietnam, the impending breakup of The Beatles, Bob Dylan's motorcycle accident, the arrest of Charles Manson, and the most famous concert The Stones ever played.

As documented in the Maysles brothers' movie *Gimme Shelter*, Jagger expected the Altamont Free Festival to top Woodstock. He confidently asserted, "It's creating a microcosm of society which is meant to set an example for the rest of America as to how one can behave in large gatherings." But by the time they came onstage, darkness had descended. Their fans had been kept waiting for almost three hours since the previous band's performance. Armed with pool cues and beer, Hell's Angels—the biker security guards—were everywhere. The Stones started playing "Sympathy for the Devil," then stopped, as a skirmish became a small brawl. "Something funny always happens when we play that number," said Jagger.

"Everybody just cool out," he pleaded. "Just cool out." But shortly after they started playing "Under My Thumb," a young

---

12 The Devil is played by Anton LaVey, author of the *Satanic Bible* and the most famous devil-worshipper of the 1960s. Typecast, he also plays the Devil in *Rosemary's Baby*.

black man, dressed in a bright green suit, flashed out of the crowd holding a gun. Hell's Angels grabbed him, stabbed him, and killed him. Bewildered, Jagger looked like a sad shivering skinny boy in a silly cape, helpless to control the frenzied, drunken bloodlust of these biker Neanderthals. The Stones finished the performance without knowing exactly what had happened.

While Altamont showed that the Sixties were over, The Stones remained saddled with their demonic reputation. "Jagger sought to covet the Devil's power and got used as a pawn to do His work" went the standard narrative. Rock critic Lester Bangs, in *Rolling Stone*, blamed more down-to-earth sins: diabolic egoism, hype, ineptitude, greed, and a lack of concern for humanity. "A man died before their eyes. Do they give a shit? Yes or No?" demanded Bangs. Responding in a radio interview with San Francisco's KSAN, Jagger stressed his helplessness in the face of monumental forces that overwhelmed him and promised that future performances would be tightly controlled. "It taught me never to do anything I wasn't on top of." According to groupie girlfriend Pamela Des Barres, Jagger cried and talked of retirement the night after the debacle. [13]

As Jagger promised, a controlled spectacle, rather than rage and chaos, marked the band's subsequent performances. Unlike Baudelaire who died of syphilis at forty-six, The Stones evolved, survived, and thrived. They turned from youthful Rock Satans to Elder Statesmen of Rock. Jagger got married and, in the 1980s, projected the image of a conventional jet-setting pop star, doing hit duets with David Bowie and Michael Jackson and briefly pursuing an unsuccessful solo career. The Stones even played the Super Bowl, the apex of mainstream acceptability.

Now, there's no more Lucifer. There's no more Prince of Darkness. In the ultimate irony, the Queen made Mick Jagger a Knight. [14]

---

[13] Quotes from Christopher Sandford, *Mick Jagger: Rebel Knight* (Omnibus Press, 2003), pp. 180–81

[14] Thanks to Maureen Musker for criticism of earlier versions of this chapter.

22
Frenzy

RANDALL E. AUXIER

> We're always having something very funny happen when we start that number.
>
> MICK JAGGER, Altamont, December 6th, 1969

In mid-June 2011 the news is dominated by images of a surprising riot in Vancouver, following their hockey team's loss to the Boston team in the Stanley Cup finals.

I suppose most people normally think of Canadians as a pretty impassive lot, stoic in the face of disappointment, mild if not really meek. West Coast Canadians are, if anything, even more laid-back than their countrymen, so everyone is taken a little off guard right now. Sort of like some were in the second half of 1969, when the New Yorkers were actually able to behave themselves for a few days in August, but on the peace-love-dope West Coast, right across the Bay from hippie central, the crowd couldn't make it through a Stones concert without violence and death. The Dionysian frenzy? War? Rape? Murder? It's just a shot away, you know?

In this case, a photographer snapped a picture of a couple engaged in a passionate kiss while lying in the middle of the street, in the midst of the riot. The picture went viral. I'm sure this will all be soon forgotten, but the photograph captured our notice for a historical moment and it reminds us of something humans have known for as long as we have existed: There is a weird connection between the build-up of group emotion, and sex, and violence. That association has vexed us for a long time, and to associate sex and violence, especially in a public setting, is still a good way to get yourself in trouble with the Man. Strangely, we can deal with violence and sex more easily when they're individualized and compartmentalized. What's up with this? And why is the build-up of group emotion so scary and so volatile?

Please Allow Me to Introduce Myself

Before we go any further, I need to make a confession. Brian Jones creeps me out, always has. He still has a weird sort of cult following of people who think he was the real genius, or that The Stones were no good without him, and so on. I certainly didn't know him and I really can't remember him at all (I was eight when he died), but I know that even on the fortieth anniversary of his death when the BBC interviewed Mick and Charlie, they couldn't come up with any kind words for Brian, and you could see them trying to. But no. He was a bad person. It isn't polite to speak ill of the dead, but Keith tells stories in his autobiography that leave people shaking their heads.

Brian was violent and cruel, and I fancy I can see that in his eyes when I study the old pictures. When I think of the embodiment of the negative energy the Sixties contained, I think of Brian Jones, and for my money, that's who Don McLean was really speaking of in the verse of "American Pie" about the disastrous Altamont concert in 1969. I know McLean said that the image in his mind was Mick Jagger, and that Brian had been dead almost four months when the concert happened, but to me, the figure "laughing with delight" at the conflagration of the world was Brian Jones.

If you are one of the Jones minions, please don't kill me. I'll recant everything if you'll just let me live. But I think the dark side of that groovy energy needs a face, and I think Brian is it, and so, what follows is a sort of meditation on what gets sacrificed on the altar of rock'n'roll, when the Dionysian frenzy turns ugly.

The Nature of My Game

No collection of folks, or even any individual, symbolizes for us more profoundly an S&D&R&R aestheticism than The Stones, and we all know that, at this late stage of history. But *why* did the Stones so reliably bring the Dionysian frenzy to the breaking point? To hear them tell it, you'd think they were more the victims of that craziness than catalyst or cause. That story isn't quite believable. The Stones may not have seen the frenzy coming, but they can't pretend to be innocent. I'm sure they never wanted anyone to be seriously hurt, and I think they were genuinely surprised at how thin the line was between a bacchanalia about pleasure and one about death.

If not in recent years, then certainly for their first twenty or so, going to a Stones concert could be, well, almost a sporting proposition (and that was part of the attraction), a little risky. You might come back preggers or even in a body bag, if you weren't careful. That includes the band themselves (on the body bag part—I'm supposing they aren't biologically right for the other). The frenzy phenomenon didn't wholly end, though, even when it did subside. You can find a vid up on Youtube where in 2005 a Pittsburgh crone attacks Keith Richards (for reasons unclear—she can't still want sex, but she certainly wants *something*), as he tries to get to his car.

Of the craze, Keith says that in the early days "what they were reacting to was being in this enclosed space with us— this illusion; me, Mick, Brian. The music might be the trigger, but the bullet, nobody knows what that is" (*Life*, p. 137). Still, I think there's something about the way the Stones have gone about crafting their personae and prosecuting their performance that taps into a deep (and disturbing) aspect of all human experience. I want to get at the bullet, if I can.

There are lots of *kinds* of crazy, so there's a very great difference between becoming schizoid, sociopathic, or individually manic, on the one hand (where I think Brian Jones belongs), and losing it with the crowd, or the mob, on the other (possibly this is the right category for the late Meredith Hunter, waving his pistol in the stage area at Altamont). Whatever takes hold when the Stones play brings people to do things in groups they wouldn't do alone, so it's more like the second kind of crazy. People don't suddenly become individually insane when Keith hits the first chord, but something happens to the crowd, for sure. It started with the girls. Keith describes it:

The '50s chicks being brought up all very jolly hockey sticks, and then somewhere there seemed to be a moment when they just decided they wanted to let themselves go. The opportunity arose for them to do that, and who's going to stop them? It was all dripping with sexual lust, though they didn't know what to do about it. But suddenly you're on the end of it. It's a frenzy. Once it's out, it's an incredible force. You stood as much chance in a fucking river full of piranhas. They were beyond what they wanted to be. They'd lost themselves. These chicks were coming out there, bleeding, clothes torn off, pissed panties, and you took that for granted every night. That was the gig. (*Life*, p. 138)

That was the gig? Okay, he knows better than I would. But it doesn't seem like you could quite *book* that gig, you know? If that's the "sex" side of the Dionysian coin, what about the "violence" side?

Reading the Riot Act

The British parliament passed the real "Riot Act" back in 1714 to make it possible for them to use the death penalty on those who refused to disperse after the Act was read aloud. Rioting breaks out periodically among all sorts of people (however tame they seem), and for a lot of different reasons, some political, some religious, and even some *purely aesthetic*. Apparently, Igor Stravinsky's ballet *The Rite of Spring* provoked a purely aesthetic riot among the Paris highbrows at its debut in 1913. That must have been very strange. The crowd started booing the bassoon solo, early on, and even the police couldn't keep the peace after intermission. Stravinsky himself just fled. The fact that it was a pagan ballet is, well, not *entirely* unrelated to what I have to say here. What the dancers were doing, and the way the orchestra was playing, had a nasty effect on the apologists of conventional taste in that crowd. These are definitely the same folks whose grandchildren would tell you that rock'n'roll is the devil's music. (And so it is, but have a little sympathy and taste, okay?)

No matter what the reason, a lot of people find it upsetting when accepted standards of public behavior (aesthetic or moral) begin to be strained by collective human emotions. That's true at a soccer match just as it is at a Stones concert, but somehow, conventional people are willing to make some room in their tiny hearts for a good sports-brawl, even if people die, in ways they won't for what happens at a Stones show gone bad. In every case where this amazing mass emotion is released, there is this moment, I think, when it seems that all order has disappeared and we come face to face with, with . . . I don't know, whatever it is "we" are *without* that imposed order. We usually don't like what we see, or at least some people don't, and those of us who do aren't making any important decisions in the world. The revelers also have difficulty remembering what happened when it's all over. The riot doesn't have enough structure to hang a memory on.

The early Stones concerts in Britain were the scene of bedlam. I can barely imagine being there. There were girls screaming, and always a few angry rednecks calling our boys faggots, and before you know it, Keith kicks some guy in the face and it's lucky nobody is killed. Here is what he says, in part, about onesuch:

> Maybe if we'd been wearing our houndstooth jackets and looking like little dolls we wouldn't have outraged the males in the audience at the Wisbech Corn Exchange. . . . And a riot was started because the local yokels, the boys, couldn't stand the fact that all of their chicks were gawping and blowing themselves out about this bunch of fags, as far as they were concerned, from London. . . . That was a good riot, which we were lucky to escape from. (*Life*, p. 131)

More in a minute about this special sort of "fags." The point is that the riots at the Stones' shows were a little different from what surrounded the Beatles. It came to the point that almost every Stones concert led to some sort of disturbance that took a toll on property and persons.

The Riot Act wasn't actually repealed in Britain until 1973, though its last "public reading" was in 1920. But I'm guessing that at least a few among the British establishment might have been happy to dust it off and try it out in 1963–65—for the Stones, not the Beatles. With the Fab Four, one didn't get the same sense of impending danger. Beatlemania wasn't much different than the fuss over Sinatra and then Elvis. When The Stones showed up, somehow things turned darker and got ratcheted up a notch or two. So, on the one hand, The Stones *per se* do seem to make a difference in what happens. The scary tone of violence seems to form itself around the sounds and the whole atmosphere of The Stones. It isn't just female lust. It harbors violence.

A Little Help from Their Friends?

It's probably a good thing that our favorite fellows headed to the USA when they did. The UK needed a rest. On their first US tour, no one in America knew who The Stones were, so the girls didn't scream and the boys didn't see the need to take any swings at anybody—even in Texas, where a long-hair limey might get a pop on the snout just for crossing the state line. Only at the end of that tour, when manager Andrew Oldham placed some teeny-bopper plants among the New York audience, did the Americans get the idea that this was supposed to be a frenzy. So on the other hand (and there's always another hand), we can see it wasn't the music alone that was causing the riots, or even The Stones, *per se*. They needed a little help from their friends, a context and a clue to tell everybody this was a moment to abandon ordinary decorum.

As a final contrast, it's interesting to think of Led Zeppelin, which had the same dark and semi-satanic brooding, and the same sex, drugs, and so on, and even the same debt to the blues aesthetic and the deal at the cross-roads, but *not* the riots. It's true that Zeppelin missed the historical window by a couple of years, but apart from timing I see no reason why Zeppelin couldn't have ended up with the albatross of Altamont just as easily as The Stones. And surely Robert Plant had the needed testosterone to do what Mick did to the girls. So maybe it was just the times and not the Stones? We'll never know for sure. With that much said, there's no question at all that the Stones pushed us past the line between light and dark, when it comes to building up collective emotion. Their sex is androgynous and forbidden, their drugs kill, and their rock and roll . . . well, all I can say is I like it.

Gimme that Old Time Religion?

It isn't quite accurate to say that the collective frenzy has a "long history" because in fact, it's *older* than history. Stuff that old is a little bit tough to *know* about, so you're onto some slippery back roads of human thought when you decide to *think* about it—can't tell what people are *making up* from what *really happened*. It's like listening to a Republican administration. The vagaries of pre-history make it especially dicey for philosophers to discuss, since we never cared too much for facts anyway, and most respectable philosophers would tell you that there was *no* philosophy back then, just irrational failures of thinking. I disagree with that, and I'm not interested in being a respectable philosopher, but I agree it's pretty hard to say what philosophy amounts to back before writing was invented. Still, even respectable philosophers need only a little encouragement and they're off into their own land of the (conceptually) lost.

The problem of the frenzy showed up early on, even in philosophy, and it has re-appeared in turns from then to now, but we should deal with it more than we do. Socrates himself was an initiate of the "Eleusinian Mysteries," which involved fertility rites and perhaps some ritual orgies. There were no human sacrifices by that time in (recorded) Mediterranean history. But even at that, the early philosophers found the sex rituals and the crowd hysteria objectionable. Plato wrote about the problem of *eros* and how it makes human beings mad with passion, like when Keith said those girls were "beyond what they wanted to be." Plato wasn't much in favor of that sort of behavior, and he used his power as a writer to absolve his teacher Socrates of any real loss of rational control in the *Symposium*. Plato was pretty dedicated to downplaying Socrates's religious leanings (this frenzy was "religion" back then). We'll never know for sure if Socrates got his rocks off at the rites. So Plato sort of got what he wanted, I guess.

By the time people like Plato and Socrates lived, the fourth century B.C.E., the Dionysian festivals were coming into poor repute. It was a time of transition, and Plato definitely opposed the old ways of the flesh, and he didn't like The Rolling Stones (they were around back then, as I will explain, they just didn't have a record deal). Plato even claimed Socrates never got drunk, no matter how much wine you gave him. I actually know a woman who's like that, so I'm sure the phenomenon exists, but I just don't think that is the real Socrates. Plato also wrote about how certain kinds of music (such as blues and rock) ignite human desires and lead us to weakness and "effeminacy" (that's what it's called in the translations). Manliness and rationality in all circumstances were associated with self-restraint by Plato, and after he'd had his say, if you still did the old rites, you were just a wimp in the thrall of women. Plato didn't want people like that around and advocated banning their favorite music. In short: no Stones concert allowed in Plato's city. Plato wanted the women to be like men, not the other way around.

I've Been Around for a Long, Long Year

And that brings me back to my earlier point about The Stones being called "fags" by the angry male element in the audience. There is a story to be told about "the boys who serve the women" and "the boys who serve the men." Some might think the Stones serve the men, but I would beg to differ. You'll see. It looks like human civilization may be a lot older than we had long believed. Well, really there's no "may be" about it. Civilization just *is* a lot older, and people who think otherwise are kidding themselves. Recent discoveries in Asia Minor indicate that highly organized communal human life goes back to 10,000 B.C.E. (that's 7,500 years older than the pyramids, and 7000 years older than Stonehenge). Google the names "Gobekli Tepe" or "Nevali Çori" and see what you find.

The world of the "ancient" Greeks is, by comparison, only yesterday. We may have had civilization *before* 10,000 B.C.E., but we don't have evidence right now. It's a murky topic. After all, even by the most conservative estimate, there have been "modern humans" (in the biological sense of the word) for at least fifty thousand years, and perhaps much, much longer. It isn't reasonable to think the humans, with brains and hands and voices just like ours, would just hang fire on the savannah all that time. They had *big* brains. They got bored. They needed some entertainment. They started beating on things. What Charlie Watts does so well isn't that much different. (Is it just me, or does Charlie bear a resemblance to those fanciful models of Neanderthal man? You know the scientists now say that some Neanderthal DNA survived in us from cross-breeding, especially in northern Europe . . .)

Once you have the groove, you also have the dance—humans had excess energies and we were dedicated to getting that out of our system. One good way to do that is sex, but even that gets old after a while (for everyone except Bill Wyman). No one knows just how the dance and the music *became* the ritual, but it seems likely that the ritual involved sex from the outset. If it were not so, it would be hard to explain why it took so many centuries to discourage the fertility cults—I say discourage, since they weren't destroyed. There are still plenty of devotees of the degraded forms of these cults, in case you haven't noticed the existence of many thousands of "gentlemen's clubs," and a billion-dollar pornography industry. I'm not at all certain I would call the debauchery of the Stones tours a "degraded" version of those cults, but rather more of an upgraded resurgence.

The fertility cults also sometimes involved death, at least by the time we can document things. Whether sacrifice is an original impulse among humans we do not know, but the ritual practice of human and animal sacrifice is very, very old. Some authorities, following Freud, say it's a basic impulse and they find analogies even among the chimps these days. Others say it isn't so, but everybody agrees that humans and animals were sacrificed in the frenzy in many of the most ancient cultures. You'll be hard pressed to compartmentalize the sex and the death as you regress into more ancient and more primal versions of these rituals—and that may explain why we don't like to look at this and think of it.

Not knowing what to do with our extra energy leads us to be diabolically creative with our nimble hands and big old brains. A French thinker (widely read by philosophers, sometimes in secret) named Georges Bataille (1897–1962) named this extra energy "the accursed share" (or *la part maudite* if you're feeling fancy) and he also expounded in most uncomfortable clinical detail the proximity of death and sensual desire. He's a scary read. Go do it, by all means, but maybe not late at night when you're alone.

I'm in Need of Some Restraint

The story of Abraham and Isaac in Genesis is a classic account of how human sacrifice was gradually replaced with symbolic sacrifices. Human sacrifice in the part of Mesopotamia Abraham left (the city-state of Ur) was already extremely old; the area had been occupied by agrarian, communal humans for thousands of years, and the rituals of human sacrifice were deeply engrained in their public life. The religious system was more stable than we can imagine these days. It endured for centuries, probably millennia.

The religion was unremarkable in many ways, but offering up the first born was required (good thing they weren't requiring that in England, since Brian, Mick, and Keith would have had to go to the gods). Sacrificing the first-born was seen as an act of humility: one gives one's best and what one loves most, to one's god, and as a result, *all* of those alive in that society are second-born, or later. The practical reason to approve such a practice is that it curbs our over-weaning "pride of place." If everyone is second-born, or lower, no one has sole inheritance, and all the other problems that go with letting the first born live. The story of Abraham and Isaac shows how a substitution method called "redemption" could be used to replace the traditional way, so that pride is curbed and the first-born can be allowed to live.

So, things did eventually change. Not just the Hebrews, but the Egyptians and the Greeks also moved "beyond" human sacrifice, independently of the Hebrews, and long before Abraham in the case of the Egyptians. But it took hundreds if not thousands of years to squash the rite, and it still lingers today, associated with the Black Mass and enacted only an infrequent teenage rebellion, as an invigorating idea among the most forbidden of the outcast fringe groups. The Stones have played on that forbidden feeling, but mainly for its shock value, I think. They are devotees of the goddess, not of the dark prince.

It's hard for people today to grasp that sacrificing the first-born was once what ordinary people did from religious piety, and that the animal sacrifices in voodoo ought to be seen as a step *away* from that. Is animal sacrifice barbarous? It's hard to understand why people are troubled by the ritual sacrifice of a chicken but don't mind eating at KFC. Which of those two, in a just world, would *really* be more inhumane? I mean, be rational about this. Treating animals as if their lives had no value at all as against treating them as individually valuable enough for sacrifice to the gods? Maybe we haven't altogether *improved* our practical, moral sensibilities in the last couple of centuries.

I think Shirley Jackson's eerie short story "The Lottery" (maybe you had to read it in high school like I did) helps us grasp the idea of human sacrifice as it might be if it existed in the present. But in her version, the sacrificial victim is chosen by chance and is reluctant. There is evidence that among the Druid's the "victim" *volunteered*, and it was a privilege to be so sacrificed. The stories of the early Christian martyrs have a lot of that same energy—read the unnerving diary of Perpetua if you doubt me.

Anyway, it is amazing what sorts of activities can be "normalized" with humans, and that includes human sacrifice. If Sarah Palin or Michele Bachmann lived back in that time, before Abraham, they'd be defending the sacrifices, because their type of conservative sensibility, about the importance of keeping traditions, along with their piety (which I think is genuine), has the same quality as the conventional worshipers in *any* age. Those gals would pretty much embrace, I'm confident, *whatever* the prevailing traditional norms were *whenever* they lived, and they would give up their own first born and condemn those who didn't if that was what their religion said. No mother wants to give up her child. But where the expectations and the practices of millennia demand it, it is done.

If Palin and Bachmann had grown up in the fertility cults of the Ba'als, even after Abraham's time, they'd also be doing the nasty with all the men at festival time just like *good girls* did back then. And it was very tough on young women who tried to choose between the traditional ways of the ancient Semitic races and the new and more modest ways of the Hebrews. If you aren't familiar with this dilemma, I suggest you read the Biblical book of Hosea. Hosea's wife Gomer was not a prostitute, she was raised in a fertility cult. God told Hosea (much to his distress) to *marry* her because he wanted His prophet to know exactly what it felt like to be the God of Israel, which kept backsliding into the fertility cults. So, if they lived in *that* later day (we're talking roughly the eighth century B.C.E.) maybe women like Bachmann and Palin would only do the seven veils in private, and only with their husbands (listening to the ancient equivalent of the Rolling Stones, on the other side of a screen). But unless you're a Southern Baptist, I think that much has been okay in almost any age.

Stole Many a Man's Soul and Faith

To give another example of a contemporary religious nut, the depiction of the Mayan human sacrifices in Mel Gibson's film *Apocalypto* is a horror in itself, but I must say, he makes no effort to understand the reasons any civilization might have for adopting the ritual. It's pretty ironic coming from the same guy who willed the world to watch the goriest depiction of human sacrifice in cinematic history (I mean *The Passion of the Christ*—a movie I'm betting Bachman and Palin endorse, since it depicts *their* favored kind of human sacrifice).

Contemporary Christians (and me among them, conventional bloke that I am) still gobble up the God and drink his blood on Sundays and somehow fail to notice the analogy to cannibalism. (Of course, it's just a symbol unless you're Catholic, but *what* a symbol, folks.) If you must be a conventional bloke like me, I hope you'll try not to be an ignorant one—eating the god is about as time-honored as any tradition can possibly be, but it *isn't* the Jewish way; that's a *pagan* survival in Christianity, more of which shortly.

As frightening as they are, these life and death rituals have always addressed a profound human need. Perhaps we know now, in the last four thousand years or so, that this need can be (at least partly) fulfilled without the bloodshed. That "need" we name with the words "religious fervor," or what they used to call "enthusiasm." There is a reason the sports stadiums are full week after week, too. We desire a release of that fervor, a kind of build up of group emotion directed at the gods, or God, or the Dallas Cowboys, or The Rolling Stones. There is a damn good reason the mainline Protestant churches are all in decline while every Sunday morning one can find enormous arenas filled with ignorant people who want to watch a preacher get possessed by the Holy Spirit while a chorus blares the same words over and over to loud ass music. If he reminds you of Mick Jagger, well, is that really surprising?

The mainline churches tried to kill the build up of group emotion in worship and it got very boring and people went elsewhere; in Europe, they went to see the soccer match, but in the US, they're still at church, plus the sports. And everybody everywhere went to the Stones concert. That is what humans always do and it's what they always have done, and

I dare to think it's what they always will do. We go where the action is.

The human race is not going to outgrow its desire for the transcendent experience of group emotion. The difference between a Stones concert and a Pentecostal revival is not huge, and there is nothing anyone can do to change that. But make no mistake, in this regard, the Christians are thoroughly pagan, and not pagan in the *civilized* way that the ancient Greeks and Romans were. Our times are closer to primitive cult than to civil religion, as practiced by elevated people like the Greeks and Romans. And the religious freaks have always been nurtured in the distant provinces of a civilization, remote places like Alaska, or the wild suburbs of Minneapolis.

Use All Your Well-learned Politesse

That brings us to the most ancient part of civilized human life where we have evidence, in places like Gobekli Tepe, and Google these too: Achelleion, Sitagroi, and Argissa Magoula. These aren't quite as old but pose the same puzzles. The debate over who these people were and how they lived will never end. We have no clear account of at least five thousand years of human civilization. That is about equal to the amount of time we *do* have in records for—the oldest writing is about 3000 B.C.E.

That's when "history" began, but there was definitely civilization of a highly complex sort *long* before there was writing. They had cities and politics and agriculture and markets and probably even rock'n'roll. I'm not kidding. Music, dance, and art came along way before writing, so if not practitioners of the oldest profession in the world, the Stones are certainly in the first five—along with the priests, politicians, and pimps (that's only one profession, if you go back far enough, or if you read between the lines in the present).

Some scholars believe that our civilized pre-history was, gasp, organized around the sense and vision of the *females* of the race. "Matriarchy" may not be quite the right word for it, since the idea that women "ruled" would be a very *manly* interpretation of what was going on. It might be truer to say that women were "civilized" and men had to be "managed"—and note that "man" is the operative location of all *man*agement. Back in the day, an otherwise sensible Swiss scholar named

Johann Jakob Bachofen (1815–1887) pretty much ruined his own life by suggesting that the evidence points to the existence of whole civilizations in which the Crone, the Mother, and the Maiden were the central figures of reverence—and of authority, such as it was. Bachofen was mainly ignored, but some took the trouble to mock him.

Frankly, I don't know whether the "civilization of the goddess" (as it was called by the archaeologist Marija Gimbutas) ever existed, and I don't need to know. What I'm sure of is that the stories of the orgiastic rites of the fertility cults that do survive point very clearly to a deep division that is still alive and well in our present civilization, a division between heavy-handed control (patriarchy), and whatever *opposes* that, which upsets the patriarchy and gets condemned and persecuted by the control freaks. Both The Beatles and The Stones tapped into that division, as had Elvis before them. Their prancing for the girls puts male insecurities on public display, but to be a man in a male-dominated civilization is to carry that division within yourself.

Bachofen had a young friend, none other than Friedrich Nietzsche, who became obsessed by this "division," which he called the Apollonian and the Dionysian energies. Nietzsche didn't care for the womanly aspects of the Dionysian, but he was fascinated by the way that the Dionysian energies kept popping up and breaking out into the frenzy. Apollonian energy is regimentation and order. Dionysian energy is the overflow of life energy, the accursed share. Every time the lovers of control get the upper hand, the cult of Dionysus springs up again, and like Keith said, there is just no stopping that energy. What happened in the 1960s has happened many, many times before. The Stones rode a wave of Dionysian energy that would not be bottled up by a heavy handed, patriarchal Cold War. But if loose lips sink ships, big lips offer a wagging tongue to the danger. The god that sacrifices himself *will* have his day. But long before this oscillation of Apollo and Dionysus, there was at least five thousand years of something else.

Mother's Little Helpers

There was a Cambridge scholar and philosopher named Jane Ellen Harrison (1850–1928) who wrote a whole bunch of books that trace the development of Greek religion from a swampy matriarchy up through the age of the Olympian gods that we all know, the age that Nietzsche talked about. The pivotal figure in her story was indeed Dionysus, the god of the vine, and yes, of the frenzy and the orgy, and he was the holy child of the Mother (the central manifestation of the goddess); the holy infant was the original man-child, the child hero, and the sacrificial victim at the rites, flayed and divided among the faithful.

If this sounds a little like the Christ story, well, you didn't really think the Christians made all that up, did you? They retold a very, very old story in a way that bridged a gap between Jews and pagans. Miss Harrison (as she was always called) ruffled more than a few Victorian feathers with her tales about the derivative (and religiously inferior) Christian version of Jesus and Mary. Like Mick Jagger, Miss Harrison is not without sympathy for the Christian story, she just sees it from a broader perspective—after all, the devilry itself is much older than Christianity. One of the things that has always impressed me about Mick Jagger is how wide his sense of history is and how very damn smart those lyrics are—not just to "Sympathy for the Devil," but in so many of the songs he wrote. He has a very keen intellect, sees things as they are, in my opinion.

And Mick knows, obviously, there is no reason to bother with being anti-Christian. You cannot successfully oppose the *kind* of story Christianity tells; it always just pops up again. It is the Dionysian story. The followers of Apollo hijacked it, as they always do, but it's the story of Dionysus. The Christian *version* of that story is a lot less objectionable than other versions we might have been saddled with. Nietzsche was right when he complained that Christianity is a puny, slave morality that renders the human race effeminate and opposes all that is mighty and virile in humans. That's exactly what I *like* about Christianity. I have always thought that slaves know more than their masters, and that over-weaning masculinity needs to be opposed with as much vigor as it takes to keep the boys from killing each other with all their stupid pointy toys.

Won't You Guess My Name?

Miss Harrison's main discovery about the Rolling Stones is in her book *Themis: A Study of the Social Origins of Greek*

Religion. The opening chapter is actually about Mick Jagger. One of his earliest songs is called the "Hymn of the Kouretes," where the island boys who serve the goddess strut around their golden child, Kouros (that was Mick's name back then), at the bidding of the goddess. The goddess likes it when the boys come to admire her perfect boy, and she gives the Maiden permission to lose it when they do. That was the gig. And that's how you book it. Ask your Mother.

Over several millennia, Mick had a lot of names. He was called Dendritis, and Nuktelios, and Isodaites, among other names, and later Bacchus, of course. It seemed he always had new albums and tours, but Mick finally surfaced in ancient Greece as Dionysus, and that was when he got the name we call him today. It takes Harrison over five hundred pages to tell the story of how Mick showed up to trouble Athens, but all her books are up on-line for free, so at least it won't cost you anything to read about it. Dionysus was eventually accepted among the Olympians, sort of like the irony of Mick Jagger becoming a Knight of the Realm. The appearance of Dionysus among the Greek gods was a real revolution, but that's a story for another time.

The story for today is about how Kouros and the Kouretes (that was the original name of the Rolling Stones) *behaved* themselves. They actually got along without too much strife back when they started out, but soon the males split off into those who like that kind of music and aren't bothered by an omnisexual, ecstatic orgy, and the males who saw that sort of behavior as weak and womanly. Those manly men didn't like being kept at the perimeter of the villages of women, and they started forming their Sour Grapes Clubs out in the woods and caves, and daring any of the girly-men to come and try their little fairy dances out where the real men are—the men who don't need women, the men who hate women for excluding them; the men who would beat women if they could get them behind a closed door; in short, the manly men. They want all the men to be like them.

But here's the thing. You really don't want to underestimate the girly-men. If you do, you may end up with Keith's boot in your face or his knife between your legs. Make no mistake, the girly-men are *men*. They are just as violent and just as dangerous. Eventually the Kouretes lived at the edge of the village and had to come and fetch Kouros to make a man of him, take him away from the women. If he didn't come with them, he was the enemy, the girly-man, the "fag." But he is irresistible isn't he?

Mick wouldn't go. Elvis went into the army, you know? That is how he became acceptable to the manly men. And didn't they love cutting off his hair? But Mick called the Kouretes to himself and kept them under his thumb. That's what Dionysus will do if you don't watch out. It really is Mick's band, as much as Keith and Charlie chafe at the suggestion. Yeah, he's no good without them, it's true, but that doesn't change the fact that She's the Boss, and Mick is her Golden Boy. No Mick, no Stones.

The story of the Dionysian frenzy is the story of the girly-men, and it isn't often well-told. But it is lived every day. So let me ask you a question: which group is *cooler*, the Beatles or the Stones? If you said the Beatles, you may not be a man at all, of either kind. The Beatles are cool, and they were girly men, but they aren't dangerous enough to be cooler than the Stones. And here's what I want you to think about for a minute. The Beatles pressed androgyny only just a bit (pretty mop-tops that they were), but as far as I can tell, they never went in drag (the closest they came was when John and Ringo borrowed their wives' coats for the rooftop concert in January of 1969, their last public performance). The Stones made a point of their femininity. Why do you suppose they did that? Let's think about it for a little bit.

"They're So Ugly It's Appealing"

This was a direct quote from a screaming teeny-bopper who was asked by a newsman outside a Stones concert in about 1965 why she liked The Stones so much. It's a fact. Those boys were just odd looking, every one of them. Big lips, square jaws, deep set eyes, pointy features—and they were all odd looking in almost the same way, except for Ian Stewart, who was sidelined from the band early because he didn't look like the rest of them (*Life*, p. 129). Ian Stewart looked like a *man*, was built like a man, and not a bad looking man at that. The others looked androgynous, like ugly, pretty, dirty things. One can barely recover from the picture they put on the cover of their single "Have You Seen Your Mother, Baby." The picture is so good it's disturbing. These guys set out to violate our gendered

expectations. On purpose. These weren't just a bunch of guys who bent the rules, they were off-sides.

The complex psychology of the Dionysian libation bearers, at least in this patriarchal day and age, involves compensation for their effeminacy. That is how I would account for the blatant misogyny of the Stones lyrics. These days you have to keep the manly men, the Dick Cheneys and George Bushes of the world, and their cops and lawyers, at arm's length. So to do that, our girly Kouretes had to bite the womanly hand that fed them—or at least that's the way it had to *look* (it appears that only Brian Jones actually abused women). Back in the bad old days, back when the women got the orgies going and no cops existed to tell them it was immoral, guys like the Stones probably didn't need to be faux-macho. They just needed an invitation to the banquet. And boys like The Stones were always welcome (well, except for Brian). They were good toys to keep around. But that was *then*, and we weren't there.

Pleased to Meet You

So, now we're getting somewhere. According to me, it's The Father of All Pissing Contests (I mean the Cold War) that obliges good English boys like Keith and Mick (who don't hate women, they *love* women) to write songs like "Stupid Girl" and "Yesterday's Papers," and "Under My Thumb" and "That Girl

Belongs to Yesterday," and two dozen others that seem, if anything, outright hostile to women. Compare it with the message in their song "Bitch," which might have been named "Under *Your* Thumb." What is the message here?

If these guys are serving the goddess, they aren't quite doing it in the limp-wristed, light-loafered way—and that, friends and neighbors, might just be the key to everything: 1. The Stones don't hate women, *this culture* hates women; and 2. the men who call the servants of the goddess "fags" are the ones who built and maintain that misogynistic culture. Even if it's impossible for a woman to win this struggle, it isn't exactly *easy* to be a man who doesn't buy into all the patriarchal bullshit. But to be secure enough in your (patriarchal) masculinity to challenge the very *need* for women, and at the same time get all the girls (see Bill Wyman's records in *Stone Alone*)? Is it possible that the supposedly macho men are unmanned by this totally twisted way the Stones present themselves? I think maybe so.

I also think that the Dionysian frenzy of the 1960s took a dark turn at just the time when we could no longer absorb the levels of testosterone being publicly exuded. We really needed to find some way out of the cultural prison built by our militarism and fear (and these are different sides of the same coin). Dionysus sprang up. There would have to be sacrifices on the altar of Western manhood. As if the Summer of Love had not already ended in a conflagration in Newark and Detroit ("love" my ass), the next year, 1968, was going to show the true face of the world the manly men had built. By the end of that awful year, over sixteen thousand American troops were dead, along with probably a hundred thousand Vietnamese (whose crime was wanting to govern themselves), and so were Martin Luther King and Robert F. Kennedy. It wasn't possible to ignore this any more. This was not about making pop records anymore. This isn't *Sgt. Pepper's Lonely Hearts Club*, this is a job for their Satanic Majesties. In the face of this melt-down, the Beatles just quit. But the Stones looked the demon square in the eye and guessed its name.

From Woodstock to Altamont

In the disastrous year of 1969, everything pretty much fell apart. The one moment people remember was Woodstock, but that wasn't the real Dionysian frenzy. That was basically a glorious and well-deserved vacation from the bullshit. The kids of New York (and Boston and Philly) had fought hard, and nobly, against the manly men. But the real thing, the genuine Dionysian frenzy was The Stones' prophetic tour of that year, ending at Altamont, and ending the Sixties. Everyone knew things would just get worse from there, but a corner had been turned, and unlike the others, the Stones would not fade away. The patriarchy doesn't give up all at once, but by December of 1969, it was on the run. Brian was gone and the Stones were reborn. I think he probably chose it. As Keith said right after his funeral, he wasn't going to live to see seventy anyway. He wasn't the kind of person who can. Empires fall too, and for about the same reasons.

I went to see the Maysles brothers' documentary *Gimme Shelter* when it was new. Before that I really had no notion of the early Stones phenomenon, being too young to grasp it until it was really over—although, like so many others my age, they, along with Springsteen, wrote the soundtrack to my own refusal of the patriarchy in the 1970s. But I have to thank my father for taking me to see that movie—rated GP in the antiquated system of the day, meaning I couldn't have seen it without a parent present. He didn't know what the movie was about beforehand, only that he had kids on the brink of teenage rebellion and The Rolling Stones were supposed to be cool, so get on board or get run over, you know?

The movie permanently formed my ideas about the Stones and the world. I think that if my pop (who was and is an apologist of the patriarchy if ever there was one), had known what we would *see* at that movie, he wouldn't have taken me and my sister. But it was the right thing to do, anyway. We lived in Memphis, one of the epicenters of the general disaster, and it had been a rough couple of years. Things were changing very fast. So he also bought me my first Beatles album, and my first Led Zeppelin album (I think that was mom's idea though).

To the parents among you, I think this is a good strategy for maintaining your influence over your kids, better than the advice you'll get from Sarah Palin or Michele Bachman. It may be better to go even further; bring them their first doobie. Dionysus will have his day, and he *will* have his time with your kids and take his accursed share, sooner or later. If you love them, make a friend of Mick Jagger; it's the only way to protect them from Brian Jones. It's just a shot away, or just a kiss away. That's the gig, so you choose.

Standing in the Shadow

RANDALL AUXIER met a few gin-soaked bar-room queens in Memphis, where he grew up. They tried to take him upstairs for a ride, but he was too busy reading Plato, which blew his mind. He now plays bass for the honky-tonk women of southern Illinois and between gigs teaches philosophy at SIU Carbondale.

MICHAEL BARILLI is currently a student at Boston College working towards a bachelor's degree in English and Finance. He has a passion for music that started from an early age, mostly influenced by his mother, Dianne, father, Ron and sister, Kristine. If he's not trying to emulate Mick's undeniable swagger, Mike can be found playing the glockenspiel or baking. He doesn't ride wild horses. He'll ride them someday and would like to thank Stephanie St. Martin, Dan Steele, and Brian Braman.

RICHARD BERGER was born in a crossfire hurricane, and has worked in journalism, broadcasting, and education. Since 2008, he has been Reader in Media and Education at The Centre for Excellence in Media Practice (CEMP), Bournemouth University, UK. Richard's work on adaptation and fan fiction writing has been published in *The Journal of Adaptation in Film and Performance* and the edited collections, *Redefining Adaptation Studies* and *Adaptation Studies: New Approaches*. Richard currently writes for *The Big Picture Magazine* and edits the *Media Education Research Journal*. He has previously contributed to *Battlestar Galactica and Philosophy: Mission Accomplished or Mission Frakked Up*, which was a gas, gas, gas!

GARY CIOCCO teaches philosophy at McDaniel College, Harrisburg Area Community College, and other schools. He wrote a chapter in *The Grateful Dead and Philosophy: Getting High Minded about Love and Haight* (2007) and has had poetry published in various journals. He has already begun using Keith Richards's *Life* as a subtext for all of his courses, and was so proud in the Nineties when his then five-year-old son was told he danced just like Mick Jagger. He remembers being nineteen and nervous, but has never tallied his breakdowns.

THERESA COTTER is a writer and editor at St Olaf College in Minnesota. She's a huge Stones fan; the album that has made the biggest impact on her is *Sticky Fingers*. Maybe this is because seven years ago she spent a month traveling in Italy with *Sticky Fingers* as her only source of music. She believes she holds the record for listening to this album ninety times in thirty days.

Some facts of LUKE DICK's New York life resemble "Some Girls." He does in fact share a small apartment with six females. That much is the God's honest truth. It's also true that only one third of those females are human, and of the two humans, one is his sweet daughter, Emily. The other is his illustrious wife, literary and domestic editor, Meredith. He teaches philosophy and is a published songwriter. Google him sometime. Spend some time together.

After his life peaked in 1966 when his bar-band friends invited him on stage to belt out "Satisfaction," DAN DINELLO wrote the book *Technophobia!* (2006); directed episodes of *Strangers With Candy*; ran the Website Shockproductions.com; and became a Professor and 2012 Distinguished Scholar at Columbia College Chicago, located on South Michigan Avenue, not too far from Chess Records.

JOSEPH J. FOY is an assistant professor in the Department of Political Science, Law, and Philosophy at the University of Wisconsin, Parkside. He's the editor of *Homer Simpson Goes to Washington: American Politics through Popular Culture* (2009) and *SpongeBob SquarePants and Philosophy: Soaking Up Secrets Under the Sea!* (2011). In his free time he likes rocking out with his young son who plays some wicked drums, but who is thankfully only addicted to milk and M&Ms.

KEEGAN GOODMAN lives in Brooklyn and is a graduate student at Stony Brook University, where he focuses on nineteenth-century German philosophy. He grew up in the country and first heard the Rolling Stones on the radio while rolling down the highway in a pick-up truck late one night. The song was "Under My Thumb," about thirty years after the Stones played it at Altamont.

For years JOHN HUSS's band, the John Huss Moderate Combo, was the voice of suburban politesse in Chicago pubs and clubs. John co-wrote the cult classic movie *Use Your Head* (1996). He co-edited (with David Werther) *Johnny Cash and Philosophy: The Burning Ring of Truth* (2008) and is now editing *Planet of the Apes and Philosophy*. In his spare time he is assistant professor of philosophy at The University of Akron.

BILL MARTIN is the author of *Avant Rock*, *Listening to the Future*, and other books about progressive rock music that have drawn praise from philosophers, music critics, and even musicians whose work he writes about, such as Robert Fripp and Chris Squire. He has contributed to *Bass Player* magazine and numerous philosophy journals, and is a professor of philosophy at DePaul University in Chicago.

RICK MAYOCK gets his fair share of abuse as a musician and songwriter in Los Angeles. He's also practiced at the art of deception, teaching philosophy at West Los Angeles College. He has contributed chapters to *The Beatles and Philosophy: Nothing You Can Think that Can't be Thunk* (2006), *The Office and Philosophy: Scenes from the Unexamined Life* (2008), and the forthcoming *The Catcher in the Rye and Philosophy*.

PHILIP MERKLINGER is professor of philosophy at the University of Alberta, Augustana Campus, in Alberta. He received his PhD from the University of Ottawa in 1991. He's the author of *Philosophy, Theology, and Hegel's Berlin Philosophy of Religion, 1821–1827* (1993). His main research interests include the philosophy of religion, the philosophy of Hegel and Heidegger, and the philosophy of spirituality. With *Get Yer Ya-Ya's Out!* presently on eternal shuffle in his office, he completing a book on the philosophy of spirituality and is preparing a course on the philosophy of rock music.

GEORGE REISCH is a historian of twentieth-century philosophy and Series Editor for the Popular Culture and Philosophy series. He teaches philosophy and intellectual history at Northwestern University, edited *Pink Floyd and Philosophy: Careful with That Axiom, Eugene!* (2007), and co-edited *Radiohead and Philosophy: Fitter Happier More Deductive* (2009). George has written about rock music for *Stereophile* magazine and Popmatters.com. He is currently writing a book about philosophy and brainwashing.

JAMES ROCHA is an assistant professor at Louisiana State University, where he teaches and researches in ethics, political philosophy, and philosophy of race. He has been searching for hidden ethical messages in supposedly Satanic songs played forwards ever since he was told as a child that one could find Satanic messages in regular songs played backwards.

STEPHANIE ST. MARTIN was born sometime between the releases of *Tattoo You* and *Dirty Work* (she's "So Young"). An Adjunct Philosophy Professor at Middlesex Community College in Bedford, Massachusetts, and a Marketing Associate at Care.com, she has a newfound respect for those adolescents who chose to be morally impotent and stayed out past curfew to listen to the Rolling Stones. When philosophy isn't giving her enough satisfaction, she enjoys going on Twitter (you can follow her @StephStMartin), struttin' and shakin' like Mick Jagger, and trying to figure out how to be immortal like Keith Richards. She credits her education at Boston College, especially her time in the late Fr. Joseph Flanagan's classroom and in his Perspectives Program, in helping her to "relish in wonder" and write her chapter. which is dedicated to Fr. Flanagan; she hopes the true Beatific Vision is even more impressive than Breyer's French Vanilla Ice Cream.

JERE O'NEILL SURBER's day gig is being a professor of philosophy and cultural theory at the University of Denver. He's also a multi-instrumentalist in the Celtic rock band Alehouse Ceilidh and has been known to pick some Irish, bluegrass, and American roots music, as well. He's published widely in nineteenth- and twentieth-century continental philosophy and has been a frequent contributor to the Popular Culture and Philosophy series. And, yep, it's always been The Stones over The Beatles . . . and Mick rules!

CRISPIN SARTWELL worked his way through graduate school in the 1980s as a rock critic for many newspapers and magazines, including *The Washington Star, High Fidelity, Record,* and *Circus.* His fifteen minutes of fame came in 1997, when he published (in the *Philadelphia Inquirer*) a decisive mathematical proof that The Stones were better than The Beatles, which landed him on Howard Stern and CNN. He teaches philosophy at Dickinson College and is the author of a number of books, including *Political Aesthetics* (2010).

CHARLES TALIAFERRO, professor of philosophy at St. Olaf College, is the author or editor of seventeen books including *The Image in Mind* (with Jil Evans, 2011) and *A Brief History of the Soul* (with Stewart Goetz, 2011). In January 1973, Charles had a bizarre day that he realized later matched almost perfectly the lyrics of "You Can't Always Get What You Want": There was a girl at a reception with a footloose man, going to a demonstration, and drinking a cherry red soda in a drugstore. Fortunately, there were no blood-stained hands.

RUTH TALLMAN is an assistant professor of philosophy at Barry University in Miami Shores, Florida. She's grateful to her brother, Joe, who helped her get some satisfaction by sharing his lifelong love of The Stones with her when she was still a tiny kid.

SETH VANNATTA is an assistant professor of Philosophy and Religious Studies at Morgan State University in Baltimore. He is the author of "The Player Prophet and the Phenomenology of Reading the Ref," in *Soccer and Philosophy: Beautiful Thoughts on the Beautiful Game* (2010) and editor of the forthcoming *Chuck Klosterman and Philosophy*. Seth writes about the intersections of philosophy with other elements of culture including law, politics, sports, and education. His favorite Stones track is "T&A." While his chapter in this volume looks at Keith's run-in with the law in Arkansas in 1975, Seth did not mention his own run-in on the way to a Stones concert in Norman, Oklahoma, in 1997. Neither Richards nor Vannatta was charged.

Index